America's Death Penalty

America's Death Penalty

Between Past and Present

EDITED BY

David Garland, Randall McGowen,
and Michael Meranze

NEW YORK UNIVERSITY PRESS
New York and London

NEW YORK UNIVERSITY PRESS
New York and London
www.nyupress.org

References to Internet websites (URLs) were accurate at the time of writing.
Neither the author nor New York University Press is responsible for URLs
that may have expired or changed since the manuscript was prepared.

Library of Congress Cataloging-in-Publication Data
America's death penalty : between past and present /
edited by David Garland, Michael Meranze, and Randall McGowen.
p. cm.
Includes bibliographical references and index.
ISBN 978-0-8147-3266-3 (cl : alk. paper) — ISBN 978-0-8147-3267-0
(pb : alk. paper) — ISBN 978-0-8147-3280-9 (e-book)
1. Capital punishment—United States. I. Garland, David. II. Meranze, Michael.
III. McGowen, Randall.
HV8699.U5A745   2010
364.660973—dc22   2010033742

New York University Press books are printed on acid-free paper,
and their binding materials are chosen for strength and durability.
We strive to use environmentally responsible suppliers and materials
to the greatest extent possible in publishing our books.

Manufactured in the United States of America
c   10 9 8 7 6 5 4 3 2 1
p   10 9 8 7 6 5 4 3 2 1

For Anthony Amsterdam and Bryan Stevenson

Contents

Acknowledgments

This book grew out of collaborative work on the relationship between capital punishment, history, and social theory that we have been developing over the past few years. On various occasions, most notably at the Law Society Association (LSA) meetings in Las Vegas in May 2005 and at a workshop at New York University (NYU) School of Law in May 2007, we drew a variety of other scholars into that discussion and greatly benefited from their ideas and advice. We take this opportunity to express our thanks.

Jonathan Simon acted as discussant at our LSA panel, and his characteristically lively and insightful reactions encouraged us to continue with our venture. Dean Ricky Revesz of New York University School of Law enabled us to develop our ideas further by agreeing to fund a two-day workshop at NYU where we were able to assemble a remarkable group of historians, sociologists, and lawyers to discuss capital punishment, past and present. We are grateful to everyone who took part in that event and whose contributions made it one of the most exciting and productive intellectual exchanges any of us can remember.

Those to whom we owe particular thanks include the contributors to the present volume—Doug Hay, Rebecca McLennan, and Jonathan Simon—as well as Grace Hale, Claudio Lomnitz, Anthony Amsterdam, Lauren Benton, Craig Calhoun, Noah Feldman, Sally Gordon, David Greenberg, Dan Hulsebosch, Bryan Stevenson, James Q. Whitman, and Tom Laqueur, all of whom prepared workshop papers or commentaries and contributed to the ideas represented here.

Finally, we express our gratitude to the people at NYU Press, particularly our editor Ilene Kalish, for their ongoing support.

Introduction

Getting the Question Right? Ways of
Thinking about the Death Penalty

RANDALL MCGOWEN

In recent years the death penalty has lost none of its power to arouse powerful emotions or to produce heated debates. Indeed, the question of capital punishment has secured greater prominence, as it has become one of the defining issues in the campaign to promote recognition of international human rights. The result has been the transformation of a debate largely taking place within national political contexts and arising mainly within Western culture into a cause that leaders of all nations feel compelled to address. Debates at the United Nations, discussions before various human rights conventions, as well as the attention of the world press have all brought a level of scrutiny of national practices that is difficult to avoid. Proponents of the abolition of the penalty assert that it violates universal human rights which transcend local traditions or circumstances. Their opponents tend to reject this claim, asserting, instead, the priority of separate and distinct national or religious identities.

Often the ethical and moral argument over capital punishment is posed as a timeless question whose fundamental shape has not, and cannot, change.[1] Yet, paradoxically, much recent scholarly discussion has centered on a particular country and its peculiar history, namely, America's retention of the death penalty. To many observers, the survival of capital punishment in this country appears both a puzzle and a provocation. The question seems simple, even if the answer has proved elusive: Why should a nation that casts itself as a leader in the battle for human rights resist so tenaciously the elimination of a practice so self-evidently a holdover from darker times? A great deal seems to be at stake in the answer to this question. The presence of capital punishment in America feels more threatening, at least to American and European scholars and activists, than its occurrence elsewhere in the world. Indeed, it often seems as if answering the riddle of the death penalty depends on solving a distinctively American enigma. Certainly this is the overwhelming impression one draws from a casual reading of the European and North American press or, indeed, from a survey of much of the recent scholarship on the topic.

This volume emerged out of a symposium convened by David Garland, Randall McGowen, and Michael Meranze (sponsored by New York University School of Law in May 2007) that sought to look at capital punishment in historical perspective, and to think again about how we might view its occurrence in our own time. The goal was to renew the debate by unsettling some of the certainties that have helped to shape its modern formulation. Our concern was that the seeming familiarity of the controversy has become an obstacle to reaching a new understanding of the issue. The strategy we followed was to examine not only the answers offered but also the questions posed in the debate. These questions often imported historical and theoretical assumptions which framed the answers that could be given. The conference drew together historians, sociologists, and legal scholars, as well as litigators engaged in the day-to-day struggles defending the condemned on death row. The conversations that went on during the meeting were wide-ranging, stretching from contemporary American death penalty litigation to the practices of capital punishment in other times and places. The longer the discussions went on, the more inadequate the insistent viewpoint of the present and the often repeated tales of the past came to seem.

Much of the initial discussion was devoted to the question of American exceptionalism, the fact that the United States seems on a different path from those countries with which its citizens usually compare themselves, especially in Europe. There was no shortage of candidates to explain this apparent disparity. Several people argued that it resulted from the country's unique judicial arrangements, and others looked to the peculiar nature of its federal system of government. There was greater consensus that the nation's tortured history of race relations was implicated in the development. Other scholars pointed to the frequency of violence in the American past and its prevalence in the country today. Finally, some participants traced the roots of the fierce retributive spirit at work in American justice to a powerful streak of religious fundamentalism that distinguishes the nation's culture.[2] It soon became clear, however, that too many candidates had the honor of explaining the American path. Every distinctive aspect of its culture and political life seemed to have a hand in producing the outcome. In sum, America retained the death penalty because it was America. This discussion of America's distinctive relationship to capital punishment soon came to feel tired, even if it kept springing to life with each new formulation of the topic. The issues it raised seemed already obvious, the questions already answered. For all the heat generated, the debate seemed to repeat what was already assumed: that America was different.

During the conference, many participants expressed dissatisfaction with the way the question was being posed. Participants increasingly agreed that we needed to de-familiarize the issue in order to restore the strangeness, rawness, and urgency of the problem. One suggestion involved the argument that focusing on the United States was too parochial and, perhaps, a shade self-indulgent. Scattered references to the situation elsewhere in the world hinted at the value of wider comparisons that did not privilege any particular region. These comments often appeared as provocations rather than settled theories. Nonetheless, even in this form, they exposed some of the unarticulated premises that marked the usual debate. The widespread use and varied forms of capital punishment today challenge many of our theories about the meaning and occurrence of the penalty. Viewed from this unconventional direction, the American experience looks less exceptional than is usually claimed. One implication of this realization is that what one can say about capital punishment in relation to modern politics and what we predict for its future may be different from that assumed in so much of the scholarly literature.

The Death Penalty Kaleidoscope

A superficial reading of American and European newspapers presents a steady stream of seemingly familiar stories of the death penalty that alternate in their tone between the scandalized, the despondent, and the triumphant. A more careful survey of press coverage, however, reveals a more complex picture. This complexity suggests a simple experiment: instead of studying the world through the lens of the American experience—as Americans are wont to do—suppose we reverse the equation and work to locate U.S. behavior in a global context. Such an exercise helps to expose the deeply held beliefs about the relationship between this extraordinary penalty and the cultural values that have helped to shape the modern debate over capital punishment. The variety of death penalty practices that prevails around the world today offers problems not so much for how one views the morality or justice of capital punishment as for how we explain the persistence of the institution, its occurrence in particular places, and the politics to which it gives rise. For different reasons, both proponents and opponents of the death penalty have presented portraits of the penalty that tend to isolate and simplify it. Both views are disturbed when we seek to explore the varied and dense elaborations of the penalty in particular situations.

Despite a tendency, when speaking of the death penalty in America, to treat the country as monolithic, even a casual observer cannot help but note the astounding variety of often contradictory experiences that characterize the nation. What really marks the country to an unusual degree is the profound interest and intense passions the controversy arouses. The American public is emotionally invested in capital punishment, and people feel a deep stake in the issue.[3] Although the nation is deeply divided, this division produces no simple pattern of political response to the topic. The result, instead, is more ambiguous and volatile. State responsibility for criminal legislation and the local election of judges and prosecutors result in what can seem a crazy quilt of possible outcomes when it comes to capital justice. Popular opinion can fluctuate considerably depending on the kinds of stories that fill the media or how the polling questions are phrased. There are committed activists on each side of the issue, but a considerable portion of the population is genuinely conflicted. One point upon which people agree is that the question is a moral one and is tangled up with the identity of the nation or a particular region. Certainly, there are few other places in the world where the practice looms so large in the national consciousness. Nor has the entire process of capital justice been subjected anywhere else to such searching examination—from police practice and issues of evidence to the capital eligibility of selected populations such as the young. The American preoccupation with the death penalty continues to produce strange and unexpected developments.

For instance, one certainty of American politics over the past thirty years has been the conviction that advocating the abolition of capital punishment meant political suicide for the candidate who pressed it. Recently, however, even this certainty has been thrown into doubt. In December 2007 New Jersey became the first state since the restoration of capital punishment in 1976 to abolish the penalty by legislation. The state had been one of many to reestablish capital punishment in the aftermath of *Gregg v. Georgia*, doing so in 1982. It also followed the national trend in legislating lethal injection as the method of execution. New Jersey courts sentenced more than forty people to death, though no executions actually took place. The last offender executed in New Jersey was in 1963. In 2004 the state appeals court held that the state's mode of managing the death penalty was unconstitutional. A state commission declared the penalty in conflict "with evolving standards of decency."

Although some legislators noted this argument in explaining their votes, more mentioned that the cost of capital justice weighed most heavily in their minds. In signing the bill, Governor Jon Corzine applauded the end of "state-endorsed killing." The measure replaced execution with life in prison with no opportunity for parole. New Mexico joined New Jersey in abolishing capital punishment in 2009. Legislatures in several other states took up the question in recent years. Only a veto by the state's governor prevented New Hampshire from overturning the death penalty, and a similar scenario played out in Connecticut. In New York the State Assembly refused to pass a measure that would have reinstated the penalty, after the state's Supreme Court ruled the existing law invalid. Polling suggested that a majority of the state's citizens would be content with life imprisonment without parole as an alternative to capital punishment.[4]

Other developments reinforced the impression that the tide in America has once more turned against capital punishment. Most significant has been the overturning of numbers of capital convictions as a result of DNA evidence. Since 1973 133 death row inmates have been exonerated, and 17 of these cases involved DNA evidence. The fear of executing an innocent person gives pause to all but the most dedicated supporters of the death penalty. News stories of innocence came to occupy as much space as tales of offenders executed for horrendous crimes. In a widely publicized instance, Illinois Governor George Ryan imposed a moratorium on capital punishment after the discovery of serious injustices in the cases of several men on death row. He also appointed a commission to investigate the operation of the penalty and, in the wake of its report, granted amnesty to everyone on the Illinois death row at that time.[5]

Even in Texas, the stronghold of the death penalty, public officials and the press expressed concerns about the conduct of capital justice. In 2001 Governor Rick Perry declared a legislative emergency after an egregious case of error resulted in an innocent man spending fifteen years in prison. The legislature passed a bill offering state funding for convicts to have DNA tests performed. Dallas district attorney Craig Watkins allowed the Innocence Project to examine 350 cases. As of April 2008 sixteen convicts have been exonerated. Such stories weakened support for death. The *Dallas Morning Post*, a longtime supporter of capital punishment, announced in an editorial that it doubted the state could guarantee "that every inmate it executes is truly guilty of murder." In 2009 Texas saw nine people sentenced to death, a sharp drop from the forty-eight condemned in 1999.[6] Still, it does not do to overstate the case for change. When the panel Governor Perry created to examine forensic evidence in capital cases heard evidence strongly suggesting that Perry had signed the death warrant for an innocent man, Cameron T. Willingham, the governor dismissed the chairman and two other members of the commission. He mocked the evidence of fire scientists who questioned the original arson finding by calling the witnesses "latter-day supposed experts." Yet, the governor's conduct did not earn him the public disapproval in Texas that one might have expected. Perry's political opponent, Kay Bailey Hutchison, criticized Perry but only for "giving liberals an argument to discredit the death penalty," clearly implying that she would do a better job of defending the practice.[7]

Texas was not the only state to experience troubling shortcomings in its legal proceedings in capital cases. The release of a death-row inmate in North Carolina, the third within six months, raised new questions about the adequacy of defense counsel in such cases.[8] State courts were also active in circumscribing the practice of death. The Ohio Supreme Court said that a mentally retarded man could not be executed, and the Nebraska Supreme Court ruled that the electric chair was cruel and unusual punishment. The Georgia Supreme Court reached the same decision in *Dawson v. State* (2001).[9] The U.S. Supreme Court displayed its concern for procedural propriety when, in March 2008, it overturned a conviction on the basis that jury selection had unfairly excluded a black man.[10]

The most surprising development of 2007–8 was a national moratorium on executions that arose from the Supreme Court's decision to rule on whether the cocktail mix of chemicals involved in lethal injection violated the Eighth Amendment injunction against cruel and unusual punishment in the case of *Baze v. Rees* (2008). As a consequence, only forty-two people were executed in the United States in 2007, the lowest total since 1994. This episode further confirmed the status of the Court as the one institution capable of shaping national policy with respect to capital punishment. The hiatus gave hope to those calling for the abolition of the death penalty even as they acknowledged that the composition of the Court was unlikely to favor their cause. It also provided cover for several governors who were inclined to suspend capital punishment because of doubts about the integrity of the process. Yet the course of the arguments before the Court in January 2008 provided scant grounds for optimism. Conservative justices made clear through their questions that they were intent on producing a decision that would forestall future litigation on the subject.[11] The subsequent vote in *Baze*, 7 to 2, to uphold the existing protocol justified the fears of liberals. Like so many Court outcomes with respect to this topic, the "splintered" decision both upheld the current mode of execution and left the door open to new challenges to specific aspects of the procedure. The division among the justices mirrored the deep and acrimonious split in the nation. Even as Justice Stevens implied he would vote to abolish capital punishment, Chief Justice Roberts suggested he would resist future appeals from the condemned unless they could prove that "the state's lethal injection protocol creates a demonstrated risk of severe pain." Justice Thomas set the bar even higher; a "method of execution violates the Eighth Amendment only if it is deliberately designed to inflict pain." In an ironic twist, the five Catholic justices on the Court, after voting to uphold the death protocol, all attended a dinner in honor of the visiting Pope Benedict XVI, a leading opponent of capital punishment.[12]

Another Supreme Court decision during the same term—*Kennedy v. Louisiana*—demonstrated just how delicately balanced the debate over capital punishment is in America. The issue concerned a Louisiana law which made it a capital crime to rape a child. The Court decided on a 5 to 4 vote that the law was unconstitutional. The deciding vote, given by Justice Kennedy, was justified on the basis of the claim that "evolving standards of decency" forbade the use of death when life had not been taken. "When the law punishes by death," he wrote, "it risks its own sudden descent into brutality, transgressing the constitutional commitment to decency and restraint." The decision appeared to be in line with recent Court rulings that served to circumscribe the application of the penalty, notably *Atkins v. Virginia* (2002) and *Roper v. Simmons* (2005) which prohibited the execution of offenders who are mentally retarded or who were juveniles at the time of their offense. Yet the closeness of the vote and the strength of the dissent suggested a Court that could easily move in the opposite direction. Chief Justice Roberts argued in his dissent that this case concerned the nature of the crime and not the characteristics of the offender, and so should not be confused with the other cases limiting the application of death. Society rightly displayed, he concluded, a particular revulsion for violence against children. The dissenters contended that the special heinousness of the crime, along with the powerful emotions it aroused, justified an extraordinary punishment. They seemed inclined to respect the wishes of the states that passed such laws. If the outcome of this case served to reinforce restrictions on capital punishment, the decision could have gone the other way. If it had, the door to the expansion of capital punishment would have been opened to other special cases, and a new kind of competition among states might well have ensued. That both presidential candidates, Barack Obama and John McCain, hastened to condemn the decision pointed once again to the potency of pro-death penalty sentiment at the national political level.[13]

The moratorium produced by the *Baze* case proved a false dawn, one that soon gave way to a race to see which state would be the first to resume executions. "We'll start playing a little bit of catch-up," an advocate for a victims' rights group announced. In early May 2009 Georgia won the competition. It executed William Lynd for the killing of his girlfriend. By late June nine men had died on death rows in six southern states (two each in Georgia, South Carolina, and Virginia, and one each in Texas, Mississippi, and Oklahoma). By the first week of December thirty-seven had been executed, twenty of whom were non-white. Eighteen were put to death in Texas, whereas only two executions (Ohio) took place outside the South. It soon appeared that the United States was likely to return to the execution rate that prevailed before the moratorium. On the other hand, the much feared torrent of executions did not occur.[14] Only fifty-two people were executed in 2009, most, once again, from the South, with Texas executing twenty-four. Indeed, the year saw a continued decline in the number of death sentences awarded, down by almost two-thirds from a peak of 328 in 1994. As so often occurred in the controversy, each side had a different explanation for the change. Proponents of abolition argued that the change was owing to jury hesitation to risk the lives of innocent defendants, and defenders of the penalty contended that the decline merely mirrored the diminution in the murder rate.[15] The national statistics, however, contained another surprise. Los Angeles County sentenced more people to death than any other state in the nation, including Texas. Thanks to a four-year hiatus in executions produced by legal challenges to lethal injection, by the end of 2009 California had 697 people on death row.[16] Just when you think you have a fix on the situation with respect to capital punishment in the United States, some unexpected twist appears. More predictably a high-profile execution at the end of the year produced a momentary surge of support for the death penalty. John A Muhammad, found guilty of the sniper killings of ten individuals in the Washington, D.C., area in 2002 was executed to general public approval.[17]

If the American scene presents an often confusing portrait, it is mirrored in reports of global developments with respect to capital punishment. At the end of 2007 the United Nations voted decisively in favor of a resolution condemning the death penalty. As many as 104 nations supported the call for a moratorium on executions, 54 voted against the proposal, and 29 abstained. Europe and Latin America provided most of the votes for the measure. America, in opposing it, was joined by a diverse group of nations, including

China, Iran, Syria, India, and North Korea. Secretary General Ban Ki-moon, who had earlier been criticized for his failure to speak out over the execution of Saddam Hussein, called the vote "a bold step." It was, he added, "further evidence of a trend towards ultimately abolishing the death penalty." The Coliseum in Rome was illuminated to celebrate the event.[18]

Human rights organizations declared the UN action a dramatic victory, and an important step toward the eventual elimination of the death penalty. But a closer look at the vote suggests a more ambiguous interpretation. Even as the resolution itself offered compelling evidence of the internationalization of the question, the vote revealed that the effort produced a potent backlash that assumed various forms. Some nations responded with anger, others with contempt, and some simply displayed disdain for the proceedings. The Indian delegate, in explaining his negative vote in the Human Rights Committee, appealed to the "sovereign right of countries to determine their own legal system." The representative, demonstrating how tangled responses to the issue can be, hastened to add that the punishment in India was rare, reserved for especially heinous offenses and was surrounded by "all requisite procedural safeguards."[19]

Several small nations aggressively challenged the right of the international organization to legislate in this area. For them the issue was a stark political question. The representative from Barbados, while stressing that his country had not executed anyone in several decades, explained that the issue was one of sovereignty as much as morality. "Capital punishment," he explained, "remains legal under international law and Barbados wishes to exercise its sovereign right to use it as a deterrent to the most serious crime."[20] The delegate from Singapore complained to the Human Rights Committee that the European Union was attempting to impose its values on the world. "There was a time," he explained, "when our views were dismissed." "Most of us here struggled for years against this. So how ironic it is that we're now being told once again that only one view is right and that all other views are wrong." Botswana's delegate echoed the complaint that some members seemed to believe "their political, cultural, and legal systems are better than those of others."[21] Several Caribbean countries opposed the motion because they interpreted the effort to abolish capital punishment as "a European-based form of neo-colonialism." Most Islamic states also resisted the change. They argued that the penalty had the sanction of their religious law, though they also displayed a scarcely concealed resentment at the European claim of the moral high ground on the issue.[22] It is noteworthy that many of the objections advanced by the retentionist states—the claims of sovereignty; the special requirements of local crime control; the concern with local culture, tradition, and belief; the resentment of laws imposed from outside; and the anger at the condescension of outsiders who regard themselves as superior— echo the attitudes and arguments advanced by southern states in their relations with the federal courts in the United States. For a variety of nations the death penalty continues to symbolize, to an almost unique degree, the sovereignty of the state and the integrity of the indigenous culture against a host of real and imagined threats.

Despite all the fanfare, the UN resolution had relatively little impact upon those states that practiced capital punishment. Aside from a few scattered editorials, Americans continued to see the issue in national terms. Indeed, the sharp criticism of Justice Kennedy for his reference to international trends with respect to the execution of juveniles in the *Roper* case demonstrated the resistance to the application of any international standards in the United States. Japan also moved resolutely along its distinctive path. In 2007 it executed nine people, and by November 2008 it had executed fifteen, the highest number since 1975. A total of 101 inmates remained on its death row. Its executions remained shrouded in mystery, at once discreet and yet frighteningly sudden for those who, after spending decades in prison, are speeded to their deaths. The only hint of unease with this process came with the broadcast of a 1955 execution. This tape, along with fresh revelations of the harsh interrogation practices used to secure confessions, sparked a brief flurry of debate.[23] In Indonesia, President Susilo Bambang Yudhoyono continued his strong support for capital punishment. In June two Nigerians were executed by firing squad for drug offenses, the first offenders to be killed for the crime in four years. Their deaths came after the Constitutional Court declared the legality of the penalty.[24] Saudi Arabia also demonstrated little sensitivity to world opinion. In May 2008 Saudi authorities beheaded a man convicted of armed robbery and rape. He was one of fifty-five people put to death up to that point in the year. Saudi authorities defend the country's practice by appealing to Islamic law and claiming that beheading is a humane method of inflicting death. They administer drugs to the condemned before the execution. Many of the executions are carried out in public.[25]

The conduct of two of the most active employers of capital punishment, Iran and China, shows just how complicated the discussion of trends and influences has become. Each, in recent actions, demonstrated concern for how its conduct appeared to the world. It is striking how nations with widely differing political institutions and philosophies of government have felt compelled to adopt the language of "civilizing" and "humanizing" reform when they explain changes in penal policies. Yet their continuing employment of capital punishment suggests the limitations of these concessions to international opinion. In January 2008 Iran's chief judge ordered that executions no longer take place in public, and he barred the reproduction of images of the event. A representative explained that the penalty "should not be carried out or publicized in a way that would create psychological tensions for the society, especially the young." The decision in no way swayed the course of capital justice, as twenty people suffered for a range of crimes stretching from murder and rape to drug dealing since the start of the year. On one day in July twenty-nine offenders, guilty of such crimes as smuggling narcotics and armed robbery, were executed. Iran executed close to three hundred people in 2007, a dramatic increase over the previous year. It continued to execute juveniles. And in the aftermath of the disputed elections in 2009, executions increased yet again. Although many of those who died were found guilty of violent crimes and smuggling, commentators saw a message being sent to the opponents of the government of President Mahmoud Ahmadinejad. In November Iran sentenced five people to death for encouraging political unrest that was held to threaten the survival of the Islamic Republic.[26]

In early 2008 China announced that it was adopting lethal injection for its executions rather than employing firing squads, in an effort to make them "more humane." China also reported a drop in the number of those executed. The Supreme People's Court, for several years, has sought to exercise greater control over lower courts, especially in the use of capital punishment. It has tried to encourage greater discretion in the application of the death sentence and has sought to impose oversight in capital cases. While China continues to lead the world in executions, killing perhaps four thousand in the "strike hard" campaign in 2006, the total for 2007, according to one estimate, may have fallen by as much as 30 percent.[27] The decline followed upon a program to "kill fewer, kill carefully" launched in 2006. Observers credited the change to the pressure of public opinion in the wake of several reported instances of obvious miscarriages of justice, as well as greater concern about world opinion in the lead up to the Olympics. Still, some commentators described these changes as cosmetic. China continues to execute people for a wide range of offenses, including economic crimes such as tax fraud, embezzlement, and bribery. Great publicity often surrounds the execution of high-profile offenders such as gangsters and corrupt government officials. China executed two men in 2009 for their roles in the contaminated milk powder scandal that rocked the country in 2008. In December 2009, amid great international attention, China executed a Briton convicted of carrying a large quantity of heroin into the country, despite pleas that the man was mentally ill. While the execution produced anger in Britain, the bulk of online comment in China supported the government's actions.[28]

The international scene offers us not only a mix of different approaches to the death penalty; it also exposes the shifting political currents that so often surround the question today. One episode, in particular, exposed the fraught and unpredictable nature of these confrontations. It offers a complex tale not only of cultures in collision but of sharply conflicting political ambitions as well. On November 6, 2006, an Iraqi court sentenced Saddam Hussein to death. The Bush administration hoped that the execution of Hussein would send several messages, that it would mark the transition from a regime of tyranny to one of orderly justice, and that it would signal the moment when the Iraqis took control of their own legal process. "It is an important milestone," President Bush announced after the event, "on Iraq's course to becoming a democracy that can govern, sustain, and defend itself." Perhaps only a former governor of Texas could with such confidence mark out an execution as a step on the road to democracy. The actions of the Iraqis, however, upset all these careful calculations. American ambitions were overwhelmed when a symbolically charged event became a contest among competing actors with contradictory goals. Although the American authorities had no qualms about employing the death penalty, they showed greater concern for careful stage management of the execution than did the Iraqi government. American officials were apprehensive about executing Hussein on a Sunni religious holiday. Some had reservations about rushing him to the gallows. Hussein was sentenced to death for ordering the execution of 148 men and boys in the Shiite town of Dujail. There had been expectations that he would also be tried for his role in the slaughter of 180,000 Kurds. The Iraqi prime minister, Nuri Kamal al-Maliki, pressed for an immediate execution of the sentence. The government secured a ruling from a Shiite cleric permitting the process to go forward despite the proximity to the religious holiday. As the hour drew nearer, the desire for vengeance against a hated oppressor dominated among Maliki's closest associates.[29] The American pretense that Hussein's death was a matter of principle and a product of due process was shattered with the exposure of U.S. hypocrisy in its bungled manipulation of Iraqi politics. The occupation authorities also failed to appreciate the level of passion they had unleashed in the country.

The actual execution was chaotic, full of the ambiguity that the Americans had hoped to avoid. It proved unseemly in violating most of the rules of modern state executions by bringing politics, sectarian conflicts, and vengeful sentiments into the open. The Iraqi state's act looked more like victor's justice than like the implementation of an impartial judicial verdict. Early on the morning of December 30, 2006, Hussein was flown from one U.S. base to another, named Camp Justice, which contained a prison with an execution chamber. Here he was handed over to Iraqi authorities. The United States sought to create the impression that it was distant from the final arrangements for Hussein's death. Advisers to President Bush emphasized that, although the president had been informed that the execution would go forward, he was asleep when it actually took place. The Americans had hoped to have the presence of international observers as a way of securing some measure of international legitimacy for the event. Instead, fourteen Shiite officials and a Sunni cleric attended. Hussein refused to lend himself to the occasion. While he thanked the American guards for looking after him, he treated the Iraqi officials with scorn. Instead of a prison uniform, he wore a white shirt and overcoat. He declined to wear the hood that was offered to him. The Shiite guards taunted him, and he answered in kind.[30]

Despite the efforts to control news of the event, an illicit cell phone video soon spread images of the execution to the world. Many newspapers carried photographs, and the video can still be seen on *YouTube*. The recording aroused uneasiness in many corners and anger in Sunni countries. The U.S. military commander in Iraq denied any American involvement in the execution: "this was a government of Iraq decision on how that whole process went down." The story of the fate of the body brought no greater comfort. After the execution it was taken to the Green Zone, where it sat in an ambulance for a number of hours while authorities debated over what to do with it. Fearful that Hussein's grave might become a shrine, Maliki and his advisers were caught up in a contest with Sunni leaders. Finally, the Americans were forced to break the impasse, thus displaying a power to interfere in events which they had been reluctant to acknowledge. Disturbed by the spectacle they observed on the video, and fearful of inspiring further unrest among the Sunni population, they handed the body over to Sunni representatives. Within a matter of days Hussein's grave became a pilgrimage site.[31] Thus the Americans' cold and calculated plans floundered in the face of the fierce sectarian passions and political ambitions that characterize postwar Iraq. This episode may sound strangely familiar to historians; it might have occurred in eighteenth-century London.[32] If it casts little light on the moral arguments surrounding capital punishment, it is more revealing of the underlying dynamic so characteristic of state executions, a crude struggle to assert sovereign command and to control a highly charged, symbolically potent moment of political power.

Lessons from an Unfamiliar Landscape

This summary of the contemporary state of capital punishment around the world is not systematic and it is certainly not complete. It is suggestive, however. It offers lessons for those caught up in the theoretical debates about the meaning of the death penalty and its place in the modern world. Situating our specific analyses in the context of a more global perspective warns us against hasty generalizations. Such a viewpoint instructs us to pay attention to the unique features of local circumstances, whether cultural, religious, or political. This approach also warns against making too much of the stark opposition between abolitionist states and those that retain capital punishment. More specifically, America looks less unusual than is generally assumed. Indeed, this realization has far-reaching consequences for how we understand the significance of American retention of the death penalty and how we estimate the future prospects for the penalty on the world stage.

It often seems as if the press in the United States and Europe has a boundless appetite for details of the ongoing saga of America's relationship with capital punishment. The succession of Supreme Court cases, the tales of innocent men rescued from death at the last minute, the spectacle of a president (George W. Bush) who, as governor, presided over more than 150 executions, all guarantee that the issue will be extensively covered. Much of the reporting uncritically adheres to the "culture wars" conventions for interpreting conflicts that are so familiar a feature of American journalism and political life. It accords a special status to the American experience, thus acceding to the culture's narcissistic assertion of its unique importance. This coverage also fosters peculiar notions of the state of the practice both in the United States and elsewhere. Yet even our rapid survey of press reports from both America and other parts of the globe destabilizes the familiar narratives about capital punishment. It no longer seems enough simply to ask whether a country has or does not have the death penalty. The answer too often produces a misleading clarity. It also raises doubts about whether we can characterize changes in capital justice as moving only in one direction, toward abolition.

Much is frequently made of the association of the United States with other major "retentionist" states such as China, Iran, Syria, Saudi Arabia, Sudan, and North Korea. American practice is thus doubly damned, by its connection with repressive regimes and, more subtly, its linkage to regions often perceived as more backward than the West, both economically and with regard to human rights. That Japan and India retain capital punishment, or that Singapore and several Caribbean nations do as well, is seldom mentioned.[33]

In this way a particular interpretation of cultural development is employed to select and organize the facts deemed relevant to understanding the phenomenon of capital punishment. The penalty is represented as a symptom of pathology and the nations that retain it as exotic. At best it seems to be an anachronism, at worst an atavistic impulse that threatens human progress. It is not surprising, then, that scholars devote volumes to searching through America's past and present in order to explain its anomalous path toward modernity. The neglect of the experience of other nations suggests the operation of deep cultural prejudices, but it also hints at an anxiety about what one might discover by taking a closer look at these cases or reconsidering the relationship between these societies and the United States or Europe.

What observations spring to mind as one looks at the mélange of stories in the preceding section? First and most obviously such a survey suggests the simple variety of death penalty stories and practices. For instance, if capital punishment in America is characterized by extensive judicial review and considerable publicity of every moment of the capital process up to the point of execution, in Japan there is much less judicial review and the execution is handled discreetly. Similarly lethal injection has become the rule in the United States, after long debate over the "humanity" of various forms of execution, while other nations continue to employ hanging, decapitation, or the firing squad. Saudi Arabia continues to execute in public. China, Iran, and the United States execute considerable numbers of people, whereas India and Japan use the death penalty sparingly. Recently China and Iran have "reformed" their procedures for carrying out executions but without seriously reducing their commitment to it. Other nations have responded to outside criticism by reaffirming traditional practices. Several American states have expressed defiance in the face of negative comment from abroad about the numbers they execute. In the United States, at least for the moment, only those convicted of aggravated murder suffer death. In China, and in much of the Islamic world, a greater variety of crimes can lead to one's execution. Even the story with respect to nations that have formally abolished capital punishment is not straightforward. The countries of Latin America have followed the path to abolition, but at different times many of these nations have seen agents of the state employ death in a semi-official but widely acknowledged manner.[34] To say that such countries have relinquished the death penalty is not untrue, but the precise meaning of the statement requires careful discussion. The same might be said of nations who preserve the penalty in law but never use it, or of those that retain it for treason or national security but have abolished it for all other offenses.

Simply acknowledging the variety of circumstances in which capital punishment is employed, and the different forms it can take, does little other than unsettle several of the more familiar claims made about the penalty. The real challenge is to discover whether these comparisons can produce fresh ways of considering the issue. The most obvious conclusion to arise from this survey is that the meaning of capital punishment, as well as the shape it assumes, is distinctive in each instance. Whether the penalty exists in a given country, and how it is used if it does, depend upon local factors and, to a considerable degree, specific historical developments. The outcome is often contingent upon the actions of individuals and groups, though these people always act within cultural and political contexts that provide them with resources and opportunities.[35]

This emphasis upon the uniqueness of each case, however, in no way denies that revealing patterns or unexpected parallels may arise out of the comparison of different national trajectories. These patterns and parallels may illuminate neglected corners of the investigation of capital punishment in the modern world. For instance, abolition, in a surprising number of cases, has followed closely upon the transition from authoritarian regimes to democracy, not only in places like Germany, Austria, Spain, and Portugal but in South America, Eastern Europe, and South Africa. In these cases the elimination of the death penalty has become a powerful statement of the repudiation of old regimes and a celebration of new beginnings. Other patterns, however, suggest more surprising avenues for investigation. The highly localized character of capital justice in China bears at least some resemblance to the decentralized nature of criminal justice in the United States. Similarly Japan and Saudi Arabia join America in displaying a marked insensitivity to world opinion when it comes to sustaining their own death penalty practices. The glare of international criticism only produces anger and defiance. This intransigence points to a process whereby social conservatives seize upon an institution like capital punishment to proclaim the autonomy and integrity of their respective cultures. The claim to have ultimate power over the life of a demonized figure, in these radically different contexts, operates in symbolically significant ways to shore up society in what are experienced as threatening times.[36]

Comparisons that might seem farfetched at first glance can provoke a fresh examination of the cultural dynamics that sustain or undermine support for capital punishment in particular societies. Thus the insistence of some religious officials in Islamic countries upon the legitimacy of the death penalty bears comparison with the importance ascribed to the punishment in Christian fundamentalist circles in the United States. Equally, the way in which some Islamic societies handle the emotional appeal to vengeance, or create special categories of concern around sexual issues, can be used to think about the clamor in America for death as a punishment for child rape. A similar approach may help to explain why drug offenders are held to be worthy of death in many of these same countries. In each of these cases, although the advocates of capital punishment appeal to religious traditions to sanction their policies, they do so in reaction to cultural struggles shaking their societies and as part of a political contest for power.[37] Even on an issue like public executions, where the path of historical development seems so secure, the gulf between Saudi Arabia and the United States narrowed slightly at the time of the execution of Timothy McVeigh in June 2001. In addition to the 10 people who observed the execution in the room next to the death chamber, 232 survivors and family members watched the event on closed-circuit television.[38]

The most promising line of inquiry arising from this analysis of international patterns in the practice of capital punishment concerns what we might call the politics of national identity. The question of the death penalty has increasingly been framed in relation to notions of sovereignty viewed in the widest sense, cultural as well as political. As in the past, the death penalty remains a particularly expressive moment for the symbolization of political authority. But it takes on a new significance in the face of increasing globalization. Where once the death penalty was directed at local audiences by a central authority all too conscious of the fragility of its ability to command obedience, it has now become a gesture presented to the world community intended to assert national importance and autonomy, as well as assuage populist or nationalist political constituencies. When national identity seems threatened or political autonomy insecure, the death penalty becomes a simple but compelling way of demonstrating independence. It is the fact of possessing the death penalty, not the spectacle of its use, which has become the central issue. Caribbean countries, including, as we have seen, Barbados, where capital punishment has not been employed in decades, have been especially strident in their explicit expression of these sentiments. These small nations, with turbulent histories, interpret the pressure for abolition as an instance of neocolonial oppression. Given the often high levels of violence in these societies, which underlines the precariousness of authority, death is seen as a necessary sanction. Yet the defense of capital punishment has been just as pronounced in Singapore, despite the fact that it is a state with a high level of internal order.

The death penalty plays a role in domestic politics as well as in the international sphere. It becomes an instrument for certain political groups to cast themselves as defenders of law and order at home, and as upholders of national integrity against outside interference. The death penalty signals a refusal to acknowledge a claim to the inherent superiority of a value system seen as foreign and condescending. Far from being embarrassed by the continuation of the death penalty, it becomes a badge of distinction, an expression of national strength and resolve. Singapore's retention of capital punishment seems to spring from this determination. Poland's vacillation over the issue builds upon internal resentment felt toward the Council of Europe and its dictates. This same dynamic seems to be at work in helping us account for the enthusiasm of Texas, and of other parts of the South, for capital punishment. As Anthony Amsterdam has remarked, the death penalty is a point of "fierce pride" in the South; it has become a rallying point for the assertion of states' rights.[39] The governor of Texas, in the summer of 2008, appealed to precisely such notions of popular sovereignty in his refusal to honor a decision of the International Court of Justice that ordered the state not to execute five Mexican nationals. Mexico bitterly protested the Texas stand. A month later the state ignored both the Court and the Bush administration when it went ahead and executed José Medellin, a Mexican citizen.[40] Thus death belongs to a national dynamic with its proponents mingling defensive and aggressive elements in staking out their position. Capital punishment, we can see, works in several registers at the same time, not only to differentiate a region from the nation or a nation from international organizations, but to valorize the distinction and create a sense of empowerment for its adherents.

The special place given to the abolition of capital punishment within the project of the European Union takes on additional meaning when seen in these terms. On the one hand, abolition as a centerpiece of a human rights agenda has proved a way of adding an idealistic dimension to the program of gradual political consolidation haltingly under way in Europe. Abolition has become the price of admission to the Union, a proof of a commitment to a European value system which proclaims itself as both new and universal. On the other hand, it gains much of its force from the distinction it draws between Europe and America, as well as the contrast it makes with Europe's own tortured past. It is not simply the death penalty in the abstract that is at issue, but the spectacle of America's embrace of death has added immeasurably to the status of the cause in Europe. This commitment thus represents a European challenge to the traditional U.S. claim of leadership in the cause of human rights. Here we see once again that the abolition of the death penalty does not represent the disappearance of the political significance of death. Rather, abolition itself takes on its meaning and importance from the continued presence of the penalty as temptation and possibility.

Several conclusions flow from this analysis. The first is that death remains a practice with extraordinary significance. Whether implemented as public spectacle or through the semi-covert protocols of lethal injection, or even if abolished, death remains singularly expressive. Its particular significance, in individual instances, depends upon the circumstances of its deployment, as well as who uses it and to what ends. Second, political factors loom large in accounting for why a state retains or abolishes capital punishment. Cultural influences may be important in shaping the form of the execution or justifying its application, but they are not the decisive element in explaining a particular state's policy.[41] Third, and following on the previous point, the temporal horizon of capital punishment policy is as much the present as it is the past. Whatever the traditions and beliefs are that throw light upon the current practice, one must begin with the present as the locus of influences explaining capital punishment policy. And, finally, a compelling case may be made for studying the United States along a continuum of death penalty practices and situations. A comparative approach is a useful antidote to the tendency for ideology to shape the question when the investigation is divorced from specific circumstances. America's relationship with capital punishment can usefully be illuminated by a comparison with other nations within the global system.

What Can We Say about Capital Punishment

The essays collected in this volume propose to broaden the discussion of the death penalty. In no sense do we want to argue that positions advanced elsewhere in the literature are wrong, and that we have the key that will expose "the truth about the death penalty." Rather, the authors represented here are united in an effort to loosen the grip of certain kinds of arguments and by a desire to step back from some of the passionate beliefs that have marked the debate. At moments in the controversy over capital punishment it seems we have the execution too much in view. Drawn to this "moment of truth" by the shock it creates or the moral challenge it embodies, we neglect other aspects of the capital punishment complex—such as the importance of enacting death penalty laws, announcing death penalty indictments, or imposing death sentences—which carry political and cultural weight whether or not they result in actual executions. In particular, these essays engage with history, either in the form of local studies or in the identification of long-term trends, as a way to achieve such distance. Their authors are committed to careful theoretical reflection upon an issue that seems to deny, because of its hard practicality and moral urgency, that such analysis is necessary, appropriate, or useful. Even as they feel the compelling summons of the death penalty issue, they recognize a danger in too quickly accepting the terms of the contemporary debate. They especially seek to create space around what seems at moments a timeless controversy that has come to feel both frozen and stale. One feature of the ongoing conflict over capital punishment is that it casts a brilliant light upon a singular moment of punishment, treating it in stark isolation from other penal arrangements, and presenting it as a simple but ominous choice for a society. By contrast, the authors of these essays approach capital punishment as a potent but shifting configuration of practices and meanings. They set out to recover the context within which the penalty operates, seeking to discover not only long-term trends but also the shifting functions that shape its changing forms and the contingent variables that influence its development.

History appears in different guises in the pages that follow. The title of the volume is meant to suggest the difficulties as well as the possibilities that arise in considering the relationship between past and present. There is nothing easy about this investigation. No stable connection exists between the two terms. The relationship between the discipline of history and the subject it investigates, the past, is caught up in this uncertainty, which becomes more acute when the topic is as controversial and emotionally laden as capital punishment. To repeat an oft-quoted phrase, the past is another country. It differs from the present in ways that constantly elude definition. The task of achieving knowledge of the past requires one to become more self-conscious about present modes of experience. In pursuit of this objective the historian may gain some measure of distance from the ideas and practice that constitute the contemporary world. In this roundabout fashion the study of the past can cast the present in a new light, making the familiar look strange and unexpected. This activity is related to but is not identical with another task of historical study: the discovery of the sources of the present in the past and the tracing of the roots that connect them. Historians have long looked for continuities between older arrangements and current practices, as well as sought to identify moments of change. In these two different aspects history has something important to contribute to our understanding of our present dilemma.

The past casts a long shadow on the present of capital punishment in a variety of ways. Deep historical associations continue to resonate in how the penalty is imagined. The themes of God's vengeance, the crucifixion of Christ, and the terror of Leviathan all echo through popular debates.[42] Medium- and short-term associations figure largely as well, providing moments of condensed collective memories that channel powerful emotions toward the subject. The names alone are enough to provoke a response—Sacco and Vanzetti, the Rosenbergs, Caryl Chessman, Gary Gilmour, Timothy McVeigh. Critical views are often freighted with historical memory, associating capital punishment with lynching, botched executions, or the drama of contests over pardon. Defenders of the penalty invoke the names of horrifying murderers. Opponents of the death penalty cite instances of miscarriages of justice or the deaths of innocent people. History is thus the unavoidable terrain for wrestling with the question of capital punishment.

Finally, history is already present in current debates over the death penalty in the form of powerful assumptions about how the penalty relates to the transformation of societies. Since at least the eighteenth century particular historical beliefs have helped to frame what is done and how it is understood by the society at large. The past often appears as a narrative told to explain, justify, or condemn capital punishment. In these accounts the penalty is located in terms of a particular temporal horizon that gives meaning to the position being put forth. The foes of the death penalty have often anchored their claim in a developmental model of historical change. They portray humanity as moving away from a brutal treatment of the body conceived as the hallmark of earlier ages. The defenders of death, for the most part, see the issue in absolute terms that transcend historical circumstances. They trace the sanction for the punishment to what they see as a legitimate human need for retribution. In the former case time is an all-important dimension; in the latter it is irrelevant. In this division we discover one reason the two sides often seem to be arguing past each other. The historical investigations offered here disrupt both assumptions, creating the possibility for finding new ways of talking about capital punishment.

Of the essays that follow, three consider the longer-term history of capital punishment, those by David Garland, Michael Meranze, and Randall McGowen. These essays share a great deal, but they also pursue different trajectories at crucial moments. They stage a debate with the goal of making more explicit the importance of theory to the arguments over capital punishment, and to offer examples of particular interpretations that might contribute to our understanding of the issue. All three essays share a sense that history is an important terrain within which to examine the question of the death penalty. They offer parallels with and contrasts to the past as a way of gaining greater understanding of what capital punishment means today and how we might imagine its future. They also explore the issue of whether there is a pattern beyond the swirl of contingent factors and individual histories. Each author argues for the importance of political considerations in shaping the history of capital punishment: but they differ as to whether they describe a style of government, a logic of governance, or a role for ideas and political commitments. In other respects as well the authors present sharply contrasting accounts. They disagree about the pattern they discover in history and what it portends for the future. Although they agree that decisive breaks have occurred in the history of the death penalty, especially between the early modern and the modern periods, they characterize these departures in diverse ways. As a result, they give different weight to the past and the extent to which it helps to explain our predicament in the present. Do we orient ourselves by looking to the past to discover what has changed or by tracing out the hidden rationale of contemporary arrangements or by close readings of what actors said and did in debating penal policy? The degree to which the authors cover much of the same ground and appeal to familiar facts is striking, and yet the evidence is located in a different theoretical space in each instance, resulting in different conclusions.

Garland contends most strongly of the three authors that history contains a general pattern from which we can derive important conclusions about the nature and development of capital punishment. In the midst of his narrative of penal change he glimpses a thread that ties together diverse national histories across time. For him the crucial framework for the investigation of the death penalty is in relation to modes of governing society. He offers a story of the growing marginalization of the penalty, identifying a profound shift in the form of capital punishment in the move from the early modern to the modern, marked most significantly by an emphasis upon restraint rather than excess. At one time the execution had been central to strategies for maintaining royal power. By the mid-nineteenth century it had been transformed into a penal issue. The practice was less central to the task of governing society. It was, perhaps, expendable. The death penalty in this later period, in almost all its aspects, reversed the terms of its earlier elaboration. Garland is circumspect about what we can claim about this pattern and is attentive to the importance of the particular and the contingent. He acknowledges that there was no one decisive factor in promoting the transformation; rather, the penalty was the focus of a number of trends—state formation, liberalization, rationalization, and the like—whose character we can identify and whose impact we can trace. Even in its late modern form, with what seems to be the emergence of contradictory developments, the death penalty can be located within a social dynamic whose direction we can discern. We should not allow ourselves, he argues, to be distracted by what appears to be the American exception. It may present us with instances of resistance to the overall pattern of radically circumscribing the death penalty, but it offers at least as many examples of conforming to the general trend of restraining and refining the penalty.

Meranze approaches capital punishment from a different direction. Rather than looking to the past to reveal the underlying logic of penal arrangements, he explores the "political and legal rationalities" operating in the present that constitute the field within which the death penalty becomes an option. Thus he resists the impulse to treat capital punishment as a unique and isolated practice, choosing instead to see it as a part of a more elaborate configuration of forces and factors. Meranze appeals to the work of Michel Foucault as a valuable resource for the investigation of the contemporary state of the question. In doing so he seeks to rescue Foucault from the misreadings that have led scholars to underestimate his significance to this debate. In particular, Meranze discovers in Foucault's notion of the biopolitical a way to talk about the new goals and principles of government, the new ambitions and mode of regulation, which developed in the modern period. The meaning of sovereignty became redefined and its place relocated. Whereas once the monarch had the right the kill, now the state celebrates its protection of life. This new configuration may or may not require the practice of capital punishment. Sovereignty, within the latter formulation, becomes a matter of the right to exercise the choice of whether to kill or preserve life. Although the biopolitical emerged at a particular point in time, its logic is discovered not from its historical roots but from a tracing of how it operates in the present. The biopolitical rationality, however, is not the only discourse in play. Issues of sovereignty continue to influence the course of the debate over capital punishment, and, in the U.S. context, the question has been shaped by constitutional considerations. Meranze concludes his essay with an examination of the Supreme Court as a focus for the struggle between the competing claims of biopolitical and legal rationalities, though most surprising may be the extent to which even within this venue the former is such a pervasive influence.

McGowen's analysis turns attention to the way in which a particular narrative of historical development was inscribed in the earliest debates over capital punishment. This means, in practical terms, that one must approach any interpretation of the death penalty with care, since so much of the discussion is shaped in overt and subtle ways by assumptions produced by this narrative. Indeed, there is tension between a historical story that may have arisen with the reformers but has become part of the more general terms in which we understand the penalty, and what the actual history of the struggle over the death penalty reveals. This struggle helped establish for Western culture the idea that modernity brought with it greater humanity. This belief has worked, at some moments and in some places, to produce the abolition of capital punishment. But the affirmation of humanity has not always resulted in this outcome. It has also been used to defend practices like the death penalty. The reality of such contrasting uses of the idea of civilized humanity sits uneasily with the tale of human progress produced through debates over slavery and penal measures in the late eighteenth and early nineteenth centuries. McGowen engages in a work of excavation in exposing this conflict. This undertaking, however, is not simply cautionary or negative. It carries implications for how we study the death penalty, signaling the importance of contingent factors in the story of abolition. It also emphasizes the influence of what people think and say about punishment on how societies wrestle with the question. And, finally, it points to the centrality of contemporary political forces and calculations in determining how a country resolves the issue of capital punishment.

The other three essays in this volume, by Jonathan Simon, Douglas Hay, and Rebecca McLennan, represent more targeted investigations of capital punishment at particular times and in relation to practices and concerns other than the death penalty itself. They remind us that death does not stand alone but rather functions in relation to other penal and governmental practices, and within specific political structures. One consequence of focusing so intently upon the penalty, taking its existence or absence as an absolute fact, is that we forget about these other relationships and fail to grasp their significance to the question of capital punishment. These practices have their own stories to tell, and they are not always the ones we see when we operate as if the debate over the abolition of the death penalty was the only issue that mattered. These essays are more sharply focused than those of Garland, Meranze, and McGowen, but the theoretical implications they present are equally wide-ranging.

Judicial and executive authorities, for instance, have long figured prominently in the operation of capital justice. Judges (the usual sentencing authority) and governors (with the power of clemency) have exercised a major influence over who dies and why. In the process, capital justice has assumed a major role in constituting and sustaining particular conceptions of authority. The discourses associated with the death penalty may, in fact, have as much to do with legitimacy and authority as they do with crime and punishment.[43] The essays by Hay and Simon take up aspects of this relationship between executive and legal officials and the operation of the death penalty. Hay charts the changing positions of English judges in relation to capital justice over the past three hundred years. Although the question of capital punishment is often analyzed as if it concerns society as a whole, Hay demonstrates the extent to which Britain's employment of death has been mediated by the ideas and conduct of a small number of judges. He insists that we not neglect the importance of legal structures and culture when we investigate the operation of the death penalty. Simon examines the politics that lie behind shifts in the conduct of governors in the exercise of executive clemency in the United States since the 1950s. In the early modern period judges and rulers advertised their majesty through the spectacle of the death penalty. More recently, at least in the United States, judges and governors have sought to present themselves as representatives of a healthy public opinion, and they are eager to permit a wider role for popular emotions in the operation of capital justice. Yet these figures also work to reconcile these changing styles with a traditional commitment to due process and a respect for the rule of law. The drama produced by these conflicting loyalties forms part of the inescapable theater of capital justice. The script may change over time but its significance for how a society represents authority to itself and its citizens remains vital.

The death penalty has always claimed a special place, even a primacy, within the penal order. Yet it is also part of an ensemble of penal practices, and it plays a vital role in relation to these other penal forms. For instance, since the rise of the modern prison, there has been a dynamic relationship between capital punishment and incarceration. In all likelihood, there would have been no reduction in the scope of the death penalty without the alternative of imprisonment. Confinement came to be the life-affirming alternative to death. The prison promised to reclaim, redeem, or reform offenders rather than wastefully or inhumanely kill them. It seemed to apply reason and moderation rather than rage to the problem of crime. This connection has been reinvigorated recently by abolitionists who accept life imprisonment without parole as an acceptable alternative to capital punishment. The compromise permits the physical survival of the condemned but at the cost of accepting a fate as absolute as the one it replaces.[44] In addition, death penalty politics has come to overshadow an even more extensive and equally disturbing phenomenon, the unparalleled rates of incarceration in America. More space and zeal is devoted to capital punishment than to the rapid proliferation of prisons and other forms of custodial control.[45] McLennan, in her essay, takes up the issue of the extent to which death has shaped life under imprisonment. The rise of the prison, she argues, did not replace the question of death; it merely transformed it. The high rates of death from neglect, mistreatment, or disease are not issues to the side of the question of capital punishment but, in an important sense, on a continuum with it. Death, in a civil as well as physical sense, continues to haunt the penal order in a way that no straightforward history of capital punishment can capture. Increasingly severe measures in prisons, such as long-term solitary confinement, as well as penalties that extend beyond the term of confinement, such as the loss of citizenship rights, draw their logic and emotional resonance from the death penalty.[46] Far from being a fixed practice with an unchanging meaning, the death penalty and the purpose of imprisonment have taken on new shades of meaning in the context of debates about security and life in the age of the "war on terror."

The essays collected in this volume, then, represent a series of experiments in writing the history of capital punishment and theorizing its significance. In seeking to approach the issue from the side, as it were, the authors do not deny the importance of the moral question and certainly do not diminish the efforts of those who struggle on behalf of the condemned every day. Capital punishment is a powerful institution, emotionally and politically, but this recognition can interfere with a critical analysis of its operation. The question of capital punishment can loom so large that we rush to judge the institution without reflecting on its power or questioning the way it demands our attention. As a practice heavily invested with meaning by both government and culture, it is also a subtle, fluid, and far-reaching form of penal practice. It is an institution that operates between past and present. Although the death penalty is anchored in beliefs, traditions, and governmental arrangements, its incidence reflects political choices and power relations within and between states at given moments. We take nothing away from the urgency of the question of death in asking more limited questions about changing practices, complex social relations, or fluctuating ideas. On the contrary, we believe that this approach will broaden our appreciation for the temptation that capital punishment represents.

1. Roger Hood and Carolyn Hoyle, *The Death Penalty: A Worldwide Perspective* (Oxford, 2008), 6–7.

2. An extensive literature addresses the question of American exceptionalism. For one summary, see Carol Steiker, "Capital Punishment and American Exceptionalism," in *American Exceptionalism and Human Rights*, ed. Michael Ignatieff (Princeton, N.J., 2005), 57–89.

3. Andrew Moravcski, "The Paradox of U.S. Human Rights Policy," in Ignatieff, *American Exceptionalism*, 175–76, and, more generally, 147–97.

4. "Death Penalty Repealed in New Jersey," *New York Times*, December 17, 2007; "N.J. Approves Abolition of Death Penalty," *Washington Post*, December 14, 2007; "In N.Y., Lawmakers Vote Not to Reinstate Capital Punishment," *Washington Post*, April 13, 2005.

5. Scott Turow, *Ultimate Punishment* (New York, 2003).

6. "In the DNA," *Economist*, April 19, 2008; "A 12th Dallas Convict is Exonerated by DNA," *New York Times*, January 18, 2007; "Texas Accounts for Half of Executions in U.S. but Now Has Doubts over Death Row," *Guardian*, November 15, 2009; "Death Sentences Decline," *Yahoo! News*, December 18, 2009.

7. "Controversy Builds in Texas over an Execution," *New York Times*, October 20, 2009; "Cameron Todd Willingham: Former Head of Texas Forensics Panel Probing 1991 Fire Says He Felt Pressured by Gov. Perry Aides," *Chicago Tribune*, October 12, 2009; David Grann, "Trial by Fire," *New Yorker*, September 7, 2009.

8. "As Executions Resume, So Do Questions of Fairness," *New York Times*, May 7, 2008.

9. "Court Overturns Ohio Death Sentence," *New York Times*, April 9, 2008; "Electrocution Is Banned in Last State to Rely on It," *New York Times*, February 9, 2008.

10. "Justices Overturn Louisiana Death Sentence," *New York Times*, March 20, 2008.

11. "Justices Chilly to Bid to Alter Death Penalty," *New York Times*, January 8, 2009.

12. "Lethal Injection Not Inhumane, Rules U.S. Court," *Guardian*, April 16, 2008; "Court OKs Lethal Injection," MSNBC, April 16, 2008.

13. "Supreme Court Rejects Death Penalty for Child Rape," *New York Times*, June 26, 2008; "Rightly Moving Away from Death Penalty," *DesMoines Register*, June 28, 2008; "Court Won't Revisit Death Penalty Case," *New York Times*, October 2, 2008.

14. "After Hiatus, States Set Wave of Executions," *New York Times*, May 3, 2008; execution count from the Death Penalty Information Center.

15. "Death Sentences Dropped, but Executions Rose in '09," *New York Times*, December 18, 2009.

16. "California's Death Row Grows as Death Sentences Decline Nationwide," *Los Angeles Times*, December 19, 2009.

17. "Sniper Who Killed 10 Is Executed in Virginia," *New York Times*, November 11, 2009.

18. "UN Assembly Calls for Moratorium on Death Penalty," Reuters, December 18, 2007; "New UN Chief's Death Penalty Flap," CBS News, January 2, 2007; "UN Adopts Death Penalty Moratorium," *Los Angeles Times*, December 19, 2007.

19. "India Defends Death Penalty in UN," *NDTV*, November 16, 2007.

20. "UN Assembly Calls for Moratorium on Death Penalty," Reuters, December 18, 2007.

21. "EU under Fire during UN Death Penalty Debate," Reuters, November 14, 2007.

22. "Milestone in Death Penalty Fight, but Still a Way to Go," *New York Times*, December 22, 2007.

23. "Japan Executes Two on Day UN Publishes Critical Report," *Guardian Weekly*, November 7, 2008; "Just Plead Guilty and Die," *Economist*, March 15, 2008; "Broadcast of Execution Forces Japan to Debate Death Penalty," *Guardian*, May 6, 2008. For additional material on Japan and other Asian countries, see a special issue of *Punishment and Society* 10 (April 2008). The election of a left-wing government in 2009, and the appointment of an anti–death penalty justice minister, has led to the "unofficial" scrapping of capital punishment. Some commentators suggest that, until Japan adopts life without parole as an alternative to death, there will be opposition to the reform (*The Times*, September 19, 2009).

24. "Indonesia Widens Use of Death Penalty," *International Herald Tribune*, July 11, 2008.

25. "Saudi Government Beheads Robber, Rapist," *Eugene Register Guard*, May 25, 2008; "Saudi Beheadings Target the Poor, Amnesty International Says," Reuters, October 14, 2008.

26. "Iran Bans Public Executions amid Death Sentence Boom," *Guardian*, January 31, 2008; "Iran's Top Judge Stops Public Executions," *New York Times*, July 30, 2008; "Iran Executes 29 Convicts in One Day," *New York Times*, July 28, 2008; "Plight of Iran's Death-Row Youngsters," BBC News, October 28, 2008; "Iran's Death Penalty Is Seen as a Political Tactic," *New York Times*, November 23, 2009; "Iran: Death Penalty for 5 in Election Unrest," *USA Today*, November 18, 2009.

27. These annual figures are mere estimates: the true figures are classified by the Chinese government as a state secret and may be much higher. See David Johnson and Franklin Zimring, *The Next Frontier: The Death Penalty in Asia* (New York, 2009).

28. "China Proclaims Big Fall in Executions after Court Reforms," *Guardian*, March 11, 2008; "With New Law, China Reports Drop in Executions," *New York Times*, June 9, 2007; "China 'Gold Medal' for Executions," BBC News, April 15, 2008; "China Switches to Lethal Injection," *Guardian*, January 4, 2008; "Two Are Executed for Roles in China Milk Scandal," *New York Times*, November 25, 2009; "Akmal Shaikh's Final Hours," "China's Execution of Akmal Shaikh Enrages British Leaders," *Guardian*, December 29, 2009. The fullest survey of world trends is that offered by Hood and Hoyle, *Death Penalty*.

29. "Dictator Who Ruled Iraq with Violence Is Hanged for Crimes against Humanity," *New York Times*, December 30, 2006; "Saddam Hussein Executed in Iran," BBC News, December 30, 2006; "In the Days before Hanging, a Push for Revenge and a Push Back from the US," *New York Times*, January 7, 2007.

30. "Saddam Hussein Executed in Iraq," BBC News, December 30, 2006.

31. "In Days Before Hanging, a Push for Revenge and a Push Back from the U.S.," *New York Times*, January 7, 2007; "Hussein Executed with 'Fear in His Face,'" *Los Angeles Times*, December 30, 2006; "Saddam Hussein Executed in Iraq," BBC News, December 30, 2006; "Guard 'Quizzed over Saddam Video,'" BBC News, January 3, 2007.

32. Peter Linebaugh, "The Tyburn Riot against the Surgeons," in *Albion's Fatal Tree*, ed. Douglas Hay et al. (New York, 1975), 64–117.

33. One notable exception to this rule is the collection of essays in a volume edited by Austin Sarat and Christian Boulanger, *The Cultural Lives of Capital Punishment* (Stanford, 2005).

34. Roger Hood refers to the paradox of abolition accompanied by extensive extrajudicial killing under military regimes in Latin America. See Hood, *The Death Penalty: A Worldwide Perspective* (Oxford, 2002), 155–56.

35. Christian Boulanger and Austin Sarat, "Putting Culture into the Picture," in Boulanger and Sarat, *Cultural Lives*, 1–45.

36. David Johnson, "The Death Penalty in Japan: Secrecy, Silence, and Salience," in Boulanger and Sarat, *Cultural Lives*, 251–73.

37. For a brief discussion of Islamic societies, see Hood and Hoyle, *Death Penalty*, 66–73.

38. "McVeigh Execution: A 'Completion of Justice,'" CNN.Com, June 11, 2001.

39. Anthony Amsterdam comment at NYU conference, May 2007. See also Agata Fijalkowski, "Capital Punishment in Poland: An Aspect of the 'Cultural Life' of Death Penalty Discourse"; and Alfred Oehlers and Nicole Tarulevicz, "Capital Punishment and the Culture of Developmentalism in Singapore," both in Boulanger and Sarat, *Cultural Lives*, 147–68, 291–307; Hood and Hoyle, *Death Penalty*, 53, 375.

40. "Texas Turns aside Pressure on Execution of 5 Mexicans," *New York Times*, July 18, 2008; "Texas Executes Mexican Despite Objections," *New York Times*, August 6, 2008.

41. See also David Garland, "Capital Punishment and American Culture," *Punishment and Society*, 7 (2005): 347-65.

42. Mitchell Merback, *The Thief, the Cross, and the Wheel: Pain and the Spectacle of Punishment in Medieval and Renaissance Europe* (London, 1999); Thomas Laqueur, "Festival of Punishment," *London Review of Books*, October 5, 2000.

43. This argument is forcefully presented by Douglas Hay, "Property, Authority, and the Criminal Law," in *Albion's Fatal Tree*, ed. D. Hay et al., 17-63 (New York, 1975). See also Randall McGowen, "The Image of Justice and Reform of the Criminal Law in Early Nineteenth-Century England," *Buffalo Law Review* 32 (1983): 89-125.

44. "Study Finds Record Number of Inmates Serving Life Terms," *New York Times*, July 23, 2009.

45. For one discussion that makes this connection, see Marie Gottschalk, *The Prison and the Gallows: The Politics of Mass Incarceration in America* (Cambridge, 2006), esp. chap. 9.

46. Atul Gawande, "Hellhole," *New Yorker*, March 30, 2009.

2

Modes of Capital Punishment

The Death Penalty in Historical Perspective

DAVID GARLAND

Capital punishment has been practiced in most known societies over the course of human history. In modern liberal democracies, however, the legitimacy and effectiveness of the institution have increasingly come into question. In these nations, with their commitment to limiting state violence, promoting social welfare, and respecting human dignity, the death penalty exists, if it does, in tension with important political institutions and cultural commitments. Where not altogether abolished—as it is throughout Europe and most of the western world—such societies now use the death penalty much less often and in forms that are increasingly restrained and refined.

This transformation is remarkable. The death penalty once formed an elementary particle of governmental power in every nation state. Today the practice is widely regarded as shameful and is prohibited throughout most of the Western world. What happened?

The death penalty can be defined as a practice whereby a properly constituted public authority puts to death a convicted offender as punishment for a crime. It is distinct from unauthorized forms of killing, such as revenge killing, murder, or lynching, and from non-penal forms of state killing, whether legal (human sacrifice, killing in war) or illegal (political killings, summary executions). Stripped to its essence, it involves nothing more elaborate than putting lawbreakers to death—an undertaking that has obvious utility for group authorities and is readily available without the need of elaborate technology, know-how, or social arrangements. These characteristics, together with its capacity to terrorize anyone who fears death, explain why the death penalty was close to a cultural universal for millennia prior to the nineteenth century.[1]

In the early modern period, newly emergent state authorities took up the death penalty and accorded it a central role in the task of state building. Elaborate public ceremonies, horrifying execution techniques, and ritual proclamations were developed as so many means to this end. By the mid-nineteenth century, in a context of increasingly well-established and rationalized states, capital punishment's primary purpose had altered, so that what had once been an instrument of rule, essential to state security, became an instrument of penal policy, focused on the narrower goals of doing justice and controlling crime.

As the institution's functions changed, so too did its forms. The death penalty came to be formatted as a penal sanction rather than a political spectacle. Its focus came to center upon criminal rather than political offenses. Its executions came to be more swiftly administered, not in the political space of the town square but in the penal space of the jail yard. By the late twentieth century, in the very different context of the modern liberal democratic welfare state, capital punishment had ceased to be a central plank in Western nations' apparatus of crime control and had become increasingly rare and controversial. By century's end, it had been abolished by most Western nations other than America, and by many non-Western nations besides.[2]

This long-term process of transformation should not be mistaken for a narrative of moral and political progress. The decline of the death penalty did not necessarily signal the diminution of punishment or the end of state violence, even in Western democracies. Nor was it the story of a "civilizing process" taking hold of capital punishment, though some of the processes highlighted by Norbert Elias certainly played a part.[3] Nor, finally, was it a narrative of the death penalty's continual decline. At the dawn of the modern period, between the fifteenth and seventeenth centuries, there was a massive increase in the use, display, and intensity of the death penalty as it became a central weapon in the armory of newly formed states struggling to establish sovereign power. And at various moments in the nineteenth and twentieth centuries, several European nations that had reduced their reliance on the death penalty, or abolished it altogether, returned to it with a vengeance, whether in response to political instability or in pursuit of totalitarian power.[4]

There was no teleological process at work in these transformations, no inexorable law that dictated the course of historical events. But the historical processes that did, in fact, unfold produced a definite developmental pattern. This pattern emerged because the forces of state formation and rationalization, liberalization and democratization, "civilization" and humanization have, for the most part, shaped modern Western history. And these political and cultural processes have had definite consequences for the shape and survival of the death penalty.

The long-term movement toward a more restrained, refined, and reduced death penalty occurred for reasons that are quite intelligible. Among the most important are: (1) the efforts of state authorities to render their use of the death penalty more effective and more legitimate in its changing contexts of use; (2) the success of liberal political forces in limiting state power and establishing legal protections for individuals; (3) the struggles of democrats to equalize punishment and to extend liberal protections to all social groups; (4) the efforts of cultural elites, disturbed by the sight of raw violence and unruly mobs, to "civilize" the institution; and (5) the efforts of anti-gallows reformers, variously motivated by religious faith, fellow feeling, or humanitarian sentiment, to reduce the suffering of convicted offenders and uphold their right to life.[5]

The historical situations in which these social processes were translated into specific reforms were often recurring ones (shifts between political regimes, the installation of left-wing governments, responses to scandals, repair of malfunctioning processes, etc.) and the actors translating them into action were typically state officials, responding to a changed political climate, to criticism, or to control problems. The final stage of complete, nation-wide abolition was typically a top-down reform legislated by a political elite in the face of popular opposition or indifference.[6]

These reforms occurred when large-scale processes of change connected with the specific concerns of well-placed actors. They failed to occur when the operation of these processes was obstructed by circumstances such as political instability, high rates of criminal violence, public insecurity, effective political resistance, and so on. Anyone wishing to understand the survival of the death penalty in the United States and the peculiar form it now exhibits—and these are the central themes of the present volume—must understand these causal forces and the situations in which they typically play out. In the present chapter I outline the major historical modalities of capital punishment, showing their relation to the form and character of the states that deployed them. The resulting analysis is intended to orient thinking about those modern liberal democratic nations—primarily the United States but also, to the extent that my account of Western history has implications outside the West, Japan and India—where the death penalty currently persists.

"Why is America not abolitionist?" is a question one hears frequently today. But just because it is often asked does not mean that it is well posed or the correct place to begin. To take abolition as our analytical focus would be to collapse a complex story into a simple one, to reduce a long-term process to a single moment, and to highlight a binary opposition (between "abolition" and "retention") in a way that obscures a continuum of different arrangements that lie between these two poles.[7] Viewed in a long-term and comparative perspective, the fundamental problem is not to explain American "retention" but to explain why the death penalty diminished and eventually disappeared from the penal and political arsenals of other Western states. First, we need to trace the rise of capital punishment in the early modern period and the causes that produced it. Then we need to trace the processes that led to its subsequent long-term decline. And, finally, we need to situate America's specific trajectory within this larger comparative history.

Abolition is now the Western norm, but for most of human history the death penalty was what anthropologists call a "cultural universal," forming an element of every organized society.[8] Even today, at the end of the late-twentieth-century wave of abolition, more than one hundred nations still retain capital punishment in some form and the vast majority of the world's population still lives under its threat.[9] The age of abolition is a decidedly Western phenomenon.

These facts should hardly surprise us. If we set aside contemporary moral qualms and political objections to its use, it is easy to see why capital punishment has been so widely embraced by ruling groups. "Death is . . . of all dreadful things the most dreadful," Dr. Johnson remarked, "an evil beyond which nothing can be threatened."[10] As a political weapon and a penal instrument, the death penalty has an irresistible power. Putting political enemies, serious wrongdoers, and dangerous individuals to death is an obvious, effective, and efficient way for authorities to eliminate the threat that such individuals represent. Imposing a death penalty on lawbreakers permits the punishing authority to proclaim its power, impress onlookers, and denounce the proscribed conduct, while simultaneously exacting revenge, undoing pollution, restoring social order, and sending a warning to would-be offenders. This very useful practice, "rife with utilitarian purposes of every kind," requires little in the way of technology or know-how and can be inflicted by states that have no apparatus of prisons and penitentiaries.[11] As a punishment, death has elemental force and meaning.

Nor has this self-evident efficacy diminished in the contemporary period. If swiftly applied, frequently utilized, and imposed with the requisite amount of pain and publicity—as it still is in places such as China, Iran, Singapore, Sudan, and Saudi Arabia—the death penalty retains much of its power as a penal and political instrument. If anything, its potential is enhanced as these societies become more developed, more affluent, and more inclined to value human life.

The Western Pattern of Transformation

The transformation of the Western death penalty has occurred as a structured, developmental change. Following a sharp increase in its use and intensity in the fifteenth and sixteenth centuries, a pattern of declining use and decreased intensity began in the late seventeenth century and continued, with rapid spurts and occasional interruptions, for three centuries thereafter. Historian Richard Evans puts it thus:

> What strikes the observer . . . is the fact that similar changes in penal practice happened virtually everywhere at roughly the same epoch. In almost all major European states, the eighteenth and nineteenth centuries saw a diminution of public punishment, the abolition of torture, the banishing of the more baroque cruelties from the scene of the scaffold, and the decisive phase in the rise of imprisonment. Everywhere, the middle of the nineteenth century saw the ending of public executions, or at least their restriction to a small number of spectators and the stripping away of the most elaborate embellishments of public ritual associated with them. . . . Right across Europe, the same period saw the culmination of a long-heralded crisis in the legitimacy of capital punishment.[12]

Historians view "developmental" claims with some skepticism, so let me stress several caveats. To identify a developmental trajectory is not to imply an inexorable movement or a teleological progress. Like any historical process, this development has definite causes and conditions of existence—it does not just happen. If these causes and conditions are absent, as they were in many non-Western nations, the death penalty transformations discussed here will not occur. If these causes cease to operate, so does the process: the pattern of change has altered and reversed in the past, and it can do so again in the future. Nor is there anything mysterious about it. Identifiable social processes and mechanisms have driven the death penalty's transformation, and their implications and effects can be clearly traced. Finally, although there is a discernible Western pattern of concurrent development across national boundaries over long periods, each nation's developmental path has been distinctive in certain respects, with its own unique concatenation of events and converging processes. Instead of thinking of a "normative" general history (with America as a deviant "exception") we should think in terms of a transnational developmental pattern composed of distinct but converging national histories—a general history within which America can certainly be included.[13]

The Three Eras of Capital Punishment

We can distinguish three eras of capital punishment in the West since the Middle Ages: the "early modern," the "modern," and the "late modern." In each of these eras the institutions of capital punishment operated rather differently, each exhibiting a distinctive modality with distinctive forms and functions.[14] Each modality is associated with a different historical period and form of social organization (early modern society, modernity, late modernity) and each one is loosely associated with a distinctive state form (the absolutist state, the nineteenth-century liberal state, the late twentieth-century liberal democratic welfare state). As we will see, the first two modalities—the "early modern" and the "modern"—are sharply differentiated in most respects, whereas the third mode—the "late modern"—is a variant of the second, though it is sufficiently distinct to warrant separate classification. Furthermore, because the present volume aims to use the past to help explain the present, it is important to highlight the distinctive characteristics of the capital punishment modality that exists in the United States in the contemporary period.

In the first two periods, capital punishment was a prominent and structurally important social practice, though its structural position changed, as did its forms and functions, as it shifted from an "early modern" to a "modern" mode. In the third period—which might be termed the "late modernity" of the last decades of the twentieth century and the first decades of the twenty-first—one sees the decline and marginalization of capital punishment as a social institution and its rapid disappearance from most Western legal codes. Where it survives—as it does in parts of the United States—the institution's forms and functions have been further altered, its use more attenuated, and its place in social organization more controversial.

The Early Modern Mode

The emergence of the modern political entity known as "the state" was a long-term process that developed at different rates in different regions. In England, state formation was apparent as early as the twelfth century; elsewhere, in Italy or Germany, for example, unified national states emerged much later. From 1400 to 1700 is the crucial period in which this process took place. By the end of that period, a European system of sovereign states had emerged, the existence of which was explicitly recognized in the 1648 Peace of Westphalia.

A critical element of state formation was the effort of nascent political authorities to exert a monopoly of power over "their" territory. This historic struggle to impose sovereign rule gave a new prominence and intensity to capital punishment. Prior to the emergence of the state, the death penalty appears to have been carried out without elaborate ceremony. Discussing the late medieval evidence from Germany, Evans says that "illustrations of executions in the fourteenth and fifteenth centuries show them as casual and unceremonial affairs, with a handful of people standing informally around while the hangman does his work." Referring to England, Sharpe writes that there "is little evidence that any elaborate ceremonial attended the execution of felons in the later middle ages." Otterbein's ethnographic survey also suggests that pre-state societies were mostly executed in secret or without fanfare.[15]

The emergence of sovereign states altered these older practices in several respects.[16] First of all, death penalties became the prerogative of state authorities who asserted their monopoly over legitimate violence and prohibited traditional practices of private vendetta and vengeance. Second, death penalties came to be imposed and administered under the auspices of the royal courts, imparting a greater degree of rule-governed formality and legal rationality. And, third, executions became more public, more elaborately ceremonial, and more violent, as the new states sought to use shock-and-awe tactics to impress the populace and strike fear in the hearts of enemies.[17] Though we sometimes describe cruel punishments as "medieval," it was, in fact, the emergence of despotic states in the late medieval and early modern period that transformed these execution events into elaborate spectacles of suffering. It was not Europe's medieval lords but the absolutist rulers who replaced them that gave capital punishment its greatest cruelty, intensity, and display.

In the states of early modern Europe—many but not all of them absolutist in form—the death penalty operated within a distinctive political and penological context.[18] Politically, the state was usually weak and unstable. It lacked any powerful infrastructure of control or any settled claim on the allegiance of its subjects. It faced the perennial threat of rebellion by internal enemies or war waged by hostile neighboring states. In respect of criminal justice, early modern states were similarly weak, lacking any well-developed criminal justice apparatus, police force, or prison system.[19] Moreover, the early modern state's communication capacity was limited, with few means other than public, theatrical displays with which to assert claims to authority. Consequently, as Esther Cohen notes, "government power was often displayed in visual theatrical form: solemn royal or urban processions, festivals, and most commonly, the execution of criminals."[20]

It is against this background that the death penalty became a vital instrument of state rule and developed its distinctive early modern, absolutist character. Later, as governmental capacities increased and a differentiated penal infrastructure was built, the death penalty's all-purpose utility began to diminish. Other sanctions—banishment, transportation, galley slavery, public works, and, above all, imprisonment—arose to take its place.

Capital Punishment's Functions in the Early Modern Era

The imposition of the death penalty is, first and foremost, an exercise of power—wherever, whenever, and however it occurs. Any account of the death penalty's development must focus, therefore, on the fundamental question of power: its dispersion and concentration; its claims to authority and the rules for its legitimate exercise; its developing techniques and their relation to social organization; and, finally, its expression through communicative symbols and cultural performance.

In the early modern era, death sentences had a variety of uses, among them the maintenance of order, the doing of justice, and the reinforcement of social hierarchies. But whatever other purposes the institution might serve, at the core of the death penalty's meaning was the assertion, preservation, and protection of the authority of the state. The elaborate cruelty and display with which state officials put enemies to death on the scaffold was driven less by a passion for punishment than by the practical need to demonstrate sovereignty to skeptics.[21]

AN ELEMENTARY PARTICLE OF STATE POWER. The early phases of state formation brought a new importance to capital punishment, as aspiring rulers shifted their efforts from military conquest to internal pacification and the production of order. Rulers staged the death penalty as a military ceremony intended to terrorize enemies and impress onlookers with spectacular displays of ritualized violence.[22] Especially in absolutist states, the execution became a structural support in the edifice of state power and a necessary concomitant of social order. As Joseph de Maistre put it: "all grandeur, all power, all subordination rests on the executioner: he is the horror and the bond of human association. Remove this incomprehensible agent from the world and at every moment order gives way to chaos, thrones topple, and society disappears. God, who has created sovereignty, has also made punishments."[23]

If the spectacular execution was the product of early modern state formation, its political utility ensured its continuing use by states keen to project an appearance of political strength. Richard Evans highlights how the regimes that emerged in continental Europe toward the end of the seventeenth century relied on capital punishment to communicate their political claims:

> In the world of Absolutism, punishment had to be seen as coming directly from the state itself, through concrete physical actions undertaken by the state's servant, the executioner, on the body of the offender. The full execution ritual, with its elaborate procession and ceremonial procedures at the scaffold, was a phenomenon of the late seventeenth and eighteenth centuries, and crowds attending it were a consequence of the state's increasing tendency to orchestrate such occasions. . . . Absolutism, from the great patrimonies of Austria and Prussia, Saxony and Bavaria, down to the petty principalities and city-states that littered Central Europe in this period, demanded that sovereignty be asserted with pomp and circumstance.[24]

The watchword here was "terror." Unable to rule by consent and close control, the early modern state sought to rule by fear. Death, being the greatest terror, became a technique of rule, and early modern states were endlessly inventive in their elaboration of scaffold torments.

The chief targets of this ferocity were enemies of the state and those who threatened public order: above all, offenders convicted of treason, *lese majesty*, riot, or sedition. The most horrendous executions were reserved not for murderers or common criminals but for political offenders. Traitors were hung, drawn, and quartered, their heads placed on spikes, their body parts displayed around the kingdom. Treasonable offenses of a lesser kind—"petit treason" against masters or husbands—also drew unusually severe punishments, such as burning at the stake.[25]

Political purposes continued to define the death penalty well into the eighteenth century, even in non-absolutist states such as England. V.A.C. Gatrell says of seventeenth-and eighteenth-century English executions that "the order of the world depended on these slaughters" and that "the sanction of the gallows and the rhetoric of the death sentence were central to all relations of authority in Georgian England."[26] Douglas Hay makes the same point when he writes that "the rulers of eighteenth-century England cherished the death penalty" and argues that "the criminal law, more than any other social institution, made it possible to govern eighteenth-century England without a police force and without a large army."[27]

Throughout this whole period, the use of the death penalty was adjusted to sustain unstable regimes in the face of insurrection. Political crises, threats to the state, acts of insubordination—all were occasions for the harsh deployment of scaffold punishments and the setting of ruthless examples. In sixteenth-century England, under the Tudors, execution ceremonies became more elaborate and traitors were singled out for especially horrific treatment.[28] But later, when the state's power was better established and its authority grounded in consent as well as coercion, the gallows became a less prominent instrument of rule. Thus in England, by the late eighteenth century, the guiding principle of state killing was more restrained: "to create examples, not a charnel house."[29] Governing authority in these more settled times was displayed by merciful pardons as well as spectacular deaths.

The predominant model of rule on the European continent in the early modern period was that of the absolute monarch. This absolutist conception of power colored the process of law, leading to secret charges, state-directed prosecutions, torture, *lettres de cachet*, and an absence of procedural protections for the individual accused. Investigative torture took place in secret, and the processes of trial and conviction were shrouded in darkness: it was not until the execution that the outcome of this process was brought into the broad daylight. Even in non-absolutist England, with its parliamentary monarchy and its tradition of the rights of freeborn individuals, it was not until the Treason Act of 1694 that any suspect was granted the right to counsel or the right to hear the charges ranged against him.[30]

In that age of faith, secular and religious forms of authority were closely integrated and state officials leaned on the church to augment their power. Like all state ceremonies of this period, the execution was also a religious event, framed in a discourse of eternal verities as well as of worldly power, presided over by clerics as well as state officials. Writing of English executions, McGowen says, "theology structure[d] and infused the gallows."[31] Discussing the German experience, Evans states, "The language by which condemned people were described emphasized above all the moral and religious aspects of their status. They were known as 'poor sinners.'" The condemned were allowed priests or pastors, and were encouraged to repent and take communion.[32]

Early modern execution ceremonies focused on the state of the condemned's soul: his every word and gesture was scrutinized by the crowd for signs of atonement and the prospect of redemption. In the ritual of state killing, larger questions of eternal judgment were also at stake. The condemned was going to die and meet his maker—a fate that every onlooker feared and that each would one day experience—and he was groomed and prepared accordingly. His last meal recalled the Last Supper. His procession to the scaffold recalled the procession to Calvary. His last words—prepared with the help of a cleric—were usually those of a remorseful penitent, offering himself up to God's mercy. His torment on the scaffold symbolically repeated that of Christ on the Cross, and suggested the fate of all believers at life's end. In addressing the themes of crime and the relation of subject to sovereign, the scaffold drama also raised the question of death and man's relation to God. The authority of one great power flowed into that of the other.[33]

Being an age of faith, the early modern period was also an age of folk superstition and magical belief.[34] Like funerals and other death rites, the scaffold was surrounded by myths and magical practices such as the drinking of the corpse's blood or the taking of relics (pieces of the rope, amputated fingers, etc.) as magical cures.[35] The execution sometimes took on the status of a totem, and practices of avoidance and respect—touching the apparatus, avoiding the site afterward, and so on—are reported from France, Germany, England, and early America.[36]

CONTROLLING CRIME AND DOING JUSTICE. If making and maintaining state power was the primary purpose of early modern capital punishment it was by no means its only one. Common criminals were also put to death for a great variety of offenses, although these "enemies of the people" were executed without the ceremony and intensity reserved for enemies of the state.[37]

In his discussion of eighteenth-century English judges, Hay describes their role as a dual one, sometimes meting out "ordinary criminal punishment," at other times assuming a more political role in the maintenance of state security. "The fine-tuning of ordinary criminal punishment was part of their semi-annual role in the assize courts, and eight times a year in the Old Bailey." Here they "adjusted the weight of the law accordingly, usually pardoning sheep and cattle thieves, always extending mercy to pickpockets, hanging coiners and deferring to the Bank's determination to hang forgers, and increasing the overall number of executions when high crime rates seemed to require more examples at the gallows." But in dangerous periods, Hay goes on to say, when faced with treason, insurrection, or dissent, these same judges functioned "in their role as rulers." They believed that in times of popular insurrection capital punishment "was the ultimate guarantee of the survival of the oligarchic, monarchical, aristocratic, and profoundly undemocratic state they served."[38]

Over the course of time, as state rule became more legitimate, state officials represented executions as the enforcement of law rather than the display of power. Authorities increasingly represented themselves as serving the broader ends of crime control, criminal justice, and public safety. Indeed, as Esther Cohen notes, "In many European languages, the term for executions was derived from the word for justice: 'faire justice' in French, 'giustiziare' in Italian, 'Hinrichtung' in German." Cohen continues by observing that "although the King's justice and the people's interests were by no means identical, the association between the two was constantly asserted."[39]

The early modern state's death penalty also had a penal function: the scaffold was used to dispatch criminal offenders as well as political ones. Terror served the purpose of deterrence, aided by the speed with which executions followed on conviction. (English statutes specified that executions take place on the next day but one following the imposition of sentence. The condemned was to be kept in solitary confinement on a bread and water diet in the interim.)[40] Early modern governments lacked much of the institutional infrastructure needed for the generalized use of penalties such as imprisonment, transportation, or public works (though each of these sanctions was used in this period), so the death penalty—supplemented by corporal and shaming punishments—formed a mainstay of the criminal justice meted out.

REINFORCING PRIVATE INTERESTS. The early modern death penalty had a further use besides shoring up state power and controlling crime—one that reached beyond the emerging public sphere into the world of private interests and market relations. The early modern state was an amalgam of public and private interests, and sections of the ruling class frequently appropriated the death penalty to their own use. Economic stability was also a state interest, and offenses such as forgery and smuggling that directly threatened the exchequer were ruthlessly suppressed.[41] But the pattern of capital legislation suggests that death was often doled out to protect the commercial interests of particular groups rather than those of the general public.

Take, for example, the notorious expansion of England's capital laws between 1688 and 1820, when the capital code grew from about fifty to more than two hundred offenses, almost all of them offenses against property forming a "Bloody Code" that shored up private interests using the state's power to kill. As Hay puts it, "the death penalty was routinely added to protect . . . investments."[42] Perhaps the most striking evidence of this can be found in instances where the intended deterrent backfired, prompting appeals from the property owners to *lessen* the severity of the law. Thus when juries began to nullify in capital cases involving theft from bleaching grounds—because they regarded the mandatory death sentence as too severe—the bleaching merchants demanded that the penalty be downgraded so that juries might convict and their property be protected.[43]

The pardon system was another mechanism that facilitated the private uses of capital punishment. As Douglas Hay has shown, the pardon process helped generate an informal system of gift giving and return benefits that amounted to a usable system of social control operating in the shadow of the scaffold.[44] The power to intercede on behalf of a servant, employee, or tenant—a power that might result in grants of mercy by the Crown—gave landowners and the propertied classes an additional claim to personal authority. "The pardon [was] important because it often put the principal instrument of legal terror—the gallows—directly in the hands of those who held power." These acts of mercy, which over time occurred with some frequency ("the papers of any large landed proprietor are peppered with appeals for pardons") helped create "the mental structures of paternalism"[45] The ability to intercede on behalf of "their people" in matters of life and death was of great importance to the eighteenth-century English gentry. It enabled them to give highly valued gifts to their subordinates and provide favors that would not easily be forgotten. The death penalty thereby provided already powerful individuals with an additional source of personalistic power and prestige.

Forms and Their Relation to Functions

MULTIPLE FORMS OF DEATH. There were many ways to die on the early modern scaffold. Judicial killings were carefully calibrated events and the form of death was modulated depending upon the condemned person's rank, status, gender, and offense. Instead of a single death for all, there were lesser deaths and greater deaths, aggravated deaths and mitigated ones. For the most serious offenders, the punishment continued beyond death, in the form of postmortem desecrations and the display of body parts.[46] For less serious offenders, the execution might be enacted in a symbolic form that stopped short of death. And for some individuals—members of the clergy, first offenders, and pregnant women—forms of relief such as "benefit of clergy" or "benefit of belly" allowed them to escape the scaffold.[47]

For those put to death, different methods were reserved for different classes. As a French legal saying put it, "The axe for the noble, the rope for the villain"[48]—a status-based distinction grounded in an old tradition that viewed hanging as "the most shameful death" and beheading as the "most honorable and mildest."[49] Such distinctions were characteristic of this period, though the symbolic connotations of each method varied from place to place. In France, according to Hunt, there were five ways to be put to death: "decapitation for nobles; hanging for common criminals; drawing and quartering for offenses against the sovereign known as *lese-majesty*; burning at the stake for heresy, magic, arson, poisoning, bestiality, and sodomy; and breaking on the wheel for murder or highway robbery."[50] In the Netherlands there were three: "the gallows, the wheel, and fire." Blok tells us that "ordinary thieves were hanged; murderers and bandit leaders were broken on the wheel; and arson and sacrilege (e.g. church robberies) were punished by various forms of burning."[51] In Italy, according to Merback, "the penalties perceived by both elites and popular culture as disgraceful included hanging, breaking with the wheel, burning and every variety of dismemberment. In contrast, decapitation by sword epitomized the honorable death; unlike its opposites, it brought no stain of infamy on either the condemned or, just as important, his or her family."[52] Death by sword—an echo of death on the battlefield—was everywhere the entitlement of noblemen and high-ranking patricians.[53]

The multi-form character of the institution expressed the stratified nature of early modern society. Even when being punished for criminal wrongdoing, the rank of a nobleman entitled him to greater respect than a commoner, just as a clergyman could expect to be treated differently than a layman, a man than a woman. But the differentiated death penalty was more than an expression of social hierarchy. The differentiation of its forms—aggravated and mitigated, with and without torture, with and without degradation, going beyond death or stopping short of death—also points to its multiple uses and the wide range of offenses for which it was prescribed. In a political context where it was essential and a penal context with few alternatives, the death penalty became varied and versatile.

THE SPECTACLE. Early modern executions were meant to be seen. They took place on elevated platforms in town centers, preceded by lengthy processions, and performed with great ceremony. Executions in Paris took place in the Place de Grève, the same public square "where fireworks celebrated births and deaths in the royal family."[54] The stress was on making examples, on demonstrating a claim, on communicating with the watching crowd. And that communication was achieved by dramatic theater and symbolic gestures encoding cultural understandings of power and authority. Executions, in short, were rituals of power and their form was designed accordingly. David Cooper's description of a London execution in the eighteenth century gives a sense of this:

Capital convicts of the City of London and the County of Middlesex were drawn in open carts, pinioned ropes dangling necklace-like from their necks, a distance of two miles from Newgate Gaol to Tyburn. A procession led by the City marshals on horseback, the under-sheriff, a group of peace officers and a body of constables with staves accompanied the convict and his executioner who rode in the open cart. A number of javelin-men brought up the rear. If the criminal was well known, the entourage had two sheriffs in their coaches, each holding his sceptre of office.[55]

Capital punishment and executions varied from place to place (more secular here, more religious there) and from time to time (more unruly on this occasion, more solemn another time). Spierenburg notes that scaffold speeches by the condemned were standard in England, Germany, and France but not in the Netherlands, where the condemned was allowed to pray or sing a psalm but not make a speech.[56] Sharpe tells us that, in England, executions after 1700 became less religious and more secular, though the evidence for this has been contested.[57] Eighteenth-century English executions also became more liable to attract unruly and resistant crowds—or so the authorities complained—until in 1783 the execution venue was moved from Tyburn Field to Newgate Prison, which permitted the authorities to impose tighter control over the event.[58]

The historical evidence from Western Europe and colonial America leaves us in some doubt about the nature of the interaction that occurred around the gallows. Historians debate over how onlookers experienced these executions and the extent to which authorities succeeded in controlling the events and their meaning. Depending on which interpretation one prefers, the execution was a solemn state theater, a pious religious ritual, or an unruly popular carnival—and any specific execution probably displayed traces of each.[59] Not in doubt, however, is that the early modern execution was enacted as a public spectacle in full view of the assembled populace.

SYMBOLIC COMMUNICATION. Rituals deal in symbolic meaning. Their staging, scripts, and performances are designed to embody ideas and to communicate with audiences. Symbols—whether in the form of words, dress, gestures, or choreographed conduct—were the medium through which these communications operated, and executions were always scenes of symbolic action and meaningful gesture. Some of the most common symbols had a standard meaning that was widely understood by people everywhere: the signs of military and religious power, for example, or the brutal significance of physical degradations and dismemberments. People understood that execution by the sword—which echoed death on the battlefield—was nobler than hanging or burning at the stake. And they understood the religious parallels between the sinner's execution and Christ on the Cross. As Esther Cohen points out, the early modern execution utilized a stock set of ritual gestures and symbols that could endure over long periods because popular culture ensured their intelligibility. "The ritual was worthless unless people knew and understood its symbolism."[60]

But if the execution's symbols had to be intelligible, they did not have to be simple. Here is Chief Justice Coke's exegesis of the capital sentence he imposed on the defendants in the English Gunpowder Plot case of 1606:

> At first, the traitor shall be drawn to the place of execution, as not being worthy any more to tread upon the face of the earth, whereof he was made; and with his head declining downwards, and as near the ground as may be though unfit to take the benefit of the common air. He shall next be hanged up by the neck between heaven and earth, as deemed unworthy of both or either, as likewise that the eyes of men may behold and their hearts condemn him. Then is he to be cut down alive, and to have his parts of generation cut off, and burnt before his face, as being unworthily begotten, and unfit to leave any race after him. His inlayed parts shall be also taken out, and burnt, for it was his heart, which harbored such horrible treason. His head shall be cut off, which imagined the mischief; and lastly, his body shall be quartered, and the quarters set up in some high and eminent place, to the view and detestation of men, and to become prey for the fowls of the air. And this is the regard due to traitors, for it is the physic of government, to let out corrupt blood.[61]

This practice of symbolic communication gave a special character to the suffering of the condemned. The torments imposed were more than just greater or lesser degrees of pain. Each specific action was designed to signify, to convey a message, to embody a statement. As Merback puts it: "the signs of the body in pain were not . . . simply a 'shameful side effect' to be tolerated for the sake of justice; they were instead the focal point of comprehension which gave the spectacle its religious meaning."[62] Randall McGowen makes the same point when he says, "The violence of punishment was a language employed by authority to write the message of justice."[63]

If these public rituals depended for their effectiveness on the existence of commonly understood symbols, they also depended on the existence of a community for whom these symbols were meaningful. Such communities existed in early modern towns and cities, and in the wider community of Christian believers, which is why rituals and symbols could be such an important aspect of secular and spiritual authority. Ritualized processions, scaffold ceremonies, choreographed performances, gallows literature, broadsheets, woodcuts, and last dying speeches—so many means of communicating to a community primed and ready to engage with the event and reflect on its meaning.[64]

REPRESENTATIONS OF THE CONDEMNED. Early modern authorities gave few signs that they felt compassion or fellow feeling toward the individuals they sentenced to die. Gatrell tells us that Edward Coke and his contemporaries cared little about the condemned man's fate and "would neither have contemplated the biographies of the humblest who hanged nor thought the worse of the law for their hanging."[65] Spierenburg describes the attitude of the Dutch authorities toward executions as "familiarity largely unhampered by feelings of repugnance."[66] But though there is scant evidence of sympathetic identification, the condemned man was not represented as alien or "other" in the way that he sometimes is today. Criminals were regarded as sinners, as lawbreakers, as individuals who had forfeited their right to live, but they were not characterized as inhuman. To members of the political class, a lower-class criminal may have been beneath notice, but he was not demonized. That came later, when a widespread commitment to the "sanctity of the individual" and the "dignity of man" rendered it more problematic to put human beings to death. For the early modern authorities, the dignity of a common criminal counted for little compared to the majesty of a monarch or the interests of state.

REPRESENTATIONS OF DEATH AND DYING. If executions were rituals of punishment they were also rituals of death. As Evans says of the early modern German institution, "The ceremony of execution would have been popularly understood, among other things, as a variant of the normal ceremony of death and burial. Both were rites of passage from life to death."[67] The killing of the offender proceeded against a background of belief that gave it a meaning rather different from that which prevails today.[68] The condemned man was not being launched into nothingness: he was going to God's judgment and perhaps to a life beyond. His death occurred within a system of belief that held out expectation of an afterlife, of heaven and of hell. That the condemned man died was less important to the watching crowd than the question of how he died. Did he confess his crimes? Did he plead for God's mercy? Did he express remorse and seek redemption? His suffering was less significant than the responses that his torments elicited and what they said about the state of his soul.[69]

In the early modern period, "the sight of decaying human bodies was more commonplace. Everyone, including children, knew what they looked like; and because everyone knew, they could be spoken of more freely."[70] No attempt was made to disguise the dying that took place on the scaffold, and there was little apparent embarrassment about the facts of pain and death it put on display. On the contrary, the death and its meaning were elaborated and amplified, vocalized by "death talk specialists" (the priests on the scaffold, the clerics who helped prepare the "last dying speech"), and memorialized by broadsheets and gallows literature. This discourse seized on the death as a cautionary moral tale and an occasion for religious reflection, as well as an affirmation of the rulers' authority.[71]

A PUNISHMENT BEYOND QUESTION. In early modern society, anyone who tested the authority of a great power could be made to pay with his life. Individual lives were valued—as they are in any society that is not a suicide club—but they were not regarded as the supreme value. The worth of a lowly individual was no match for an angered God or an injured sovereign.[72] There was therefore no deep controversy about the state's right to kill lawbreakers. Writing of seventeenth-century England, Beattie notes that "[t]here is little evidence of a serious disagreement in society about capital punishment itself. It was justified on grounds of both social utility and religious authority."[73] Radzinowicz suggests the same when he notes that practically all capital offenses enacted by the British Parliament in the seventeenth and eighteenth centuries "were created more or less as a matter of course by a placid and uninterested Parliament. In nine cases out of ten there was no debate and no opposition."[74] And, according to Banner, no one seriously proposed that capital punishment be abolished in colonial America: "It fulfilled the moral expectations of most colonial Americans most of the time.... Hardly anyone suggested that it be used more sparingly, much less that it be abandoned."[75]

Nor was capital punishment cause for anxiety or embarrassment on the part of the authorities. "The rulers of English society in the early modern period were . . . unembarrassed by the violence of their punishments," McGowen tells us. "Hanging, branding, flogging, the pillory, drawing and quartering, burning alive—all were accepted as legitimate forms."[76] In contrast to late modern Western society, where death penalties are controver-

sial and executions take place in semi-secret, laden with anxiety, the absolutist execution was highly integrated into the social fabric of early modern
societies.[77]

A GRAND TRAGEDY. Early modern capital punishment had the character
of a tragedy. Having been convicted of a capital offense, and in the absence
of any merciful intercession, the rebellious lawbreaker would inevitably be
killed. His death on the scaffold was a tragic necessity, compelled by the
scheme of things, ordained by the way the world was put together. "What is
a public execution?" Jeremy Bentham asked at the end of the eighteenth century. "It is a solemn tragedy which the legislator presents to the assembled
community; a tragedy made truly important, truly pathetic, by its sad reality
and the grandeur of its object." [78]

The early modern era was the heyday of capital punishment, the period
in which it had greatest importance in the organization of social and
political life. In an unstable political environment, constantly on the edge
of violence, with a barely elaborated criminal justice system offering few
practical alternatives, the death penalty was, for rulers, a vital means to
secure important political, religious, and penological ends. It is this social
context and these functional purposes that shaped the institution's forms,
providing it with richly symbolic rituals and representations, rendering it
continuous with cultural assumptions, and silencing all questions about its
legitimacy.

This classical moment in death penalty history left a deep cultural legacy,
a lasting mark in the collective memory. Divine justice, sovereign power, terror and death, a sinner facing his fate, awesome engagements with higher
powers staged before an enraptured crowd—all these images have come
down to us from the early modern era, indelibly associated with the penalty
of death. Subsequent modes of capital punishment are less explicit in their
engagement with these larger issues, more focused on crime, criminal justice, and public protection. But the connotations remain in the background.
Think of the persistent scramble for mementos of the execution when Rainey
Bethea was put to death in Owensboro, Kentucky, in 1936; or the continuing tradition of the last meal; or Governor Mario Cuomo's references to the
sacred, transcendental dimensions of the death penalty—which invoke this
classical legacy.[79] If Terror, Death, and God are nowadays the private night-
time fears of the condemned, in the early modern period they were exhibited
in the bright light of day for all to see.

The Modern Mode

The old death penalty, early modern style, had disappeared from most parts of Europe and America by the early nineteenth century. Several jurisdictions—Tuscany, Prussia, Austria, and Pennsylvania—had reformed their capital codes in the last decades of the eighteenth century, either abolishing the penalty or else drastically limiting its use. Others made the shift later: England's Bloody Code, for example, was not reformed until the 1830s. There was a spectacular reprise of the grand ritual in Paris in 1757, when the execution of Robert Damiens, the regicide, revived the fading genre for a memorable last performance.[80] But by 1800 the shift was already well under way and by 1900 it was virtually complete.

The transition from one mode of capital punishment to another occurred within a larger arc of development: the transformation of the European state system. The newly stabilized states of the late seventeenth century gave way to the enlightened monarchies of the eighteenth century and eventually to the unified and bureaucratized nation states of nineteenth-century Europe. But the reform of capital punishment was also reinforced by developments internal to criminal justice, notably the development of alternative punishments such as transportation and imprisonment, and later the rise of a progressive penology.

During the last part of the eighteenth century rulers regularly commuted death sentences, substituting transportation to the colonies, forced service on public works, or even long-term confinement in the new penitentiaries that were beginning to appear.[81] Within a few decades, and all across the West, the new disciplinary prisons became the courts' punishment of choice for all kind of offenses, from the most trivial to the most serious. The nineteenth century would become the age of the penitentiary and, with the decline of transportation and public works, long-term imprisonment—rather than death on the scaffold—became the punishment for all but the most serious criminals.[82] Out of the penitentiary experience grew a new penology that rejected retribution, embraced reform, and stressed the positive, utilitarian character of penal sanctions. These ideas—which quickly spread across Europe and America—reinforced the shift away from the old death penalty and raised questions about the value of capital punishment in a reformed criminal justice system. As national prison systems developed, becoming more secure and more disciplinary, and often, in the process, more austere, penal reformers pressed the idea of imprisonment as punishment for serious crime. During the course of the nineteenth century execution numbers in many Western nations declined—at first because of ad hoc commutations but later through the substitution of "life sentences" of imprisonment for death sentences. By the 1890s Western governments had begun to establish criminal justice institutions (probation, reformatory prisons, parole, and indeterminate sentencing) that stressed reformatory and even welfarist goals—a development that placed new ideological pressure on an already embattled institution of capital punishment.[83]

By the start of the twentieth century capital punishment in the West was operating in a transformed political and penological context. Changes in the structures of political power and penal control had rendered death sentences less "necessary," while changes in the dominant culture rendered them less legitimate. During the course of the nineteenth century most Western states consolidated their monopolies of violence, disarmed and pacified the population, and created standing armies and extensive police forces. The new nation-states institutionalized their social control capacities—through taxation, government bureaucracies, and legal regulation—and fostered new sources of popular consent such as nationalism, limited democracy, and citizenship. By the 1890s some were providing rudimentary social insurance and welfare benefits.

The result was that terroristic displays of state violence ceased to be a vital tool in the armory of many Western states. As Lamartine declared, "Today society is armed with powers of repression and punishment that do not require the shedding of blood."[84] And such displays, being less vital, came to seem less legitimate. They clashed with the new liberal-democratic politics that defined the state's relationship to citizens and with the civilized, humanitarian sentiments that increasingly shaped the self-image of the ruling elites. As states became more secure, political restraints on violence more robust, and individual lives more valuable, the institution of state killing began to lose its moorings.

The rise of the rational, bureaucratic state brought with it a more developed criminal justice apparatus of professional police and prosecutors, adult and juvenile courts, and a penal system of prisons, reformatories, probation, and parole. This, in turn, moved decision making about punishment away from political actors and placed it increasingly in the hands of criminal justice professionals who were more oriented toward properly criminal justice goals. Over time capital punishment was gradually transformed from a state-controlled political institution geared to state maintenance to a legally controlled criminal justice institution geared to crime control and penal justice.

And with this institutional reorientation came new rationales and representations. "Justice" continued as a central purpose, but that value came increasingly to be phrased in terms of the protection of individual life and public security rather than the king's justice or the maintenance of state rule.[85] What had once been an explicitly political exercise of state power came to represent itself as a form of apolitical penal practice.

By the end of the nineteenth century the ancient rites of state killing had largely disappeared and been replaced by an "enlightened" death penalty, a criminal punishment forming one penal sanction among others in an increasingly professionalized criminal justice system. This new death penalty was less a ceremonial of power and a technique of rule than a policy instrument, rationally adapted to the ends of criminal justice and crime control. But having lost its grounding in absolutist *raison d'état* and the imperatives of divine justice, the death penalty's rationale now became more controversial, more subject to moral debate and utilitarian dispute. The modern death penalty was no longer an unquestionable expression of sovereign power but a policy tool like any other. If it was deployed, in the face of ideological doubts, it was because it was seen to serve human purposes: to deter crime, save innocent lives, inflict pain with a view to creating benefits. What had once been a tragic necessity now became contingent and conditional.

The Functions of Capital Punishment in the Modern Era

CRIMINAL JUSTICE AND CRIME CONTROL. The modern death penalty functioned primarily as an instrument of criminal justice, an "ultimate" penalty reserved for the most serious criminal offenses. Its purposes were represented in penological rather than political terms—as a matter of justice and crime control rather than an exercise of state power. It took place in a penal space, inside the prison, rather than the political space of the public square. Its chief targets were criminal wrongdoers rather than political enemies. New perceptions of the institution as inessential and controversial led to a greater concern with questions of justification, and considerations of social welfare and criminal justice framed these legitimacy debates. Executions were no longer discussed as a means of securing secular or religious power but instead as a means of doing justice and reducing crime.

POLITICAL USES. If modern capital punishment was located within what one might call "ordinary" penal policy and, for the most part, administered accordingly, this did not mean that it lost its connection to the political process. In contrast to other criminal sanctions, which were routinely imposed without any direct involvement on the part of government ministers, the execution of death sentences typically required the approval of some high-ranking government official—the home secretary, the chancellor, the minister of justice, the state governor, and so on. As a result, political considerations always played a role in decisions about executions and pardons. But the political character of these questions had changed. The considerations involved were now matters of party advantage rather than anxieties about the preservation of state power. "If a government wished to signal its determination to crack down on crime and disorder and to brook no opposition to its policies, what better way of doing so than to consign the majority of capital offenders to the block?" writes Richard Evans, discussing the German institution in the nineteenth century. "On the other hand if, perhaps, under liberal pressure, a government wished to signal its humane and benevolent intent, an increase in the number of capital offenders granted the royal clemency was a simple and striking way of doing so." The result was that "the number of executions mirrored with astonishing accuracy successive waves of liberalism and authoritarianism in German history."[86]

"Political uses" are different in important ways from "state functions." Politicians might manipulate modern death penalty laws for partisan political purposes—and the state might sometimes use it against traitors and domestic enemies—but stable Western nation-states no longer treated it as an important tool in state maintenance. These party political uses should also be distinguished from the "private uses" common in the early modern institution. In the modern mode, pardons and commutations were no longer triggered by private interventions, nor were they used as forms of giving and getting linked directly into private hierarchies of status and deference.

NARROWED USE, FEWER VARIETIES, AND GREATER RESTRAINT. The modern death penalty was used for a much narrower range of offenses than hitherto. Property crime, moral offenses, and crimes against religion were no longer punishable by death, which was reserved for the most serious crimes against the person—above all for murder. Its chief targets were individuals who harmed other individuals or threatened public safety, not individuals who threatened the state.[87] Treason remained a capital offense, as did other crimes against the state, but these were rarely prosecuted outside of wartime. Capital punishment was now deployed in the name of the public, not as an expression of a ruler's power. It became an "ultimate" penalty, an exceptional measure of last resort, not a multipurpose sanction to be routinely deployed across a wide range of offenses. Justified only at the extremes of criminal wickedness, incorrigibility, and danger, it was now regarded as much too severe for the property offenders and public order violators who had previously mounted the gallows.

By the modern era executions had come to be administered in a single format, with the same uniform death for everyone. This change resulted not just from the leveling of status distinctions in nineteenth- and twentieth-century Western society but also because a variety of other sanctions were now available to deal with the range of offenses. And, of course, modern sensibilities acted as a barrier to the use of torture, postmortem torments, and other forms of aggravated death sentences.

SECULAR NOT RELIGIOUS. Over the course of the nineteenth century the Western death penalty lost much of its religious character and became predominantly secular in orientation and organization. "Penal policy was rationalized," writes Richard Evans of the German institution, "Enlightenment monarchs and bureaucrats . . . rejected the divine aspect of punishment as irrelevant, even counter-productive. Punishment was to be based on a rational degree of pain, a calculus of terror, a system of punishment graded according to the degree of deterrence required."[88]

Clerics remained at the scene of modern executions and the traditional rites of the "last meal" and the "last words" continued to be administered. But these were less a mark of presiding religious authority than a private consolation to the condemned and a means of smoothing the execution process. Wherever religious traditions clashed with the more secular objectives of the modernized institution, the former tended to give way.[89] Arrangements once regarded as politically and culturally essential came to seem counterproductive as the institution adapted to its new context and purposes.

According to Lynn Hunt, the secularization of the scaffold was well under way in much of Europe by the end of the eighteenth century: "Pain, punishment, and the public spectacle of suffering all gradually lost their religious moorings in the second half of the eighteenth century. . . . In the emerging individualistic and secular view, pains belonged only to the sufferer in the here and now."[90] By the mid-nineteenth century the religious justifications traditionally offered in support of capital punishment had become much less frequent and much less persuasive. William Wordsworth's "Sonnets upon the Punishment of Death" expressed a religious justification for the institution, but by the time they were published in 1841 such arguments had lost much of their power. As Randall McGowen tells us, sentiments such as these "were seldom voiced in the mid-century debates," making Wordsworth's defense of capital punishment seem "dated."[91]

The fading of capital punishment's religious aspects had implications for the cultural status of the institution and for the experience of the condemned offender—a change Haltunnen traces in her history of gallows literature. Describing New England executions in the seventeenth and early eighteenth centuries, she writes: "The execution sermon was a sacred narrative which focused . . . on the spiritual condition of the condemned criminal. What course of smaller sins had brought the sinner to the terrible transgression for which she or he was about to be hanged? What was her spiritual state now, and where would she spend eternity?" One hundred years later the focus had changed: "[The] sacred narrative was gradually replaced by a variety of secular accounts . . . which turned attention to the crime itself unfolding within worldly time. What was the nature of the violence; when and where had the crime taken place, what were the murderer's motives; and just how had he or she been brought to worldly justice?"[92]

Secularization deprived the event of many of its larger meanings. It reduced the execution to a state killing, pursuant to a contingent decision by fallible social actors rather than an instantiation of God's justice. At the same time the fate of the condemned came to seem more grimly horrifying, since he was now being condemned to nothingness rather than commended to God's mercy. "Gone . . . is the construction of the hanging as a drama of salvation."[93] In its place is a bureaucratic procedure that offers the soul little solace or hope of redemption.

In a discussion of two New York execution reports, one in 1825 and the other in 1892, Michael Madow captures something of this ongoing shift. The earlier report depicted the execution as a drama of sin and atonement in which the offender's spiritual fate was in the balance: "It was Reynold's soul, not his body that claimed the narrative's center." In contrast, the 1892 report focused on the physical aspects of the event. "[W]hen Charles McElvaine was privately executed at Sing Sing some sixty-six years later, physicians, not clergy, dominated the scene, and the question posed by journalists assembled outside the penitentiary all presumed this event's medicalized construction: 'Exactly when did McElvaine die? When did he lose consciousness? Did he feel any pain? Was there any burning of the flesh?'"[94]

HUMANITY NOT HORROR. The modern execution aimed not to terrorize onlookers with a spectacle of suffering but to carry out the court's death sentence in an efficient, humane manner. The sights, sounds, and smells of the body in pain ceased to be an essential part of the institution and became a problem to be minimized out of concern for the offender and for witnesses.

Death, and death alone, became the punishment. The offender's life was to be terminated but, beyond that, no supplementary suffering was to be imposed. All additional torments, degradations, or postmortem aggravations were avoided. In a secular world, the finality of death meant that additional, postmortem punishments were harmful superstitions. As a German appeal court put it in 1853: "Death expiates all guilt here on earth; the human judge's hand should not stretch out beyond it."[95]

SPEED NOT CEREMONY. The shift from an extended ritual of death to a curt termination of life meant that the modern execution would become increasingly oriented toward speed and efficiency. As Evans observes in his discussion of nineteenth-century German executions, "the emphasis was above all on speed." Modern executions were "simple straightforward affairs, with a minimum of speechifying," their "formulaic brevity" standing in stark contrast to the "spectacular, semi-sacral procedures of an earlier day."[96] As Simon Schama writes, discussing the introduction of the guillotine in France, "for the crowds accustomed to the prolonged and emotionally rich ritual of penitential processions, loud public confessions, the climactic jump of the body on the gibbet, the exposure of the hanging remains, even in some rare cases the prolonged ordeal of breaking on the wheel, the *machine* was a distinct disappointment." As a public ceremony, the execution was now too expeditious to be satisfying. "A swish, a thud; sometimes not even a display of the head; the executioner reduced to a low-grade mechanic like some flunkey pulling a bell rope." But, of course, as Schama observes, "this austere compression of the spectacle of punishment was exactly what the designers of the *machine* had in mind"[97]

PRIVATE NOT PUBLIC. The modern execution withdrew from public view. As early as the late seventeenth century, permanent stone scaffolds were replaced with temporary structures that were removed from sight when not in use. The procession to the gallows was first shortened then abolished altogether. The scaffold was partly covered so that the dangling corpse would not be visible. Later the scaffold was moved from the public square to the closed jail yard. The large hanging day crowd disappeared, replaced at first by an invited audience given access to the jail yard, eventually by a smaller number of "witnesses" whose access was closely controlled. By moving the event from the public square to the interior of a state prison the authorities were, as Elias would phrase it, putting the execution "behind the scenes of social life," rendering it distinct from the everyday life with which it had previously been integrated. The execution ritual became "defensive not demonstrative," its visibility and audibility greatly diminished, its performative character changed from noisy public event to silent, backstage procedure.[98]

As Michael Madow sums up the transformation, the modern execution was thrice removed from the life of the community: *spatially*—from an outdoor open space to the interior of a high-walled prison; *geographically*—from the local county where the murder occurred to a state prison that might be many miles away; and *epistemologically*—from "the domain of first-hand, everyday experience," where people apprehended capital punishment with their own eyes and ears, to the sphere of "abstract consciousness," where people learned of the event indirectly through newspaper reports and cultural stereotypes.[99]

RESTRICTED COMMUNICATION. As the early modern death penalty developed into the modern one, its symbolic communications changed. The offender's death and the staging and discourse surrounding it were no longer designed to evoke images of a soul in torment or metaphors of the body social. By the early nineteenth century the institution had become disenchanted, stripped of its religious character and its status as communal ritual. Allusive, metaphoric communication was increasingly shut down. The execution came to be merely about itself, a matter of imposing death without further ado.[100]

Some traces of the older religious practices survived, of course—the "last meal" and "last words" continue right up to the present—but without much collective meaning other than a bland sense of tradition. And where the early modern execution had been an occasion for extensive and elaborate discourse, the modern execution generated few official statements and permitted little in the way of speech making or narrative performances. To some extent the press took up the slack, providing a steady stream of sensationalist reports, putting the event into the "abstract consciousness" of the cultural imaginary. Journalists represented the execution as a horror, a terror, a fate to be avoided . . . but no longer as a symbolic communication about man, the state, and the cosmos. Stories about modern executions concerned themselves with the physical details of the procedure and the legal process that led up to it. Little space was given to larger political or religious lessons that might be drawn from the event.[101]

CONTROVERSY AND LEGITIMATION. If the early modern institution was legitimate, confident, and taken for granted, modern capital punishment operated in a more troubled environment. In the modern era, capital punishment came to be regarded as inherently problematic, the more so as nations moved toward liberal democracy and later to welfarism. From the Enlightenment on, the liberal ideas and humanitarian sentiments of the professional and middle classes and their religious and political leaders have challenged the death penalty. Whereas the early modern institution had been continuous with the background assumptions of political and cultural life, the modern institution came to seem increasingly incongruous, caught in a contradiction between traditional conceptions of absolutist justice and a newer insistence that state violence should be strictly limited and human life preserved.

Throughout the modern period this contradiction between absolutist tradition and liberal modernity exerted a steady background pressure for reform. But its most immediate effect was to give rise to a critical discourse challenging the institution, which, in turn, prompted new and more elaborate efforts to justify it. The late eighteenth and early nineteenth centuries became a period of forceful critique and normative debate. In 1764 Cesare Beccaria published his treatise, *Dei delitti e delle pene*, an Enlightenment critique of the death penalty and absolutist criminal justice that resounded across Europe and America and quickly became a standard reference for reformers everywhere.[102] The critical challenge launched by Beccaria energized a conservative reaction, moving death penalty supporters to an intensified concern with justification. In England, for example, William Paley mounted a powerful defense of the institution that took nothing for granted. Leaving behind the "uncomplicated vindictiveness" of earlier writings such as the early-eighteenth-century pamphlet *Hanging Not Punishment Enough,* "Paley advanced the political and moral justifications for capital punishment with unprecedented ambition." As Gatrell comments, Paley's "elaborate pleading" was necessary "because older certainties had become uneasy."[103]

Rationales that had previously gone unstated were now made explicit, and new justificatory arguments were developed in response to the institution's Enlightenment critics. The modern philosophy of punishment mostly dates from this time, with the writings of Kant, Hegel, Bentham, and Mill serving as its foundations. Among the institution's supporters, the death penalty was no longer discussed as an unquestioned necessity. Henceforth its use would be framed as a moral duty that treated individuals as ends or a utilitarian deterrent that saved human lives—each account striving to represent state killing as somehow aligned with the cause of humanity.[104] For the first time the death penalty came to be represented as a humanitarian institution. To condemn killers to death was, so its supporters said, a way of expressing respect for human life. The executioner took lives in order to save lives. The savage will of the sovereign had become a means of social welfare.

At the same time and for the same reasons the institution came increasingly to be surrounded by anxiety and embarrassment. By the 1960s and the beginning of what I will term the "late modern" contemporary era, this ambivalence had become quite pronounced. "No one dares speak directly of the ceremony," Albert Camus observed in 1961. "[We] read at breakfast time in a corner of the newspaper that the condemned has 'paid his debt to society' or that he has 'atoned' or that 'at five a.m. justice was done.' The officials call the condemned 'the interested party' or 'the patient' or refer to him by a number." What had once been a demonstrative public ritual had become a topic for reticence and euphemism. "People write of capital punishment as if they were whispering."[105]

REPRESENTATIONS OF THE CONDEMNED. The waning of religious understandings, together with renewed efforts to justify the institution, prompted new representations of the condemned. In his discussion of nineteenth-century Germany, Richard Evans notes the emergence of a new language of justification centered upon the dangerousness, bestiality, and inhumanity of the murderer.[106] Foucault reports similar developments in nineteenth-century France, noting that the "monstrosity" of the offender now became a key justification. In order to kill the condemned person, it had become necessary to distance him from the human race.[107] Haltunnen observes the same occurrence even earlier in the United States: "by the end of the [eighteenth] century, the cult of horror was replacing an earlier, sympathetic view of the condemned criminal as moral exemplum with a view of the murderer as moral alien."[108] And in nineteenth-century England, according to Gatrell, "it seems also to have been necessary to insist on the 'otherness' of the hanged man or woman. . . . [henceforth] the condemned were to be defined with increasing explicitness as social others (poor people and thieves) or political others (subversives or traitors) or psychological others (monsters, murderers)."[109] To see hanged men or women as human was to increase the friction between capital punishment and modern culture. Rendering them monstrous served to reduce dissonance and lubricate the machinery of death. Medicine, psychiatry, abnormal psychology, and positive criminology—the new human sciences that emerged in this period—helped by supplying a new language of monstrosity, each of them providing a positive source of scientific legitimacy for the institution, much as they do in the capital trial penalty phase in America today.

The Late Modern Mode

If the modern era of Western capital punishment began in the early decades of the nineteenth century, 150 years later that era had begun to draw to a close.

By the 1960s, the political contradictions that had long affected capital punishment in its modern mode had grown more intense, the cultural environment in which it operated, less hospitable. Why? Because by that time, the politics of liberalism, democracy, and welfarism had become dominant across most of the Western nations and these governmental rationalities rendered the death penalty increasingly outmoded and illegitimate. Of course, these developments unfolded unevenly, their timing and extent determined by the balance of political forces in the different nations and by the contingency of events. While most of Europe moved toward social democracy in the postwar decades, Spain, Portugal, and Greece were under military rule until the 1970s, during which time they retained capital punishment. And although America added to its New Deal welfare state with President Johnson's Great Society programs of the 1960s, the nation remained decidedly less welfarist and egalitarian than its European equivalents. And instead of European-style social democracy, with citizenship, solidarity, and redistribution organized in and through a powerful state apparatus, the United States sustained its long-standing commitment to radical local democracy, devolving most social and penal policy decisions to local political actors—an arrangement that fostered local variation and populist politics rather than uniform national governance by professional elites. But in general, compared to the prior period, and across the whole of the West, this era saw the enhancement of liberal democracy, the growth of welfare states, and the further decline of capital punishment.

In the wake of two world wars, the experience of fascism, and the searing horror of the Holocaust, Western societies set themselves on a path toward a new form of social organization. All across the West there emerged liberal-democratic institutions, developed welfare states, anti-authoritarian cultures, and international institutions dedicated to the cause of human rights. In this context the death penalty began to appear increasingly transgressive and anachronistic, increasingly at odds with the "politics of life" and the humanistic culture that were defining feature of welfare state societies. At the same time the professionalization of police and criminal justice, and the rise to dominance of a more correctionalist style of penal policy, exerted new pressure on capital punishment as an institution. If the proper purpose of penal sanctions was not retribution but reform, as most penal experts now insisted, then the death penalty was an outmoded anomaly. In this developing context, the death penalty grew increasingly marginal. By the 1960s many nations—the United States, Britain, and France among them—reported sharp declines in their annual execution toll.

An institution that had been contested ever since the Enlightenment now became more controversial than ever. Schoolchildren everywhere debated the subject, and most adult citizens came to have an opinion on the "issue."[110] Governments in every Western nation were pressed to end the institution once and for all. For cultural elites and for increasingly large sections of the public, being in favor of capital punishment was regarded not as a sign of common sense or moral rectitude but of a social and political conservatism.

By 1965 the death penalty had been completely abolished in only a handful of nations, but its use had declined everywhere and no Western nation routinely deployed it any longer as a normal penal sanction. Those nations that continued to impose and execute death sentences did so rarely and somewhat reluctantly, and only for the worst crimes of violence, usually heinous cases of intentional murder. And when executions did take place—which happened more and more rarely—they were surrounded not just by solemnity, as before, but by intense controversy and palpable discomfort.[111]

One by one, the Western nations resolved these contradictions by means of national legislation that abolished the institution. And as the postwar wave of abolitions took hold, that movement changed the context in which the death penalty existed elsewhere. Each new act of abolition made each subsequent one easier to accomplish—and each refusal to abolish more difficult to justify. In nations where the death penalty survived into the 1960s and 1970s, its use became ever more controversial and problem-laden. In one Western nation after another, executions no longer occurred.

The majority of abolitions occurred in the second half of the twentieth century, either in the years immediately after the Second World War or else in the 1960s and 1970s. Italy, Germany, and Austria included abolitionist provisions in the new liberal constitutions they enacted following the end of the war and the collapse of fascism. In several nations where capital punishment had long been abolished for "ordinary" crimes, the death penalty remained on the books for political offenses against the state—a reminder that capital punishment is a last-resort power to defend against attacks upon the state that governments have sought to retain. In the relative stability of Western Europe in the postwar years, these "extraordinary" penalties were never invoked, and they, too, were eventually abolished: by Portugal in 1976, Denmark in 1978, Luxembourg and Norway in 1979, the Netherlands in 1982, Australia in 1985, New Zealand in 1989, Ireland in 1990, Italy in 1994, Spain in 1995, Belgium in 1996, and Canada and the United Kingdom in 1998.[112]

Between the 1980s and the present anti-death penalty provisions were increasingly embodied in human rights conventions, transnational treaties, and international law. Protocols 6 and 13 of the European Convention on Human Rights (adopted in 1983 and 2002, respectively) prohibit the death penalty, as does the United Nations' Second Optional Protocol to the International Covenant on Civil and Political Rights (ICCPR) (passed in 1989) as well as the American Convention on Human Rights Protocol to Abolish the Death Penalty, adopted in 1990 by the General Assembly of the Organization of American States.[113] The emergence of these international legal norms has had various effects. Their existence exerts abolitionist pressure on other states and in some cases provides national governments with political and economic incentives to abandon the death penalty. They have internationalized death penalty politics, transforming a domestic matter into an issue that has a bearing on international relations. They "lock in" death penalty abolition in those nations that are signatories to the ICCPR or members of the European Union and the Council of Europe, making continued abolition an international obligation rather than merely a domestic policy choice. Consequently capital punishment has tended to fade from national political debate in these nations, and popular opinion in some countries has begun to loosen its attachment to the death penalty.[114] The new reform movement has largely succeeded in elevating death penalty abolition to the status of an international human rights principle, giving this "age of abolition" an international legal backing. The long-term history of the death penalty in the West thus approaches its absolute antithesis: what was once an unproblematic institution, universally embraced, is fast becoming a violation of human rights, universally prohibited.

The death penalty systems that operated during this late modern period—in Britain until 1965, Spain until 1976, France until 1981, and the United States still today—were still structured in much the same way as before. The discourses that framed their operation—with their rationales and critiques, their formulaic arguments and textbook debates—were still recognizably the ones that emerged in the eighteenth century, though by the 1960s the American debates had begun to focus on questions of constitutional law. The cultural and political forces that challenged the death penalty's legitimacy continued to operate, rendering its use ever more narrow, restrained, and refined. In short, these death penalties were still recognizably modern. But all the earlier contradictions grew more intense. The institution became increasingly at odds with the political and cultural institutions that surrounded it. Alternatives—especially life imprisonment or life imprisonment without parole—became more routinely available. Legal reforms narrowed capital codes still further, until only aggravated murders attracted a death sentence. Mandatory capital punishment disappeared. Homicide was reclassified into capital and noncapital offenses. Capital cases attracted more legal process, more appeals, and thus generated greater delays. Sentences were more often commuted so that executions became rarer than before.

The growing rarefaction of death sentences and executions increased the institution's marginality and further diminished its effectiveness as a means of crime control or retributive justice, thus providing more fuel for the critics. Where executions did occur, they attracted a great deal of negative publicity and criticism—now from foreign audiences and international authorities as well as from domestic critics. Each event was carefully scrutinized by opponents for the least sign of inhumanity, watched anxiously by ambivalent authorities for fear of mishap or a botched result. Increasingly the death penalty became a divisive issue rather a functioning institution.[115]

In nations such as the United Kingdom and France that retained their old execution methods—the noose and the guillotine—capital punishment came to seem especially archaic and outmoded.[116] In the United States, where most states had already "updated" their execution technologies in the course of the twentieth century, setting aside the noose in favor of the electric chair or the gas chamber, most of them did so again in the 1980s and 1990s, when the lethal injection provided a way to make the death penalty seem less objectionable. But even the reformed institution—used sparingly, for the most unpopular murderers, after an elaborate show of due process and administrative review—could not avoid appearing increasingly transgressive in the new context. Indeed, in the context of late modernity, the continued practice of capital punishment places officials and their supporters in a cultural contradiction: they are obliged to behave in ways that are at once lawful and transgressive. It traps them in the uncomfortable space between the cultural norms of liberal humanism and the legal practice of state killing. This transgressive status marked death off as different. Other criminal penalties might sometimes become a subject of dispute, but by the end of the twentieth century the death penalty was always and everywhere controversial. Whenever and wherever a death sentence was imposed, the legitimacy of the institution was liable to be called into question.

Eventually all the major European nations became abolitionist, with Britain making a provisional abolition permanent in 1969, Spain repealing its capital laws in 1975, Portugal in 1976, and finally France in 1981.[117] Each of these national abolitions was brought about by reform forces internal to the society in question, with only occasional reference to the experiences or preferences of other nations.[118] But once all the major European nations had come into line, they proceeded to regard the new abolitionist consensus as a transnational norm, a human rights principle that ought to be observed by all nations everywhere. Nations that were once retentionist holdouts now became abolitionist proselytizers, thereby increasing the pressure on states that had not yet abolished the death penalty. By the 1980s the United States—or, rather, a majority of American states plus the federal government—was left as the only remaining retentionist nation in the West.

Western capital punishment in the late modern era no longer performs the functions associated with the institution in its modernist modality, or at least not to the same degree or with the same effectiveness. Too rare and uncertain to deter, too averse to bodily violence to deliver harsh retribution, the late modern death penalty has lost much of its modern *raison d'être*. Where it still exists as a legal sanction—which by now is only in the United States, although European laggards such as France and Britain displayed similar patterns in the 1960s and 1970s, as do non-Western retentionist democracies such as Japan and India today—we observe a great deal of institutional ambivalence surrounding its use. The visible signs of this ambivalence are laws that go unenforced, sentences that go unexecuted, legal proceedings that create endless delays, and a great deal of discomfort on the part of judges, government ministers, and penal functionaries charged with administering the punishment. The death penalty that exists in the public imagination and in justificatory argument grows ever more distant from the death penalty as it is actually administered. What was once a practical instrument of penal policy has become something rather different. As a U.S. federal judge declared in 1995: "[We] have the worst of all worlds. We have capital punishment, and the enormously expensive machinery to support it, but we don't really have the death penalty."[119]

NOTES

This essay is drawn from David Garland, *Peculiar Institution: America's Death Penalty in an Age of Abolition* (Cambridge, Mass., and Oxford England, 2010). I am grateful to my co-editors, Randall McGowen and Michael Meranze, for their help with this chapter.

1. Keith Otterbein, *The Ultimate Coercive Sanction: A Cross-Cultural Study of Capital Punishment* (New Haven, 1986). As Beccaria observed, "almost all nations, in all ages, have punished certain crimes with death." Cesare Beccaria, *On Crimes and Punishments and other Writings* (New York, 1995 [1775]), 49. The death penalty's place in the ancient world is well attested by legal documents from the Code of Hammurabi, Mosaic law, and the Pentateuch to the laws of classical antiquity (e.g., Draco's Athenian Code of 621 BC, the Roman Republic's Law of the XII Tablets) and ancient Judaic practice.

2. See Roger Hood and Carolyn Holye, *The Death Penalty: A Worldwide Perspective*, 4th ed. (Oxford, 2008); and David Greenberg and Valerie West, "Siting the Death Penalty Internationally." *Law and Social Inquiry* 33, 2 (2008): 295–343.

3. On Elias, see David Garland, *Punishment and Modern Society: A Study in Social Theory* (Oxford, 1990) chap. 10.

4. The Black Acts in eighteenth-century England involved a major reversal of an earlier trend. See Leon Radzinowicz, *A History of the English Criminal Law*, Vol. 1, *The Movement for Reform* (London, 1948). For several examples of such reversals in nineteenth- and twentieth-century Germany, see Richard Evans, *Rituals of Retribution: Capital Punishment in Germany 1600–1987* (Oxford, 1996). Charles Duff, in *A Handbook on Hanging* (New York, 2001), 41, discusses Italy's return to capital punishment under Mussolini. America's return to capital punishment in 1976, following a ten-year hiatus, is another key example.

5. My evidence comes chiefly from the United States, the United Kingdom, Canada, Australia, New Zealand, and the continental European nations, especially France, Germany, and the Netherlands. The pattern of change in the rest of the world is not addressed here, though future research might usefully broaden the range of analysis by studying non-Western nations. David Johnson and Franklin Zimring, *The Next Frontier: National Development, Political Change and the Death Penalty in Asia* (New York, 2009).

6. Franklin Zimring, *The Contradictions of American Capital Punishment* (New York, 2003).

7. It seems to me that we should distinguish jurisdictions that have the death penalty, but use it rarely or never, from others where executions are a regular event. The movement toward abolition is typically a gradual one in which the death penalty becomes increasingly restricted and restrained before finally being abolished. Moreover, in any history of the death penalty, "abolition" may not be the actual end point. Many nations subsequently reintroduce capital punishment, and, for long periods after the abolition, the death penalty may be invoked as a desirable policy option. International treaties—such as the European Convention on Human Rights—or constitutional codes such as South Africa's—may "lock in" abolition and make reenactment less likely. But a realism about state power would lead one to believe that the death penalty will never entirely disappear, remaining forever the "ultimate" resource in the state's repertory of rule.

8. Otterbein, *The Ultimate*. See also UN Department of Economic and Social Affairs, *Capital Punishment*, Part I: Report, 1960; Part II: Developments, 1961–1965 (New York, 1968), 31: "There are practically no countries where the death penalty has never existed."

9. Hood and Hoyle, in *Death Penalty*, report that there were, as of 2007, forty-eight nations that retain the death penalty; eight retain it for extraordinary crimes; and forty-five have capital punishment laws that have not recently been enforced. See also Austin Sarat and Christian Boulanger, eds., *The Cultural Lives of Capital Punishment: Comparative Perspectives* (Stanford, 2005), 3. On capital punishment in Asia, see Johnson and Zimring *Next Frontier*.

10. Samuel Johnson, *Rambler*, 114, April 20, 1751. See also *Michigan Legislature Report of the Proceedings and Debates in the Convention to Revise the Constitution of the State of Michigan* (Detroit, 1850), 743: "the fear of death and the love of life are the most powerful motives in the human breast."

11. The quoted phrase in the previous sentence is from Friedrich Nietzsche, *The Genealogy of Morals* (New York, 1967), 214. Charles Tilly, in *Coercion, Capital and European States, AD 990–1992* (Cambridge, 1992), 70, makes a similar point in his discussion of why wars occur: "The central, tragic fact is simple: coercion works: those who apply substantial force to their fellows get compliance, and from that compliance draw the multiple advantages of money, goods, deference, access to pleasures denied to less powerful people."

12. Evans, *Rituals*, 894–95.

13. See David Garland, "Capital Punishment and American Culture," *Punishment and Society* 7, 4 (2005), where I argue this point.

14. In this usage, a mode or modality of capital punishment is an ideal type that groups together the institutional arrangements characteristic of a particular period— institutions that have more in common with one another than with institutions in later or earlier modes. By grouping institutions together in this way, I do not deny the specificity of particular institutions in particular places at particular times. My concern is, instead, to point to the characteristics that these specific institutions share and their roots in a certain form of social organization. No one would deny that the political history of England is quite different from that of France or Germany in ways that matter to the shape and use of the death penalty. But my concern here is not with variation—of which there was no doubt a great deal. It is with the generic form, or ideal type, insofar as we can specify it. The analytical purpose of these types is not to understand the details of capital punishment in the past but to produce contrastive types that help us better understand it in the present. As always, such classifications are generated by the specific character of the inquiry. A historian interested in early modern capital punishment might be inclined to identify variants within the absolutist mode.

15. Evans, *Rituals*, 50; James Sharpe, *Judicial Punishment in England* (London, 1990), 31; Otterbein, *Ultimate*.

16. Pieter Spierenburg, *The Spectacle of Suffering: Executions and the Evolution of Repression: From a Preindustrial Metropolis to the European Experience* (Cambridge, 1984), 1.

17. Katherine Royer, "The Body in Parts: Reading the Execution in Late Medieval England." *Historical Reflections* 29, 2 (2003): 319–40 at 323.

18. Absolutist monarchs—unrestrained by other institutions, such as churches, legislatures, or social elites—ruled in Europe from the seventeenth to the nineteenth century. Absolutism was a political system that emerged following the decline of feudalism, in which the monarch's power was concentrated and consolidated, state laws unified, and the power of the nobles decreased. The classic example was Louis XIV of France, but the monarchies of Austria, Spain, Italy, Poland, Prussia, Russia, Denmark, and Sweden were also absolutist in form (Perry Anderson, *Lineages of the Absolutist State* [London, 1974]). The "absolute" nature of that power was, of course, relative: these monarchs had limits, above all financial limits, on their capacities. Despite important differences in their political institutions, the forms of capital punishment used in continental Europe by absolutist rulers were similar in most respects to those used in England, with its oligarchic, constitutional regime, and in England's American colonies.

19. Radzinowicz, *History*, 28, 32.

20. Esther Cohen, "Symbols of Culpability and the Universal Language of Justice: The Ritual of Public Execution in Late Medieval Europe." *History of European Ideas* 11 (1989): 407–16 at 407.

21. The last phrase is taken from Clifford Geertz's account of the Negara state and its theatrical display of political power in nineteenth-century Bali; see Geertz, *Negara: The Theater State in Nineteenth-Century Bali* (Princeton, N.J., 1980). Even the liberal abolitionist Beccaria recognized the death penalty's necessity where the stability of the early modern state was in jeopardy: "The death of a citizen cannot be necessary except in one case. When, though deprived of his liberty he has such power and connections as may endanger the security of the nation; when his existence may produce a dangerous revolution in the established form of government. But even in this case, it can only be necessary when a nation is on the verge of recovering or losing its liberty; or in times of absolute anarchy, when the disorders themselves hold the place of laws" (Beccaria, *On Crimes*, 45). The pattern of abolition in Europe and South America shows a clear tendency to abolish for "ordinary" crime while retaining for "extraordinary crime"—that is, for political offenses, crimes in wartime, offense against the security of the state, treason, and so on; see Hood and Hoyle, *Death Penalty*. The retention of capital punishment for crimes against the state—despite its abandonment for ordinary crime—is an echo of the institution's original and fundamental purpose.

22. On this, see Douglas Hay, "Property, Authority and the Criminal Law," in Hay et al., eds., *Albion's Fatal Tree: Crime and Society in Eighteenth-Century England* (Harmondsworth, 1975); Spierenberg, *Spectacle*; Evans, *Rituals*; Mitchell Merback, *The Thief, the Cross, and the Wheel: Pain and the Spectacle of Punishment in Medieval and Renaissance Europe* (Chicago, 1999); and Randall McGowen, "The Body and Punishment in the Eighteenth Century," *Journal of Modern History* 59 (1987): 651–79.

23. Joseph de Maistre, from the St. Petersburg dialogues of 1821, page 192 of Lively's 1965 edition. On the absolutist state, see Anderson, *Lineages*.

24. Evans, *Rituals*, at 50. In England, where the absolutist aspirations of monarchs like James I and Charles I were undone by a powerful Parliament and the merchants and nobles that supported it, capital punishment was less closely and visibly linked to sovereign power, except in cases of treason. Nevertheless, English executions exhibited most of the key features of the "absolutist" mode.

25. Anton Blok, "The Symbolic Vocabulary of Public Executions," in June Starr and Jane Collier, eds., *History and Power in the Study of Law: New Directions in Legal Anthropology* (Ithaca, N.Y., 1989), 47; Richard Van Dulmen, *Theatre of Horror: Crime and Punishment in Early Modern Germany* (Oxford, 1990); Spierenburg, *Spectacle*; Merback, *The Thief*; John Langbein, *Torture and the Law of Proof* (Chicago, 1976); Hay (this volume) notes the extraordinary severity of the executions staged for the Jacobin rebels and the Cato Street conspirators.

26. V. A. C. Gatrell, *The Hanging Tree: Executions and the English People, 1770–1868* (Oxford, 1994), 2, 32.

27. Hay, "Property," 17, 56. See also John McManners, *Death and the Enlightenment: Changing Attitudes to Death among Christians and Unbelievers in Eighteenth-Century France* (New York, 1981), 379–80.

28. Sharpe, *Judicial Punishment*, 32.

29. Douglas Hay, "Hanging and the English Judges" (this volume).

30. For more on this, see Hay, "Property"; and E. P. Thompson, *Whigs and Hunters: The Origins of the Black Act* (Harmondsworth, 1975).

31. Randall McGowen, "Punishing Violence, Sentencing Crime," in *The Violence of Representation: Literature and the History of Violence,* ed. Nancy Armstrong and Leonard Tennenhouse, 92 (London, 1989). Evans notes that in Germany in the same period, "public executions contained a mixture of sacred and secular images of authority" (*Rituals*, 98).

32. Evans, *Rituals*, 65, 66.

33. Michel Foucault, *Society Must Be Defended: Lectures at the College de France, 1975–1976* (New York, 2003), 247. See also McGowen, "Punishing Violence,"143; Sharpe, *Judicial Punishments*, 33); Stuart Banner, *The Death Penalty: An American History* (Cambridge, 2002), 14; Louis Masur, *Rites of Execution: Capital Punishment and the Transformation of American Culture, 1776–1865* (New York, 1989), 5, 26.

34. Keith Thomas, *Religion and the Decline of Magic* (Harmondsworth, 1991).

35. Evans, *Rituals*, 93–96.

36. Philip Smith, *Punishment and Culture* (Chicago, 2008); Evans, *Rituals*; and Banner, *The Death Penalty.*

37. McGowen, "The Body," 665: "Death served a useful purpose: the criminal's miserable end served as a terror and warning to all others not to offend."

38. Hay, "Hanging." Hay gives examples of how the judges (sometimes with direct guidance from the government) used the death penalty tactically to quell riots and incipient rebellion.

39. Cohen, "Symbols," 409.

40. See the 1752 Act for Better Preventing the Horrid Crime of Murder (25 geo. 2, c.37) quoted in *Pratt v. Att Gen for Jamaica*, Privy Council Appeals No. 10 of 1993, appendix, p 10. This regime of immediate execution was relaxed in 1836 in order to allow post-conviction review.

41. Randall McGowen, "Managing the Gallows: The Bank of England and the Death Penalty, 1797–1821." *Law and History Review* 25 (2) (2007): 241–82.

42. Hay, "Property," 18, 21. See also Thompson, *Whigs.*

43. See Radzinowicz, *History.*

44. Hay, "Property." For an account of similar functions in Japan, see also Daniel Botsman, *Punishment and Power in the Making of Modern Japan* (Princeton, N.J., 2005).

45. Hay, "Property," 42, 48.

46. See John Lofland's description of gibbeting: "However killed, the corpse was treated by boiling or tarring and hung up in a chain or wicker suit at the scene of the crime, along heavily traveled roads and rivers, or at a special gibbet place. The preservative retarded decay and the chain or wicker suit prevented large parts of the corpse from detaching. By such means the corpse's public display was prolonged until carrion birds eventually picked the bones clean." Lofland, "The Dramaturgy of State Executions," in H. Bleakley and J. Lofland, *State Executions Viewed Historically and Sociologically* (Montclair, N.J., 1977), 316.

47. The traditional "neck verse" was Psalm 51: "Have mercy upon me, O God, according to thy loving kindness: according to the multitude of thy tender mercies, blot out my transgressions." Lawrence Friedman, *Crime and Punishment in American History* (New York, 1993), 43.

48. Quoted in Gene Ogle, "Slaves of Justice: Saint Domingue's Executioners and the Production of Shame," in *Historical Reflections* 29, 2 (2003): 275–294 at 283.

49. James Whitman, *Harsh Justice: Criminal Punishment and the Widening Gap between America and Europe* (New York, 2003), 103.

50. Lynn Hunt, *Inventing Human Rights: A History* (New York, 2007), 80.

51. Blok, "Symbolic Vocabulary," 47.

52. Merback, *The Thief*, 141. England's death penalties were less differentiated by rank, with hanging being the standard punishment for most offenders. But even England made an exception for the execution of traitors, and, after 1752, the courts could aggravate a death sentence by imposing dissection or hanging in chains.

53. Echoes of this tradition continue in modern military executions. According to the UN Department of Economic and Social Affairs (*Capital Punishment*, 24) "in the great majority of countries there are two methods of carrying out a death sentence: one for crimes tried by the ordinary courts, and the other in military cases; the latter is nearly always carried out by firing squad."

54. Hunt, *Inventing*, 94.

55. David Cooper, *The Lesson of the Scaffold: The Public Execution Controversy in Victorian England* (Athens, 1974), 5. See also Blok, "Symbolic Vocabulary," 47.

56. Spierenburg, *Spectacle*, 63.

57. Sharpe, *Judicial Punishments*, 36; Evans, *Rituals*, 105; van Dulmen, in *Theatre*, notes a similar trend in Germany. Andrea McKenzie suggests that theological themes continued to be a prominent part of London's Tyburn executions until at least the end of the eighteenth century (McKenzie, *Tyburn's Martyrs: Execution in England, 1675-1775* [London, 2007]).

58. For a detailed discussion of this development, see Simon Devereaux, "Recasting the Theatre of Execution: The Abolition of the Tyburn Ritual." *Past & Present* 202 , 1 (2009): 127-74.

59. On the first interpretation, see Hay, "Property"; Michel Foucault, *Discipline and Punish: The Birth of the Prison* (New York, 1977); and Spierenburg, *Spectacle*. On the second, see McGowen, "The Body"; and Banner, *The Death Penalty*. On the third, see Thomas Laqueur, "Crowds, Carnival and the State in English Executions, 1604-1868," in *The First Modern Society: Essays in Honor of Lawrence Stone*, ed. A. L. Beier, David Cannadine, and James Rosenheim (New York, 1989); and Gatrell, *Hanging Tree*. Laqueur is criticized in turn by Evans, *Rituals*, 104.

60. Cohen, "Symbols," at 410. The same symbols could mean quite different things in different cultures. Cohen suggests that, in early modern Europe, women were rarely hanged for reasons of modesty. In ancient Greece and Rome, hanging was a punishment specifically reserved for women. See Eva Cantarella, *Les Supplices Capitaux en Grece et a Rome* (Paris, 2001).

61. Sir Edward Coke, *State Trials*, 1:23.5. Quoted in Radzinowicz, *History;* and also in Basil Montagu, *The Opinions of Different Authors upon the Punishment of Death* (London, 1816).

62. Merback, *The Thief*, 157.

63. McGowen, "Punishing Violence," 143. McGowen's "The Body" presents a brilliant analysis of the metaphor of the body social in early modern executions.

64. On gallows literature, see James Sharpe, "Last Dying Speeches: Religion, Ideology, and Public Execution in Seventeenth-Century England" *Past and Present* 107, 1 (1985): 144-67; Karen Halttunen, *Murder Most Foul: The Killer and the American Gothic Imagination* (Cambridge, 1998); McGowen, "The Body"; and Masur, *Rites*.

65. Gatrell, *Hanging Tree*, 2.

66. Spierenburg, *Spectacle*, 98.

67. Evans, *Rituals*, 99.

68. On late-twentieth-century American attitudes to death, see James Farrell, *Inventing the American Way of Death, 1830–1920* (Philadelphia, 1980).

69. On cultural understandings of pain and the body in seventeenth-century capital punishment, see McGowen, "The Body."

70. Norbert Elias, *The Loneliness of the Dying* (New York, 2001), 23.

71. Lofland, "Dramaturgy."

72. Emile Durkheim makes this point in "Two Laws of Penal Evolution," *Economy and Society* 2, 3 (1973).

73. John Beattie, *Crime and the Courts in England, 1660–1800* (Princeton, N.J., 1986), 453.

74. Radzinowicz, *History*, 35.

75. Banner, *The Death Penalty*, 23.

76. McGowen, "Punishing Violence, Sentencing Crime," 142.

77. Lofland, "Dramaturgy."

78. Jeremy Bentham, *Rationales of Punishment* (Edinburgh, 1799).

79. Banner, *The Death Penalty*, 156.

80. On the execution of Damiens, see Michel Foucault, *Discipline and Punish* (New York, 1977); and John McManners, *Death and the Enlightenment: Changing Attitudes to Death among Christians and Unbelievers in Eighteenth-Century France* (New York, 1981). The sentence imposed on Damiens copied, virtually to the letter, the sentence imposed on Francois Ravaillac in 1610 for the assassination of Henry IV and therefore included the elaborate scaffold tortures that had been designed to force Ravaillac to name his co-conspirators. For an account of Ravaillac's execution, see Orest Ranum, "The French Ritual of Tyrannicide in the Late Sixteenth Century," *Sixteenth Century Journal* 11, 1 (1980): 63–82.

81. John Beattie, *Crime and the Courts in England, 1660–1800* (Princeton, N.J., 1986).

82. As Randall McGowen observes, this was not a simple substitution in which the prison replaces death. "Rather it is that the prison replaces a regime centered on death, but with many forms of mitigation that are crucially related to the character of the overall regime, such as flogging, branding, the stocks, transportation, the galleys and even fines. So while the prison represented a diminution of punishment for some offenders, for many others it represents an increase in punishment" (McGowen, personal communication, December 2009).

83. On nineteenth-century developments in criminology and penology, see David Garland. *Punishment and Welfare* (Aldershot, U.K., 1985) and *The Culture of Control* (Chicago, 2001).

84. Alphonse de Lamartine, from a speech to the French Chamber of Deputies, 1837, quoted in James Megivern, *The Death Penalty: An Historical and Theological Survey* (New York, 1997), 236. See also Beccaria, *On Crimes*, at 45: "In peace-time, in a form of government approved by the united wishes of the nation; in a state well fortified from enemies without and supported by strength within . . . there can be no necessity for taking away the life of a subject."

85. This corresponds with the process that Michel Foucault terms the "governmentalization of the state" (Foucault, "Governmentality," in *The Foucault Effect*, ed. C. Gordon et al. (Chicago, 1981)).

86. Evans, *Rituals*, 231.

87. See Karen Halttunen, *Murder Most Foul: The Killer and the American Gothic Imagination* (Cambridge, 1998), 10: "The crimes considered most heinous in the Middle Ages had been heresy against God and treason against the state. But by the sixteenth and seventeenth centuries, the murder of an individual had largely surpassed these as the most serious crime." See also Durkheim, "Two Laws."

88. Evans, *Rituals*, 146.

89. Evans quotes a statement of the Bavarian Ministry of Justice criticizing the old religious aspects of the execution for getting in the way of the state's crime control objectives. Ministry officials were afraid, they wrote in 1854, "that the clergymen often take a different point of view in these admonitory sermons from that which is required in the interests of the state. . . . The cleric often interprets the criminal from a subjective point of view, and thus it can happen that a man condemned to death for a terrible crime is portrayed as a penitent and remorseful converted sinner, who is sure of God's forgiveness. This is not the way to achieve fear of the death penalty and deterrence from crime" (ibid., 310).

90. Hunt, *Inventing*, 95–96. See also Halttunen, *Murder*. McGowen suggests that, in the nineteenth century, religion ceased to be publicly expressed on the gallows but continued to be felt in the privacy of the death cell where the condemned man feared for his soul ("The Body," 93).

91. Randall McGowen, "History, Culture and the Death Penalty: The British Debates, 1840–70," *Historical Reflections* 29, 2 (2003): 229–49 at 232.

92. Halttunen, *Murder*, 2.

93. Timothy Kaufman-Osborn, *From Noose to Needle: Capital Punishment and the Late Liberal State* (Ann Arbor, Mich., 2002), 92.

94. Michael Madow, "Forbidden Spectacle: Executions, the Public and the Press in Nineteenth-Century New York." *Buffalo Law Review* 43 (1995): 461–562 at 486.

95. Evans, *Rituals*, 246.

96. Ibid., 397.

97. Simon Schama, *Citizens: A Chronicle of the French Revolution* (New York, 1989), 619.

98. The distinction is attributed to Herb Haines, quoted by Kaufman-Osborn, *Noose*, at 108. Lofland says: "To contrast English and American state executions circa 1950 with those circa 1700 is virtually to contrast pure strategies of dramaturgical concealment and openness" ("Dramaturgy," 283).

99. Madow, "Forbidden Spectacle."

100. McGowen writes that "the gallows no longer participated in a complex metaphorical discourse" ("The Body," 673). Madow likewise observes that the modern event was "shorn of imagery and symbolism" ("Forbidden Spectacle," 482).

101. Masur, *Rites*.

102. Masur reports that within a few years of its publication Beccaria's essay was being serialized in local newspapers in America (ibid., 52).

103. Paley quoted in Gatrell, *Hanging Tree*, 263.

104. See Randall McGowen, "Through the Wrong End of the Telescope" (this volume), on death penalty proponents' use of the tropes of humanity and civilization.

105. Albert Camus, "Reflections on the Guillotine," in Camus, *Resistance, Rebellion and Death* (New York, 1961), 176.

106. Evans, *Rituals*, 367.

107. Michel Foucault, *The History of Sexuality*, Vol. 1, *An Introduction* (New York, 1978), 138ff.

108. Halttunen, *Murder*, 57.

109. Gatrell, *Hanging Tree*, 263; Evans, *Rituals*; Karen Halttunen, "Humanitarianism and the Pornography of Pain in Anglo-American Culture," *American Historical Review* 100, 2 (1995): 303–34.

110. Banner, *The Death Penalty*, at 242: "Learning to have an opinion about capital punishment was becoming part of public education. . . . Similar debates were taking place all over the world."

111. See Robert Badinter, *Abolition: One Man's Battle against the Death Penalty* (Boston, 2008); Terence Morris, *Crime and Criminal Justice since 1945* (Oxford, 1989); Banner, *The Death Penalty*.

112. Hood and Hoyle, *Death Penalty*.

113. Hood and Hoyle, *Death Penalty*; William Schabas, *The Abolition of the Death Penalty in International Law* (Cambridge, 2002); William Schabas, "International Law and the Death Penalty: Reflecting or Promoting Change?" in *Capital Punishment: Strategies for Abolition*, ed. Peter Hodgkinson and William Schabas (Cambridge, 2004). The Asian Human Rights Charter, adopted in 1998, declares that "all states must abolish the death penalty," and in November 1999 the African Commission on Human and People's Rights urged states to "envisage a moratorium on the death penalty." The Arab Charter of Human Rights, adopted by the League of Arab States in 2005, permits the imposition of the death penalty if allowed under national laws. See Hood and Hoyle, *Death Penalty*, 24.

114. See ibid..

115. One also sees this in non-Western retentionist democracies such as India and Japan. Both nations rarely use the punishment and only after much delay. India has a large death row, a delay of many years while reviews occur, and most death sentences are commuted by the higher courts. The Caribbean nations that still have the death penalty also seem ambivalent about its use, and they also exhibit the death row phenomenon.

116. Badinter, *Abolition*; Morris, *Crime and Criminal Justice*.

117. As for the non-European Western nations, New Zealand abolished the death penalty for ordinary crime in 1961, Canada in 1976, and the last state in Australia in 1984.

118. Franklin Zimring, *The Contradictions of American Capital Punishment* (New York, 2003).

119. Alex Kozinski and Sean Gallacher, "Death: The Ultimate Run-On Sentence." *Case Western Reserve Law Review* 46, 1 (1995): 1–32 at 20.

3

The Death Penalty

Between Law, Sovereignty, and Biopolitics

MICHAEL MERANZE

For several decades the penal practices and policies of the United States and the countries of Western Europe have diverged in surprising and notable ways. With the relative exception of Great Britain, none of the European countries has taken so strenuously the path of mass imprisonment. Nor have any European countries continued to deploy the death penalty. Indeed, the European Union now makes the abolition of the death penalty a condition of membership and officers of the Union press for the extension of abolition throughout the world. In the realm of common penality at least, European identity has turned on claims to human rights in matters of punishment and to the restoration of some sense of dignity to offenders.[1]

In the United States, on the other hand, American politicians, states, counties, and cities have vied with one another to prove that they were the toughest on crime, the most committed to punitive treatment in criminal justice, and the least sympathetic to the claims of convicts. The reach of the criminal justice system in the United States has consistently expanded: whole communities have been fractured by the experience of incarceration; the line between adult and juvenile offenders is increasingly blurred; and public shaming penalties have, albeit sporadically, reemerged as an active penal option. Capital punishment, in many states, remains entrenched, and the effort of both political parties and the Supreme Court to speed up the process of judicial review has exacerbated the problematic character of death penalty counsel and jurisprudence.[2] Under the Bush administration, efforts were made to centralize the decision making, and expand the practice, of the federal death penalty.[3]

Among these disparities, the death penalty has emerged as a flashpoint of domestic and international controversy. Europe redefined itself as a death penalty–free zone and seventy countries around the globe abolished the death penalty since 1976, whereas the United States not only reinstated capital punishment but thirty-six states and the federal government expanded its use and provenance.[4] In so doing, the United States appears to have broken with a nearly two-hundred-year trajectory of the gradual overcoming of capital punishment and the lessening of state punishment more generally. Given the United States' traditional self-perception as leader in the realms of human rights and penal reform, these growing gaps between Europe and the United States, indeed between the United States and most of its leading allies (with the notable exception of Japan), have triggered intense debate and denunciation. Between "abolitionist" and "retentionist" countries internationally and between anti– and pro–death penalty individuals and groups domestically, a huge, seemingly insurmountable, moral gap has emerged.

Not surprisingly, the transformation of the American penal system in general and its redeployment of the death penalty in particular have stimulated a wide range of analyses. Scholars and scholar-activists have offered interpretations rooted in deep structural conditions to understand the disparity between the United States and most of the other advanced liberal democracies.[5] Others have stressed either the contingencies or the structural components of recent political and social developments.[6] Unfortunately neither of these approaches can explain both the continuities *and* the discontinuities in the entangled penal histories of Europe and the United States.

Moreover, these interpretations suffer from interconnected flaws beginning with their historical vision, moving through their theoretical frames, and ending with the political and moral implications of their analyses. First, they treat recent European history as a norm modeled on the successful eighteenth- and nineteenth-century struggles against slavery and the slave trade; second, they interpret that norm through the lens of a totalizing historical sociology; and, finally, they draw from these positions a sense of the vestigial character of the death penalty. These analytical assumptions remain trapped within the present structure of death penalty politics; mistaking opposition for critique, critics end up replicating only one side in the ongoing arguments within and about the rationality of the death penalty. They do away with the particularity and contingency of history while overlooking their own historical rootedness. It is as if they were writing from a future where Europe set the terms and controlled the history of the death penalty.

I proceed here in a different manner. Rather than privileging Europe and the trope of abolition, I argue that we need to consider the death penalty as one among many highly complex and dispersed fields of practices and debates. Although there are several common elements in the histories of the death penalty—the relationship to sovereignty for one—we cannot assume that there is any teleology, either moral or political, that organizes the history of the modern death penalty. Second, against the tendencies to explain the trajectory of the death penalty by reference to "society" and the categories of historical sociology, I treat the contemporary American death penalty in terms of its political and legal rationalities. In doing so, I draw upon the work of Michel Foucault and, in particular, his evolving notion of "biopower"— that is, a politics that takes the problem of life and of the norm as its central themes. Finally, I argue that through this biopolitical lens we can make sense of the Supreme Court's death penalty jurisprudence and its political implications and effects. The Supreme Court's effort (first in *McGautha*[7] and then in *Furman*[8]) to meet the challenge of biopower within constitutional law opened the contemporary history of the American death penalty. But in an unanticipated way, the Court's decisions triggered a reassertion of sovereignty claims of the states and the U.S. Congress. In this way the continual re-presentation of new challenges to the death penalty implicates some of the oldest dilemmas of American constitutional law. In turn, a consistently divided Court has articulated the range of moral and legal positions on the death penalty but has done so within a context of constitutional limits and rules.

Through these arguments I hope to show that the American death penalty is not a vestige of the past but an important moment of some of the most pressing dilemmas of contemporary (international and domestic) politics. I do not draw any comfort from these positions. But if we are to understand the true implications of the death penalty in the contemporary world, then we need new analytical instruments and narratives.

The Paradoxes of the European Model

Discussions of the progress of the "abolition" of the death penalty conjure up another process of legal "abolition": that of the slave trade and slavery in the nineteenth century. Indeed, the entire structure of the European/American comparison is built upon this referent: from the use of the term "abolitionist" for countries that have discarded the death penalty, through the sense that European (and other) abolitions are irrevocable, to the notion that America is peculiarly laggard in a situation where the Europeans have first incorporated a revolution (in that case, democratic; in this case, human rights) that will eventually conquer another archaic institution. In this context, the movement to abolish capital punishment becomes analogous with the movement to abolish slavery—not simply on ethical grounds but on historically normative grounds. In other words, the successful abolition of slavery allows death penalty opponents to assume that their position replicates that of anti-slavery figures, and, as presumably was the case with anti-slavery, that the course of history is on its side.[9] This analogy is deeply problematic. Leaving aside the complexities of the actual history of anti-slavery which might complicate this understanding, there is an inherent problem in equating an ethically normative position (abolition) with the historical process itself, an equation which implies that the eventual triumph of the cause, however delayed, is historically normative.[10]

There are, to be sure, reasons for making these assumptions. From the late eighteenth to the late twentieth centuries there existed a common historical experience between Europe and the United States marked by a gradually decreasing reliance on the death penalty. From that perspective it appears reasonable to assume that abolition is the logical end point of the process. But is it?

The act of faith involved in assuming that abolition will inevitably follow from decreased use cannot be hidden either by talking about the marginalization of the death penalty or, as Amnesty International does, about "de facto" abolition states. Making the European disavowal of the death penalty normative creates a sort of tautological loop: because it has decreased in use it is a vestigial form, and because it is a vestigial form it is unnecessary and doomed.

Instead of this normative and tautological loop, I would argue that the rush to abolition in Europe after World War II was the historical anomaly— albeit one with undeniable political and ethical importance. The European example, and European pressure, certainly contributes to the growing human rights critique of the death penalty. But can we be sure that the condition of European abolition (i.e., the capacity of liberal modernist elites to withstand populist pressures in the name of an ethical ideal) is unquestionably stable, can be generalized, or even that it will last in Europe? Or was it historically a special case, a result of a momentary stabilizing of liberal modernism in the face of the Cold War combined with particular European commitments to the discourse of Human Rights in the aftermath of two world wars triggered on European soil? During the long period that Tony Judt has recently termed "Post-War," European states and societies (both East and West) designed social apparatuses (of varying effectiveness) to maximize security (social and economic as much as military) while minimizing the risks faced by individuals (at least outside the systems of national and political destruction).[11] At least in the Western half of the continent, these security systems offered a historically unprecedented, and arguably never equaled, practical application of government designed to direct, maintain, and intensify the life of a population.

A second reason to be cautious about the European case is religion. Here we might heed Albert Camus. Camus, after all, prominently declared that "capital judgment upsets the only indisputable human solidarity—our solidarity against death—and it can be legitimized only by a truth or a principle that is superior to man." From which he concluded: "The supreme punishment has always been, throughout the ages, a religious penalty."[12] Camus' point, of course, was that this fact, in an age without transcendence, condemned the death penalty (a point that Walter Berns, in his defense of capital punishment, takes to condemn both Camus and the lack of transcendence).[13] I think that we need to take Camus' confident assertion quite seriously—precisely because it is an assertion of the European 1950s. Today it is hard to have his faith in secularization. Europe's situation, rather than pointing out the future, appears to be running on its own peculiar path. Around the world the resurgence of religion, especially fundamentalist religion, and the insertion of religion into politics is a significant cultural mark of our time. One clear indication of the passing of the Cold War world has been the explosion of religious conflicts, not only between religions, whether Christian, Jewish, or Islamic, but even within them (as in the conflict between the Catholic Church and evangelical Protestant groups in Latin America). The relative absence of religion and religious conflict in Cold War Europe helped make possible the success of European elites in eliminating the death penalty. Whether they will be able to maintain the abolition of the death penalty, in a world of religious conflicts, remains to be seen. In this regard, again, it is the peculiarities of the Europeans that need to be stressed. That so many Americans believe in angels or that religion in the United States is such a divide may not be as unusual as the scholarship assumes.

Both these contentions, in turn, point to a third. The death penalty and its abolition in Europe, particularly, are situated in a wider context of discourses and practices of "national security." Much of the discussion of capital punishment relates it solely to the juridical or, at best, social discipline. But the politics of the death penalty is one of sovereignty, of national defense, and of the relationship between international laws and national laws. Even in Europe we run the risk of misrecognizing the sovereign dimensions of abolition. Although it is true that the history of abolition in Western Europe preceded in a highly contingent and national basis (and, indeed, the death penalty was temporarily eliminated in the United States while certain European nations such as France and Spain still exercised the power), it is the case that the economic power of the European Union and its ability to compel new members to abolish the death penalty has created the death penalty–free zone of Europe.[14] This situation, I think, raises the paradoxical relationship between the Cold War and European abolition even higher: for if the Cold War allowed both the bracketing of religion and the consolidation of liberal welfare states that enabled national abolition without populist pressure, it was the *end* of the Cold War and the hegemonic manner in which the West integrated the Soviet Union's client regimes into the Union which gave the impression that morality and civilization were playing themselves out on the European stage. Prior to the end of the Cold War, after all, the abolition of the death penalty had proceeded in piecemeal fashion in Europe and was justified largely in terms of the death penalty's necessity (or lack thereof) for fighting crime. But in the 1990s the contingent development of individual states was transformed into a moral imperative of the new Europe—here the death penalty became a marker for Europe's claim to regain its centrality for world history.

Indeed, the recent reopening of debate about torture (in both Europe and the United States) should give us additional pause in assuming that humanitarian law and assumptions are particularly stable.[15] To be sure, torture takes place in hiding and is justified by euphemism—it has not been truly re-legitimated. But the willingness of European nations to partake in extraordinary renditions or to accept CIA prisons, and of European and American intellectuals and lawyers to probe the means by which torture can once again become an ongoing part of our constitutional orders cannot be overlooked or separated from our understanding of the place of capital punishment in the contemporary world. After all, the disavowal of state torture would seem to be far more universal and unquestioned than the deployment of the death penalty. If the former is able to make a comeback under new historical considerations, how can we be certain that the latter has been banished even from the European community?

From the European perspective, the United States may look anomalous; compared to other nations that emerged out of European colonialism it is less so. If one looks at the British Caribbean, for instance, the death penalty is firmly defended by the island states. India persists in the death penalty, as do many of the nations of the Middle East. Japan maintains the death penalty as, of course, does China. Moreover, if we were to calculate what portion of the world's population is subject to the death penalty, which would seem anomalous—Europe or the United States? Of course, this is not the way that

Americans or American analysts (even death penalty critics) normally like to situate the United States. But that is precisely the point. American exceptionalism is a means to remove the United States from history—but putting it back into history means deciding which history to put it in.

Moreover, the colonial context allows us to draw more connections between the death penalty and other issues (high crime patterns, systems of racial and labor discrimination and violence, histories of extralegal punishments, etc). The importance of colonialism remains, admittedly, an open question. A colonial past cannot explain the history of capital punishment itself. Not all regimes with colonial pasts continue to deploy capital punishment: Brazil, to name only one, abolished capital punishment in the nineteenth century. But the colonial inheritance opens us up to histories and to the particularity of legal regimes in shaping contemporary penal practices. In the United States, to take the relevant point, several of the crucial characteristics of American penal life (its juridical diversity, its legalism, its intersection between religious moralism and penal practice; its complex racial conflicts; its anomalous systems of sovereignty) emerged during its colonial period.[16] Just as important for the history of American punishment, the presence of chattel slavery organized through race—in the midst of a series of unfree labor systems and powerfully patriarchal familial orders—meant that the issue of corporal punishment as simultaneously an issue of racial distinction, and of competing sovereignties, would haunt the American order in ways different from many other metropolitan and postcolonial contexts.

As even these cursory discussions of secularization, bureaucracy, and teleology may indicate, I suggest that underlying the assumption that Europe is normative and that the United States lags behind is an unacknowledged modernization theory. The assumption presumes that there is some shared, irrevocable process that underlies the history of penal forms. One symptom of these unacknowledged assumptions is the very instability of the justifications for the comparison. How is the question framed? Sometimes it is shared traditions, sometimes common membership in the "West," sometimes "advanced democracies" or "industrial democracies," and sometimes even a gesture toward those countries to which the United States is "normally" compared (a tautological definition if there ever was one). These bases of comparison all stand in for something else—sociological assumptions about the shared characteristics of a "modern" industrialized nation-state. The problem is that these assumptions preclude us from understanding specific historical processes, indeed specific histories. As a result, analysts smuggle in analytical and ethical norms and transform them into historical ones. Instead of an analysis of the structured contingencies of different histories, we get an implicitly normative account of (hoped-for) inevitability.[17]

All these points suggest recognizing that European abolition is a remarkable historical accomplishment. It is a significant historical fact. It may provide inspiration for activists. It may provide crucial leverage for worldwide abolition of the death penalty. But it cannot provide a starting point for analysts. Instead, we must look elsewhere for the coordinates of the history of the death penalty.

Biopower, Sovereignty, and the Law

Michel Foucault, in his work of the mid-1970s, aimed to critique an understanding of politics rooted in the controlling values of law and rights. During this period he treated the law as an essentially negative system of order, one that concealed at least as much as it revealed. In *Discipline and Punish* he sought to show that the disciplines had effectively infected and displaced the law and legal systems. Whereas we tend to think of penal practice as guided by statute and our liberty as defended by rights, Foucault insisted that historically our notion of the law was the remains of an absolutist strategy for conquering alternative loci of authority; consequently our recourse to law and rights failed to capture a form of power (discipline) that acted according to an entirely different logic. In the *History of Sexuality* he challenged the assumption that the problem with modern sexuality was that it was repressed by the law (whether state law or psychic law). Instead, he insisted, the power that shaped sexuality was productive. Modern sexuality, he argued, was an endlessly expanding cycle of discursive and non-discursive incitements to speech. If his prison book challenged the law as a locus of rights, the sexuality book challenged psychoanalysis (especially Lacanian psychoanalysis) and its notion that the "Law" functioned to suppress desire. Indeed, sex rooted in natural desire is what makes it possible for us "to conceive power solely as law and taboo."[18] As Foucault put it in one of his most famous phrases: "In political thought and analysis, we still have not cut off the head of the king."[19]

If the law was essentially negative, and power was productive, then the history of the law could not explain modern governance. Foucault argued that we live within a regime of "biopower" instead.[20] He contended that early modern Europeans developed new rationalities for approaching the questions of life and death. This modern politics of life, he argued, approaches the human body through two distinct but interrelated systems. On the one hand, there exists what he referred to as "*the disciplines: an anatomo-politics of the human body,"* and, on the other, *"regulatory controls: a biopolitics of the population."* The disciplines concerned the individual body—above all, as a "machine." They train and shape bodies, work to increase their productive capabilities, tone down their resistance, and place them within carefully divided and organized spaces of production and restraint.[21] Regulation, on the other hand, concerns itself not with individuals but with populations—population as the site of the reproduction of the mass organism. "Biopolitics" identified the problem of statistical regularities within populations, patterns of disease, of birth and death, the organization and defense of health in order to ensure that populations would grow in strength, health, and numbers. As he put it:

> The disciplines of the body and the regulations of the population constituted the two poles around which the organization of power over life was deployed. The setting up, in the course of the classical age, of this great bipolar technology—anatomic and biological, individualizing and specifying, directed toward the performances of the body, with attention to the processes of life—characterized a power whose highest function was perhaps no longer to kill, but to invest life through and through.[22]

This technology of life, aimed to link the training of individual bodies to the project of the regulated growth of a population. From the seventeenth century on, Foucault argued, life itself became a central object of political calculation and strategy. It was the development of techniques of calculation and strategy that moved Europe and the United States into the realm of *"biopower"* where "the life of the species is wagered on its own political strategies."[23]

Given the dual technology of modern biopolitics it is not surprising that Foucault approached the politics of life through the topic of sexuality. As the intersection of the desires of the subject and the reproduction of the population, sexuality offered the meeting place for disciplines and regulations. Sexuality, Foucault insisted, was a seemingly natural object that was actually a constructed historical object. Once constructed it became open to investigation in the name of knowledge and subject to direction in the name of the norm. Within what he called the "deployment of sexuality" scientists, doctors, public officials, and others produced knowledge; professional groups and governments developed institutions; experts, families, and businesses expanded interests; religious and political figures, parents and doctors, men and women asserted the necessity to control the sexuality of others; and those situated to extract profits from this new system derived material benefits while those excluded from profits (both financial, political, and subjective) bore the costs. The material reality of this network meant that struggles over sexuality were ongoing and that these conflicts, knowledge, and institutions helped shape and produce bodies and experiences. Individuals in the midst of modern sexuality gained a means to imagine themselves as deep selves, containing an interiority that allowed them to exercise self-control (or self-expression), a new sense of personal destiny and meaning.

But even the deployment of sexuality was itself a link in a large chain—the chain of biopower. As politics attended to life itself, Foucault argued, sexuality became a key means to link together the disciplinary training of individual bodies with the collective management of human populations; the structures of knowledge and power with the subjective organization of the person. Forging this chain took time. Foucault suggested that sexuality was originally a bourgeois invention that gradually gravitated to the working classes. At first, class experiences took different shape: the working classes were disciplined and the bourgeois classes were sexualized. But by the end of the nineteenth century discipline and sexuality had crossed class lines and formed a grid that traversed class distinctions.

In his *History of Sexuality* Foucault suggested that this new biopower "supplanted" an older regime organized around the problem of sovereignty.[24] Under the reign of the absolutist monarchies, power—following a structure descended from the authority of a Roman patriarch—could simply "*take* life or *let* live." Foucault meant that, ultimately, the sovereign's power over life and death was circumscribed: "Power in this instance was essentially a right of seizure: of things, time, bodies, and ultimately life itself; it culminated in the privilege to seize hold of life in order to suppress it."[25] Here, he was essentially following his account of the public execution in *Discipline and Punish*.[26] Power under the logic of sovereignty was modeled on the law of the Monarch and supported by violence. This power reached its ultimate violence in warfare and the death penalty and was essentially negative: it functioned primarily by forbidding things, overawing opposition, and marking boundaries. It could not penetrate and direct life itself, instead it achieved its own limit at life—its greatest assertion of authority (the power to kill) was also the point at which its effective power disappeared.

In such an era of biopower the death penalty would appear—and indeed has appeared for many people—as an embarrassment. From within the logic of the new biopolitics, the death penalty—one of the great symbols of the overweening might of the sovereign—appears excessive and counterproductive: "How could power exercise its highest prerogatives by putting people to death, when its main role was to ensure, sustain, and multiply life, to put this life in order? For such a power, execution was at the same time a limit, a scandal, and a contradiction."[27] Hence governments increasingly hid the death penalty behind prison walls, legislators minimized its use and lessened the reach of capital crimes, and reformers sought newer more "humane" means of death from the guillotine, to the electric chair, the gas chamber, and the lethal injection. But still the penalty persists and Foucault turned to the interplay between race and biopolitics to explain this persistence. "One had the right to kill," he declared, "those who represented a kind of biological danger to others."[28]

Consequently, despite the rhetoric of biopolitics "supplanting" sovereignty, this intersection of the death penalty, race, and biopower indicated—within Foucault's analysis—the persistence of the logics of sovereignty. Put another way, the tactics of sovereignty (like the death penalty) took up a new position in the wider field of government. In both the first volume of his *History of Sexuality* and in the final lecture of his *Society Must Be Defended*, Foucault offered an account of the transformation of sovereignty in an age of "biopower." In this telling, while the symbolic centrality of the death penalty (as symbol of sovereign power) declined, the death penalty did not disappear. Instead, it became linked in new ways to the nationally and racially organized technologies of mass destruction—particularly those of warfare. As Foucault put it: "The justification of—or the way biopower functions through—the old sovereign power of life and death implies the workings, the introduction and activation of racism. And it is, I think, here that we find the actual roots of racism."[29] But we must be careful here, for Foucault's notion of racism is broader than how it is conventionally understood, especially in the United States:

> What in fact is racism? It is primarily a way of introducing a break into the domain of life that is under power's control: the break between what must live and what must die. The appearance within the biological continuum of the human race or races, the distinction among races, the hierarchy of races, the fact that certain races are described as good and that others, in contrast, are described as inferior: all this is a way of fragmenting the field of the biological that power controls. It is a way of separating out the groups that exist within a population. It is, in short, a way of establishing a biological-type caesura within a population that appears to be a biological domain.[30]

Put this way, Foucault did not ignore the commonsense notions of race and racial politics. Instead, he complicated them. For if, on the one hand, warfare and social struggle could be fought between opponents conceived of as different races, then, on the other hand, individuals could be removed from the general population and condemned to death or unending coercion as part of a race of "monsters." Too many accounts of Foucault's reasoning have avoided a confrontation with this persistent place of the "Right of Death" in his account of the biopolitical regime; instead, they have focused on the interventions into the "Power over Life."[31] But this is a fundamental mistake: the power over life has not supplanted the right of death; whether taking the form of a living tomb unto death or the deliberate act of state killing, the penal system remains rooted in this moment of dismembering the social body.[32]

From this perspective, sovereignty, discipline, biopower, and governmentality do not mark societies (or refer to the entire social field) or even institutions per se but are ways of identifying, intervening, and rationalizing. Biopolitics, to take only the most pressing example, is the problem of the population as a natural and self-regulating problem that is also subject to the intervention of knowledge and government. And with the emergence of new problems, old ones do not necessarily disappear but are displaced (not replaced) and take up a new place in a reconfigured level of social and political practices. As he put it in 1978, "we should not see things as the replacement of a society of sovereignty by a society of discipline, and then of a society of discipline by a society, say, of government. In fact, we have a triangle: sovereignty, discipline, and governmental management, which has population as its main target and apparatuses of security as its essential mechanism."[33]

Over time the field of sovereignty (organized around the defense of territory and the subordination of families and subjects to the state) became enmeshed with the logic of biopolitics (organized around the organization and regulation of the population). The complexities of modern politics emerge out of the intersection and intertwining of these serial rationalities (and one could imagine others as well). From *Discipline and Punish* forward, Foucault was concerned with the identification and analysis of different aspects of the practices of government. Whether characterized as "rationalities," "technologies," or "problematizations," the target of Foucault's work was a series of discrete, if dispersed, ways of marking, reflecting upon, and subjecting a problem or domain in reality, discrete ways that have come to define modern politics.[34] Sovereignty was, one might say, both here and there. The real question is how to understand this reconfigured situation.

Paradoxically the emergence of a politics of life has thereby heightened the importance of the death penalty as an act of sovereignty precisely *because it has made capital punishment even more an act of self-reflective political judgment*. If the early modern death penalty was a taken for granted aspect of state power, now the death penalty is a highly significant point in an evolving political rationality. No longer assumed, its significance has grown because it must be chosen.

If the body—its desires, its reproduction, and its complex embeddedness in families, themselves open to pedagogy and medicine—marked one pole of the domain of biopower, there was another equally crucial pole. Liberalism and the politics of security grounded this other pole. In his discussion of liberalism and security, Foucault was most concerned with the different rationalities that came to critique and direct the operations of government. In part, liberalism and security were one moment in a far longer and wider history of the governing of people by themselves and others. It is possible, for instance, to construct a long history from the ancient arts of the self to the modern theories of *Homo oeconomicus*. But for our purposes, the crucial moment in the construction of liberal security was the transformation of governing that accompanied the political, social, and imperial struggles of the early modern West. In Foucault's optic, techniques devised to govern specific groups, religious orders, families, schools—what he termed the conduct of conduct[35]—transformed state practice beginning in the sixteenth century. In particular, this problem of conduct has led to a greater emphasis on the open and reflective nature of the "arts" of government—a recognition that governance exists beyond the state and that even the most repressive state actions are part of a wider web of political strategies.[36]

But most distinctive about Foucault's treatment of liberalism—and this is only one of a series of significant differences between an analysis rooted in biopower and a more conventional accounting of the growth of the welfare state—is that liberalism (even in its modern forms) was not simply the transposition of these new techniques of governance into the state but a way of marking the space between them. From one angle, the biopolitical regime witnessed an expansion in multiple forms of governance that traversed relationships between people. From another angle, liberalism defined itself through its search for the precise point at which the State should operate within those multiple fields of governance. "Public" and "private" then, name relationships between different modes and relations of governing.

One can see this process clearly in the case of what Foucault called "security." Put simply, Foucault defines "security" in relation to the emergence (in the seventeenth and eighteenth centuries) of techniques to study the "normal" or regular occurrences of births, deaths, illnesses, and so on, as well as the overall growth of population and the movement of people and commodities. Security then becomes the governmental rationality that—taking account of these seeming natural movements of populations and commodities—creates governmental policies designed to ensure that actual events approach normal conditions. People, states, and capital, according to the logic of security, should be able to operate without unnecessary restraint on their movements *and* without fear of crisis. Perhaps not surprisingly, Foucault points to the central place that political economy comes to play within this technology of security. Classical political economy worked to naturalize the conditions of the market and the population, and to offer a liberal rationale for minimum state intervention against the mercantilist and police states of early modern Europe. With its powerful critique of absolutism in the name of utility, political economy—and here Foucault is clearly offering a rewriting of his earlier account of political economy's place in the birth of the episteme of man[37]—brought political rationality to the threshold of the biopolitical. Indeed, this treatment of political economy and its descendant, utilitarianism, allowed Foucault to bring together liberalism, governmentality, and biopolitical rationality for the first time.

Indeed, these concepts allowed Foucault to understand both the specificities of liberalism and neoliberalism. If early liberalism helped define the politics of security, the problem of security reemerged transformed with *neoliberalism* understood as a critique of the state in the mid-twentieth century. Focusing on the German and American variants of neoliberalism, Foucault showed how neoliberalism radicalized political economy's emphasis on the rationality of the market to make market rationality the ordering principle of the social field. Whereas liberalism imagined society on the basis of the individual as entrepreneur, neoliberalism left the individual behind in focusing on the individual enterprise. Neoliberalism insisted not only that the economy should be allowed to function freely no matter the immediate cost but that the rest of society should be imagined as functioning according to the logic of the economy. Neoliberalism was not a return to classical liberalism but a redefinition of liberalism from a technique of governmental restraint to a program of market domination.[38] But left implicit in this account was the recognition that liberalism was a critique of mercantilist and police rationalities, neoliberalism a critique of biopolitical rationality. Neoliberalism does not forget the use of statistical models or ignore the importance of norms of behaviors—in fact, as "rational choice" theory exemplifies, neoliberalism extends the economic to new dimensions. But neoliberalism is a technique that intensifies risk for individuals rather than minimizes it; it provides security for the economy but not for the population.[39] In this way the economy, originally a means to rationalize government in the interest of population, now becomes the end to which populations and techniques of security are subordinated.

Left out of this account—yet central to any understanding of the American death penalty—is a consideration of the specificity of the law. In large part, of course, this lacuna is a result of Foucault's conception of the law as the remnant of Absolutist centralization. Telling in this regard was his characterization of constitutional questions. As Foucault saw it, "the problem of the constitution" had been central to political reflection during the seventeenth and eighteenth centuries but lost its centrality to the question of utility and governmental limitation in the nineteenth.[40] But to make this argument is to ignore the long history of modern juridical and political debate over constitutional forms as well as the varied forms of constitutionalism that continue to coexist with liberal governmentality. Put another way, Foucault's powerful historicism—combined with his reduction of the law—led him to underplay the multitude of struggles that surround law, constitutions, and the juridical in contemporary societies.[41] As a result, by the end of the lectures titled *The Birth of Biopolitics* he had reached something of a dead end. But it was a dead end related not—as conventional wisdom has it—to his treatment of the subject but rather to his treatment of the law.

Foucault's insistence that at stake in the history of political rationality was the transfer of the reflective arts of government into the state (and their transformation of the state) rather than the transformation of the arts of government when they entered the sphere of the law, legal regulation, and the state, then, prevented his account from providing a meaningful history of the development of biopower and a concrete account of the emergence and meaning of neoliberalism as its critique. It is only by seeing the latter phenomenon that we can begin to understand the history of biopolitics in general, and the relationship of the death penalty to biopolitics in particular.[42] Biopolitics must be set against, and within, a history of the law. In the United States, in particular, it is the uneasy intersection between biopolitical consideration and constitutional arguments that accounts for the peculiarly obsessive centrality of the death penalty not only to our politics but to our constitutional thinking. But first let me sketch out a larger historical context for understanding the contemporary American scene.

Capital Punishment and the History of Biopolitics

The history of biopower and the law, of course, remains to be written. And I can only offer a few general signposts here, limited for the most part to the North Atlantic and particularly the Anglo-American worlds. But looking at the long-term intersection between changing political rationalities, law, and state practices will help us situate the recent divergences in the history of capital punishment more effectively than the use of the categories of either historical sociology or recourse to ideas of moral progress.

It is clear that—on both sides of the North Atlantic—the theory and practice of social intervention and organization changed dramatically in the late eighteenth and early nineteenth centuries. Not only were there growing efforts to measure the utility of governmental and charitable programs, and increasing arguments in favor of removing legal restraints on the movement of capital and commodities, but social organizations and governments engaged in new and more systematic investigations of social and economic conditions. One need only read the annual reports of societies that dealt with pauperism or charity, working conditions or urban health, industry and agriculture, to recognize the widespread effort to quantify and display the shape of society. In the British Parliament, to name only one example, the vast accumulation of information through parliamentary investigations revealed that this impulse was not limited to private actors. All told, the age of political economy and of "security" inaugurated an age of information.

If this explosion of investigation and intervention was true in general, it was also true in two particular domains: anti-slavery and anti–death penalty activity. In both these domains, a discourse of humanity combined with a discourse of utility to promote not only moral outrage but political commitment and, in the case of anti-slavery at least, a powerful social movement. Each of these movements drew simultaneously upon the individualizing rhetoric of sentiment and the collectivizing rhetoric of charts, graphs, and blueprints (for anti-slavery, the representation of slave ship holds; for anti–death penalty, the representation of idealized prison spaces of repentance).[43] By effectively bringing together questions of utility, sentiment, and dignity, both these efforts marked a transition to a new politics of life. For what anti-slave trade, anti-slavery, and anti–death penalty activities shared above all was a critique of both inefficiency and the absolute power over life and death.

Yet the examples of the slave trade, slavery, and death penalty issues should remind us that the new politics of life and death was actually limited at the turn of the nineteenth century. Whereas the North Atlantic slave trade was abolished early in the nineteenth century (it continued to flourish to South America through much of the century), the American South resisted the abolition of slavery through political confrontation and force of arms until the U.S. Civil War (Britain, of course, abolished slavery in her colonies earlier, as did France). And although the focus of the death penalty shifted from crimes of property and public display to crimes against persons and increasingly segregated performances, the death penalty did not disappear in any of the nations making up the North Atlantic world. Moreover, the nineteenth century also witnessed the diffusion of new notions and images of dangerous individuals, moral monsters, cruel sadists, gothic villains, and others deserving of the ultimate penalties.[44] The emergence of race as a crucial mechanism for disqualifying individuals from civic standing (most directly in the American South but also in the American North and throughout the European empires) revealed that the new biopolitics had more success in intervening in society than in remaking sovereignty. In the cases of the slave trade, slavery, and the death penalty, the successful political struggles convinced the sovereign power to eliminate alternate sources of sovereignty (in the slaveholder) or to withdraw legal sanction from a practice (in the slave trade) but only to modify the exercise of its own power (in capital punishment).

That the practice and theory of the death penalty would come repeatedly into question in conjunction with wars and revolutions only sharpens this point. The first systematic political questioning of the death penalty took place within the context of the American and French Revolutions, and the crises of the British Empire and British representation. In the United States, the aftermath of the Civil War and the intensification of industrialization and mass immigration led to a hardening of attitudes toward the death penalty as well as the emergence of lynching as a systematic effort to regain Southern sovereignty. In France, the possibility of death penalty abolition accompanied the first socialist regime in the early twentieth century, and, in Britain, the death penalty, though continuously debated in the aftermath of World War II, was only abolished under a Labor government. I stress these moments not because they provide some sort of continual history but as a reminder that the sphere of sovereignty remained central to the question of the politics of life and death.

If war, revolution, and the persistence of the death penalty remind us of the continued importance of the problem of sovereignty, we should not lose sight of the extent of the "governmentalization" of the state during the same period. From the late eighteenth-century on, liberal critics and governmental officials attacked the traditional organization of police powers—operating in an older regime of morally just regulation—and sought to replace them with market-based approaches.[45] Poor laws on both sides of the Atlantic placed ever greater emphasis on the distinction between "deserving" and "undeserving" poor, efforts were made to force the poor into the job market for their subsistence, and reformers and the state took the family—both in its sexuality and in its organization of child labor—as a prime target for intervention.[46] The growing intersection between the state and private groups worked to raise the reflexivity of government policy on society, and the spread of moral reform societies and institutions created a new web of organized interventions into social problems. And, of course, from the late nineteenth century on, governments on both sides of the Atlantic expanded their regulatory powers and welfare systems—even if in the United States these systems tended to remain local.

In the realm of criminal law and punishment two moments stand out. The most dramatic was the initial turn toward reformative incarceration between 1780 and 1840. However one construes the motivations for this shift (growing humanization, the spread of the disciplines, or utility) it is undeniable that the elaboration of penal regimes (and other secondary institutions such as reformed workhouses, new spaces to hold juveniles and lesser offenders, etc.) meant the importation of new forms of governing into the state apparatus. With the growth of reformative incarceration, the state took hold of the lives of individuals for long periods (longer, in many cases, than military terms of service), and prison officials devised systems of labor, oversight, punishment, and individual reformation. Arguably the state's adoption of these practices and tasks not only transformed the state but the practices as well. As they become embedded within the law, their legal deployment legitimized their spread into non-state institutions.[47] A second governmental earthquake occurred in the late nineteenth and early twentieth centuries. If the first movement toward the governmentalization of criminal law and punishment had been centered on the problem of the structuring of the prison, the second was centered on the question of structuring the individual offender. Both in the United States and Europe new forms of knowledge that took the offender as their prime object (e.g., criminal anthropology, criminology, and urban sociology) developed their own arguments, journals, and approaches articulating a basis for a eugenicist notion of criminality, on the one hand, and an environmental notion of criminality, on the other. Reformers constructed and reconstructed large-scale organizational networks to investigate criminal justice, to communicate ideas across state and national lines, and to lobby for new approaches to the question of crime. Coupled, in the United States at least, with a late-century crisis of penal labor, these new intellectual disciplines and social organizations pushed for a growing "progressive" emphasis on the cultural and educational in punishment. The result was a growing "socialization" of justice—to borrow a phrase from Michael Willrich—that deemphasized individual responsibility for crime and instead stressed either social or hereditary causes.[48]

The biopolitical notion that human scientific knowledge was available to separate the corrigible from the incorrigible was an essential element of these transformations. The institutional innovations of the late nineteenth and early twentieth centuries (e.g., juvenile courts, parole, probation, and the growing emphasis of psychology within punishment) all presumed that professionals could be entrusted with the task of reorganizing penal decisions—that a second tier of experts could make certain that jurors did not err in their punitive judgments. Likewise and moving deeper into the twentieth century, the administrative restraint placed upon the death penalty (either through court review, commutation, pardon, or indeed jurors themselves) intersected with the notion that those deserving death were a statistical few whose incorrigibility or evil could be clearly identified and articulated.[49] Here, however, in an anticipation of the crises of the latter twentieth century, this decline in the use of the death penalty did not extend fully either to African Americans in the American South or to colonial subjects during decolonization. And, of course, the Nazi regime should caution us against any sort of confidence in a long-term, unidirectional civilizing process. But even with these acknowledgments the introduction of biopolitical rationales into both judicial sentencing and penal practice clearly reconfigured the juridical on both sides of the Atlantic.

Still, despite the widespread use of biopolitical technologies and rationalities, only with the great crisis of the mid-twentieth century did full biopolitical regimes emerge in Europe. Ironically the first biopolitical regime was a negative one—that of Nazi Germany where biopower was turned in upon itself and produced an outwardly destructive and inwardly self-devouring system based on racial distinctions.[50] But from the 1930s on, and with growing intensity in the aftermath of the Second World War, biopolitical and welfare states spread rapidly in Europe. In the United States federal and state officials also began construction of a biopolitical order. Social security, unemployment insurance, rudimentary welfare mechanisms, and expanded regulatory systems for the economy are all indications of the web of security that underlay the politics of life. The United States joined, indeed shaped, the international institutions—from the United Nations to the Bretton Woods

Accords, and later the International Monetary Fund and the World Bank—that the Western industrial powers developed to stabilize postwar global relations. From the 1950s on, increased state funding for education, scientific research, and various campaigns (against poverty, cancer, smoking, etc.) reshaped the relationships between public and private in a biopolitical direction, deploying not only newfound scientific capabilities but also the models of statistical regularity to identify and intervene in society in new ways.

The structures of American society limited the institutionalization of biopolitics in at least three distinct ways. First, let us consider the racial politics in the United States. For Europe, at least once Nazi Germany was defeated and until the renewed immigration problems at the end of the twentieth century, the politics of race could be contained largely in a colonial setting. But in the United States the problem of race lay at the core of American politics, and thus it is no surprise that opponents were able to limit biopolitics in its welfare mode along racial terms. The American system of federalism only strengthened the hands of opponents—racial domination systematically trumped the implementation of structures of shared security on the local and state levels (just as the emergence of a more active Civil Rights movement would lead to the dismantling of large sectors of the biopolitical order in the 1960s and 1970s). Second, the architects of the new biopolitical regime had to confront constitutional questions and oppositions almost immediately. The New Dealers may have been able to triumph in their showdown with the Supreme Court, but the structures of federalism and opposition within the judiciary meant that the New Deal and its successors (in particular, the Great Society) were haunted by constitutional challenges and difficulties. The racial and constitutional issues, combined with a more powerful ideological and economic opposition, led to the third difference: the generally less-developed welfare and regulatory regimes of the United States compared to postwar Europe. Despite the growing power of the federal government, the divided sovereignties of the United States allowed state and local officials to circumscribe the shape of regulation and security—deploying their old claims of police power against the federal government.

But the contrary situation existed in terms of national security and the power to kill. Here the United States quickly outstripped its European counterparts and—rhetoric aside—its Soviet challengers as well. The United States' unmatched economic power and huge nuclear arsenal, along with its unparalleled capacity to deliver it, placed the choice of life and death at the center of American politics. Put another way, if Foucault's original account of biopolitical rationality took as its stage nineteenth-century continental

Europe and its entry point the question of sexuality, in looking at the history of biopolitical practices and their institutional embodiment, the United States in the latter half of the twentieth century stands at the forefront of the history and contradictions of biopower, for it was here above all other places where "the life of the species is wagered on its own political strategies."[51]

Here it is important to stress that "biopolitical" is not simply another name for "welfare" and that a "biopolitical order" cannot be equated with questions of a "weak" or "strong" state. For one thing, biopolitics is not a social and institutional formation. Unlike the welfare state with which it sometimes overlaps, biopolitics is not rooted in institutions but instead marks a set of rationalities that cut across institutions and guide their decisions. But perhaps more important, there is no "outside" to the biopolitical. Unlike discussions of welfare or the state in which confident statements can be made about strength and weakness in order to delimit the range or reach of institutions, biopolitics defines the system of rationality that determines what will be included or left out, what will be private or public—and, especially in the nuclear age, what will be an acceptable level of destruction and indifference to suffering. Biopolitical rationalities define the state; they cannot be reduced to it or equated with it.

The American biopolitical state was thrust almost immediately into struggles and contradictions. Although the national security apparatus and, with it, the powers of the executive branch expanded with little check (at least until the twin crises of Vietnam and Watergate) the conflicts over internal sovereignty were less easily settled and increasingly took the form of constitutional questions before the Supreme Court. From the 1950s on, the Supreme Court became a flashpoint within U.S. politics. The Warren Court, after all, famously tangled with federal and state legislatures over issues regarding racial segregation, civil rights, voting rights, representation, and internal security. Although the Warren Court's commitments fluctuated over time (allowing for a slowing down of desegregation, reversing itself on internal security matters, vacillating on its commitments to civil rights and criminal law reform), the basic thrust of the Court remained a liberal modernist one, its decisions regularly enraging the South, and, as a result, the opposition to the liberal modernist state as embodied in the New Deal and Great Society took the form of opposition to the Supreme Court.[52]

Nowhere perhaps was the centrality of the Court as clear as in the area of criminal justice. The obvious lack of a political base opposed to the death penalty, combined with the continual effects of racial prejudice on the practice of capital punishment, caused the federal judiciary to become the central front in anti–death penalty activism. In particular, the Legal Defense Fund attorneys of the National Association for the Advancement of Colored People (NAACP) creatively challenged the death penalty on a variety of constitutional grounds—including, but not limited to, the question of racial prejudice.[53] But if the Court was crucial in efforts to control police conduct, ensure defendant's rights, improve the possibilities of counsel, and regulate the imposition of punishment, particularly capital punishment, its actions not only stimulated challenges to its own authority but also to the entire biopolitical project in its Great Society form. The growing fear of crime—culminating in the Omnibus Crime Control and Safe Streets Act of 1968, itself an attack on the Court's decisions—made the Supreme Court a central symbol in the emerging culture wars.[54] By the early 1970s the Court found itself at the limit of the administrative compromises that had governed capital punishment for several decades.

The Constitution and the Crisis of the American Death Penalty

The recent history of the death penalty in the United States crystallized during the early 1970s in the string of Supreme Court decisions that began with *McGautha* and concluded with *Gregg* and *Woodson*. Although *Furman* and *Gregg* remain the most famous—and crucial—of the cases, they all share the same historical problematic: What is the proper relationship of biopolitics and constitutional law? The elevation of the death penalty to a question of constitutional struggle was a startling development. Before the 1970s the Supreme Court rarely addressed the death penalty, and, when it did, it handled the issue without questioning its fundamental constitutional status. But now the death penalty became a central aspect of constitutional jurisprudence, and the Supreme Court has returned repeatedly to the issue. The Court did so, of course, partly because of the continual and skillful challenges made to capital punishment. But that the Court accepted these challenges, and struggled both to acknowledge and contain them, demonstrates the intense problem that biopolitical rationalities posed for constitutional law and thinking—at least in the context of the United States.

The cases of the early 1970s all shared the same trigger: Could juror discretion be regulated enough to meet the requirements of a biopolitical constitutionality? And they all confronted the same political question: Where did sovereignty lie in making this decision? Regularity, discretion, and sovereignty—these issues provoked the continuing politics of capital punishment in the contemporary United States.

When the Court took up the constitutionality of the death penalty in *McGautha* and *Furman,* it did so at the intersection of two separate ideas of race. On one side stood a biopolitical notion of race (i.e., the delineation of a subpopulation that could be killed) and, on the other, the deeply established sociopolitical notion of race (i.e., the question of racial prejudice against African Americans within the judicial system). Implicitly *McGautha* and *Furman* posed the question of whether the death penalty was so profoundly intertwined with the sociopolitical problem of race that it could not be rationalized according to the logic of the biopolitical notion of race. In constitutional terms this question took the form of the demands placed upon Eighth Amendment jurisprudence by the due process demands of the Fourteenth Amendment.[55] Put in terms of this essay, determining the relationship between the Eighth (cruel and unusual) and Fourteenth Amendments (due process) meant addressing the relationship between biopolitical and constitutional logics.

The opening salvos in this problem were the twinned cases *McGautha v. California* and *Crampton v. Ohio.*[56] At issue in *McGautha* was California's refusal to provide guidance to jurors in deciding whether to sentence McGautha to death. In *Crampton* the issue was Ohio's system of death penalty trials, in particular the state's practice of holding a single trial to determine both guilt and sentencing. McGautha's attorneys argued that the lack of direction prevented any meaningful (and constitutionally required) judicial review of the sentence, and Crampton's attorneys argued that the lack of a two-stage capital trial system placed the defendant in the position of sacrificing the ability to introduce exculpatory autobiographical evidence or else conceding the Fifth Amendment rights against self-incrimination.

Despite the obvious differences in the cases, the Court chose to rule on them jointly and to reject their challenges (both biopolitical and constitutional) to the death penalty. Indeed, John Harlan, in writing for the Court, made three interlocking arguments that, while treating the singularity of each case, brought them under a common rubric in defense of the constitutionality of the death penalty. First, he sought to separate constitutional demands from wider currents of thought. As he put it, "Our function is not to impose on the States, *ex cathedra,* what might seem to us a better system for dealing with capital cases. Rather it is to decide whether the Federal Constitution proscribes the present procedures of these two States in such cases."[57] And that Constitution, he insisted, was restrained in its demands upon criminal justice: "the Federal Constitution, which marks the limits of our authority in these cases, does not guarantee trial procedures that are the best of all worlds, or that accord with the most enlightened ideas of students of the infant science of criminology, or even those that measure up to the predilections of members of this Court."[58] This self-restraint, in turn, imposed upon the Court a particular mode of anti-progressive history. Turning to the history of death penalty legislation, Harlan argued that all efforts to legislatively determine degrees of guilt within murder, or to offer juries precise instructions for their decisions, have failed.[59] Indeed, the structure of Harlan's historical reconstruction emphasized the historically limited reach of due process and treated that precedential history as constitutionally binding. "The procedures which petitioners challenge," Harlan declared, "are those by which most capital trials in this country are conducted, and by which all were conducted until a few years ago. We have determined that these procedures are consistent with the rights to which petitioners were constitutionally entitled, and that their trials were entirely fair.[60] Having reached these conclusions we have performed our task of measuring the State's process by federal constitutional standards, and accordingly the judgment in each of these cases is Affirmed."[61]

Yet, almost immediately, Harlan transformed this seemingly constitutional and precedential claim into a claim about knowledge. Not only have efforts to guide the decisions of juries failed, he argued, but they are doomed to fail. Directly challenging those who had argued for standards in capital cases, Harlan pronounced that

> Those who have come to grips with the hard task of actually attempting to draft means of channeling capital sentencing discretion have confirmed the lesson taught by the history recounted above. To identify before the fact those characteristics of criminal homicides and their perpetrators which call for the death penalty, and to express these characteristics in language which can be fairly understood and applied by the sentencing authority, appear to be tasks which are beyond present human ability.[62]

If this move from the historical to the epistemological was relevant, if excessive, in the context of *McGautha*'s due process challenge to standardless trials, its reappearance in *Crampton*'s self-incrimination challenge was powerfully symptomatic. Harlan was at pains to insist that there was no difference between how Fifth Amendment rights operated in capital and noncapital trials. Guilt was guilt, and the nature of the sentence might have a "peculiar poignancy" in capital cases but not a constitutional importance. But having addressed the claim that death was different Harlan concluded this piece of his argument on an entirely different note: "Even in noncapital sentencing," he declared, "the sciences of penology, sociology, and psychology have not advanced to the point that sentencing is wholly a matter of scientific calculation from objectively verifiable facts."[63] How the state of these "sciences" was relevant to the question of self-incrimination Harlan never stated.

With this opinion Harlan, and the Court for whom he spoke, rejected extending the biopolitical organization of criminal justice to the death penalty system. Whereas the socialization of justice, the expansion of parole and probation, the creation of separate tiers of special courts for the juvenile, and the introduction of psychological services into prisons had all served to modify criminal justice and bring it, to some extent at least, under the sway of expert knowledge organized around different notions of the normal and the healthy, Harlan—despite declaring that death was not different—drew a line at capital punishment. There juries could remain unbound and defendants unheard. The biopolitical had no place; instead law (in the form of judicial review of procedural questions) and sovereignty (in the form of a governor's pardons) would continue to hold sway.[64]

McGautha did not stand for long. The following year *Furman* effectively abolished the death penalty as practiced in the United States. Furman's attorneys famously linked the Fourteenth and Eighth Amendments together to argue that the intrusion of the biopolitical politics of life into capital punishment (e.g., the administrative and practical tendency not to actually execute individuals, the tendency to hide executions when they occur, and the death penalty's controversial status in society) made clear that, despite the statutory presence of the death penalty, capital punishment was itself contrary to "evolving standards of decency." The reason the death penalty persisted, they argued, was that it was so rarely imposed; the precondition of the death penalty system was that the death penalty was unusual. It survived by being imposed not on any rational basis but only on marginal and "outcast" individuals. Put another way, the death penalty could continue only by violating the Eighth Amendment.[65] To make matters worse, Furman was mentally ill, and his execution would violate long-standing norms (biopolitical norms at that) about the execution of the mentally ill.

Effectively Furman's attorneys argued that the spread of a new politics of life had transformed the meaning of the Eighth and Fourteenth Amendments and at the same time insisted that the new biopolitics should thereby attain constitutional status. Had they succeeded, the politics of life would have trumped the politics of death (governmentality over sovereignty), and the death penalty would have become merely historical. But, of course, they did not succeed in that way.

Instead, the Court met their arguments halfway. *Furman* is a notoriously difficult case to determine, as there was no single Court opinion; instead, the five justices who voted to abolish the death penalty chose to provide individual opinions in support of the Court's judgment. Of the five, William Brennan and Thurgood Marshall, although offering complex tests of constitutionality, essentially accepted the biopolitical logic of Furman's attorneys. Brennan argued that the severity of the death penalty, its controversial status, as well as its arbitrariness and excessiveness relative to legitimate penal aims (having ruled out retribution) meant that it was no longer a "punishment [that] comports with human dignity."[66] Marshall, arguing from "evolving standards of justice," pointed out the inconsistency in the notion of who should live and who should die, and concluded that the death penalty could not be sustained in face of all the facts and trends of history (as well as its racial politics).[67] William O. Douglas was prepared to strike down capital punishment given the rules established in *McGautha*. But these three had dissented in *McGautha*.

The crucial votes against the death penalty were cast by Potter Stewart and Byron White, and their opinions opened up the difficult task of incorporating the biopolitical into the Court's death penalty jurisprudence. Stewart refused to reach the ultimate question of the constitutionality of the death penalty (and "put . . . to one side"[68] the question of racial discrimination). Instead, he focused on the singular cases that appeared before the Court and deemed the sentence of death in these cases to be "cruel and unusual in the same way that being struck by lightning is cruel and unusual."[69] Whereas Harlan had earlier valorized the autonomy of juries, Stewart (and in this he was aligned with Douglas) opined that the lack of any rational method for determining those few who would be executed from the much larger number of those convicted of capital crimes meant that the actual penalty had become cruel through its unpredictability and rarity. White was even more explicit in limiting the reach of his decision: "In joining the Court's judgments, therefore, I do not at all intimate that the death penalty is unconstitutional *per se* or that there is no system of capital punishment that would comport with the Eighth Amendment." Instead, he insisted that he was only ruling on cases where a state has authorized the death penalty but has left its actual imposition to judges and juries and where the result was highly infrequent executions. In those cases, he argued, the death penalty had achieved cruel and unusual status.[70]

Furman, then, reconfigured the place of the biopolitical in the death penalty system. In *McGautha* Harlan, speaking for the Court, rejected any biopolitical criteria for the imposition of the death penalty. He had little trouble with either randomness or a rule-less jury. In fact, he welcomed that randomness, for he thought that such randomness indicated that juries were indeed acting according to community mores and treating each case by its individuality. Nor was he troubled by the absence of effective knowledge-based oversight (either of a professional or juridical nature). The following year a majority of the Court rejected Harlan's position and brought the biopolitical into the organization of the death penalty. But the majority did so from the vantage point of two different positions within a biopolitical logic. From the liberal side, Brennan and Marshall took the position (since then taken by so many anti–death penalty activists and advocates) that the changes in the valuation of life (the "evolving standards of decency") meant that the death penalty had become inherently demeaning and barbaric. They took the effects of the institutionalization of biopolitics as a symptom of moral progress and then assumed that these effects were an independent, indeed causal, variable. Stewart and White, from the conservative side, assumed the perspective of biopolitical technique. They adopted the biopolitical approach to the means and mechanisms of judgment and execution. The crucial question, for them, was how to separate out those who deserved to die from those who did not deserve to die and subjecting that decision to a norm. As indicated above, techniques for making these decisions had spread throughout "common" criminal justice. Stewart and White insisted that the death penalty was unconstitutional if it lacked similar mechanisms. The constitutionality of the death penalty would depend on biopolitical mechanisms, not on values that had been produced out of those mechanisms. Both the liberal and conservative wings of the Court had incorporated the biopolitical within constitutional law.

Furman thus marked a caesura in the history of the death penalty in the United States. While abolishing the penalty and transforming all death sentences into life sentences, the Court (especially Stewart and White) offered the states clear hints about how to restart the death penalty in the future. And the states responded. Within a matter of years, thirty-five states had reinstituted the death penalty. Moreover, the number of actual sentences also skyrocketed.[71] The seeming triumph of the anti–death penalty movement had been transformed into a historical defeat: abolition had led to a renewed penalty practiced with a vengeance and in far greater numbers than in the decades before *Furman*. The Court affirmed the renewed system in *Gregg v. Georgia*, when it accepted Georgia's revised system because it provided written instructions and a two-stage capital trial.[72] The Court also set new limits to the death penalty system by overturning North Carolina's mandatory death sentence for certain crimes and, in the process, commanding that there be a two-stage capital trial system.[73] With these decisions the contemporary American death penalty was established. At the time it did not stand out from Europe.

Coda: Toward Baze v. Rees

The series of decisions from *McGautha* through *Gregg* and *Woodson* not only marked a transition from one capital punishment system to another, but it also reconfigured the relationship between biopower, law, and sovereignty (at least in criminal justice). The incorporation of the biopolitical into the death penalty system not only transformed the logic of "cruel and unusual" punishment but also effectively made the biopolitical one point within a wider set of constitutional traditions and arguments. *Gregg* may have allowed the reestablishment of the death penalty, but it did so on biopolitical grounds—and the meaning of those grounds (and, indeed, how important those grounds should be) have continued to structure the jurisprudence of capital punishment in the United States. But just as important, the transition from *Furman* to *Gregg*, and the struggles it produced, made the question of sovereignty central to the death penalty in new ways. The rapid response of the states (and the federal government, for that matter) in the aftermath of *Furman* indicated a reassertion of the sovereign power to legislate and to kill. A majority of the Court in *Gregg* acceded to that sovereign claim (once the system had incorporated the biopolitical). That the death penalty has been most prominent in southern states that had born the fullest brunt of the Supreme Court's efforts to limit their sovereignty is no surprise. Nor is the continued struggle (as witnessed in *Roper* and *Atkins*) over the question of the constitutional importance of international law and opinion.[74]

But there is a larger question of sovereignty involved. As I suggested earlier, the death penalty today may be less important as a sovereign display than it was in the eighteenth century, but it is more important today as a sovereign decision—precisely because it has been so challenged. It is not coincidental that the resurgence of the penalty in the United States coincided so closely with the reassertion of sovereignty and militarization in the aftermath of Vietnam. Nor is it a coincidence that the dramatic movement to make Europe a death penalty–free zone took place when large portions of European sovereignty were being disengaged from the nation-state while the United States was seeking to extend its national sovereignty as the "last superpower."[75] What appears to some as a deep-rooted or structural difference between the United States and its European counterparts is a result of a differently organized constitutional system (with different demands) and a contingent distinction arising out of different geopolitical realities.

At the same time it is clear that the different organization of biopolitical states is absolutely central here. In the United States, which always placed greater stress on the logic of national security and less on the logic of social security, neoliberalism found a much easier point of entry. With the ascent of Reagan and his followers, the logic of neoliberalism came to the fore in its full grandeur and brutality. Whereas classical liberalism had aimed to secure the rights of individuals, neoliberalism aimed to ensure the security of markets. In this latter vision the casting off of individuals (often from marginal groups to begin with) caused no great moral reflection. In a political economy willing to enable unprecedented degrees of inequality among the general population and subordinate the lives of the working to the profits of investments, and in a nation reasserting its pride in its ability to dominate or destroy the globe militarily, populating death row seemed of minor consequence.

The biopolitical constitutionalism put in place during the 1970s has been both contested and stable for several decades. And, indeed, there is no reason to believe that it will change in the near future. The fiscal crises affecting state governments may alter the latter's commitment to mass incarceration, and the growing impact of DNA and other evidence of false conviction may ultimately shift the politics of punishment in the legislatures. It is unlikely, however, that any dramatic change will come out of the courts. Indeed, the effort to treat the effects of biopolitics in punishment as evidence of moral transformation may have less potential in the courts than even its limited reach has suggested so far. In his decision for the Court in *Baze v. Rees*, Chief Justice Roberts turned down a challenge to Kentucky's lethal injection practice partly because Kentucky's lethal injection protocol served the state's "interest in preserving the dignity of the procedure, especially where convulsions or seizures could be misperceived as signs of consciousness or distress."[76] With this statement, Roberts inverted Brennan's original effort to use a politics of life to condemn the death penalty. In Brennan's formulation, "A punishment is 'cruel and unusual,' therefore, if it does not comport with human dignity."[77] For Brennan, the dignity of the person was the standard. For Roberts, it is the dignity of the State.

I deeply appreciate the help of my co-editors, David Garland and Randall McGowen, in writing this essay.

1. On this European value system, see James Q. Whitman, *Harsh Justice: Criminal Punishment and the Widening Divide between America and Europe* (New York, 2003); Eva Girling, "European Identity and the Mission against the Death Penalty," in *The Cultural Lives of Capital Punishment: Comparative Perspectives*, ed. Austin Sarat and Christian Boulanger (Stanford, Calif., 2005), 112–28.

2. For the two, now leading analyses of these developments, see David Garland, *The Culture of Control* (Chicago, 2001); and Jonathan Simon, *Governing through Crime* (New York, 2006).

3. See Christopher Conkey and Gary Fields, "Federal Prosecutors Widen Pursuit of Death Penalty as States Ease Off," *Wall Street Journal Online*, February 3, 2007, http://proquest.umi.com/pqdweb?did=1209939411&sid=1&Fmt=3&clientId=48051&RQT=309&VName=PQD (accessed May 10, 2010).

4. For information on countries that have abolished the death penalty, see http://www.amnesty.org/en/death-penalty/abolitionist-and-retentionist-countries (accessed September 10, 2008).

5. For two examples among many, see James Q. Whitman, *Harsh Justice,* ; and Franklin E. Zimring, *The Contradictions of American Capital Punishment* (New York, 2003).

6. See Garland, *The Culture of Control;* and Simon, *Governing through Crime.*

7. *McGautha v. California* 402 U.S. 183 (1971).

8. *Furman v. Georgia* 408 U.S. 238 (1972).

9. For a discussion of the sense of the inevitability of historical progress on this issue that, although it does not make the connection with the abolition of slavery directly, does raise some of the problems with any assumption of historical teleology, see Randall McGowen, "History, Culture, and the Death Penalty: The British Debates, 1840–1870," *Historical Reflections/Reflexions Historiques* 29 (2003): 229–50.

10. The classic account of the international abolition of slavery remains David Brion Davis, *The Problem of Slavery in the Age of Revolution, 1770–1823* (Ithaca, N.Y., 1975)

11. Tony Judt, *Postwar: A History of Europe since 1945* (New York, 2005).

12. Albert Camus, *Resistance, Rebellion, and Death* (New York, 1995), 222.

13. Walter Berns, *For Capital Punishment: Crime and the Morality of the Death Penalty* (New York, 1979).

14. On the contingent nature of Western European abolition, see McGowen, "Through the Wrong End of the Telescope," this volume.

15. Susanne Krasmann, "Folter im Ausnahmezustand?" in *Rationalitaten der Gewalt,* ed. Susanne Krasmann and Jurgen Martschukat (Bielefeld: Transcript, 2007), 75–96.

16. On this issue, see my "Penality and the Colonial Project: Crime, Punishment, and the Regulation of Morals in Early America," in *Cambridge History of Law in America,* ed. Christopher Tomlins and Michael Grossberg, vol. 1 (New York, 2008), 178–210.

17. I argued this case in greater detail in "Michel Foucault, the Death Penalty, and the Crisis of Historical Understanding," *Historical Reflections/Reflexions Historiques,* 29 (2003): 191–209.

18. Michel Foucault, *History of Sexuality,* Vol. 1, *An Introduction* (New York, 1978), 155.

19. Ibid., 1:88–89.

20. Ibid., 1:140.

21. Michel Foucault, *Discipline and Punish: The Birth of the Prison* (New York, 1978), 135–94

22. Foucault, *History of Sexuality*, 1:139. I should note that when Foucault used the term technology here he was using the term in a neo-Heideggerian sense to indicate a set of practices that made objects open to knowledge and power. Technologies in this way isolate things so that humans can perceive (in some cases create) them and therefore actually become objects that subjects can address, alter, control, investigate, or even worship.

23. Ibid., 1:143.

24. Ibid., 1:140.

25. Ibid., 1:135–136 at 136.

26. Foucault, *Discipline and Punish*, 3–69.

27. Foucault, *History of Sexuality*, 1:138.

28. Ibid.

29. Michel Foucault, *"Society Must Be Defended": Lectures at the Collège De France, 1975–1976* (New York, 2003), 258.

30. Ibid., 254–55.

31. This, of course, is the title of the absolutely central part 5 of Foucault's *History of Sexuality*.

32. This logic of repositioning means that the death penalty can be marginalized and still persist; there is no necessity for biopolitics to eliminate capital punishment.

33. Michel Foucault, *Security, Territory, Population: Lectures at the College De France, 1977-78*, trans. Graham Burchell (New York, 2007), 107–8.

34. I should make clear that—on my reading at least—Foucault here is making a historical and not a structural argument; that is, he is arguing that the interconnection of biopower and sovereignty occurred not by some logical necessity but as a matter of historical reality. This interconnection becomes clear in his detailed arguments if not in some of his quick summaries.

35. Foucault, *Security, Territory, Population*, 193–95, 230–31.

36. For discussions of this theme in Foucault's work, the two most important collections are *The Foucault Effect: Studies in Governmentality*, ed. Graham Burchell, Colin Gordon, and Peter Miller (Chicago, 1991); and *Foucault and Political Reason: Liberalism, Neo-liberalism, and Rationalities of government*, ed. Andrew Barry, Thomas Osborne, and Nikolas Rose (Chicago, 1996).

37. Michel Foucault, *The Order of Things: An Archaeology of the Human Sciences* (New York, 303–87).

38. This "swerve" forms the heart of Foucault's lecture series, *The Birth of Biopolitics*.

39. I should make clear that here I am, as was Foucault, discussing neoliberalism as theory or critique, not as practice. As evidenced by the financial meltdown of 2008, neoliberal regimes in practice socialize the risk of financial institutions while privatizing their profits. Of course, the reverse is true for the poor.

40. Foucault, *The Birth of Biopolitics*, 28–29.

41. It is also the case that some of his positions on the law can be related to the different juridical cultures of the continent and of Anglo-America. But even if that is so, it points to the importance of the juridical in understanding the course of biopolitics.

42. He did begin to recognize this problem empirically. On the one hand, he stressed the use of the law to combat Absolutism in seventeenth-century England, and, on the other, he offered a long meditation on the liberal effort to use legal means as a way to contain state power from within. See Foucault, *The Birth of Biopolitics*, 8–22. However, he never was able to translate these empirical reconsiderations into his concepts.

43. For the rhetorics of anti-slavery activity, see, especially, Ian Baucom, *Specters of the Atlantic: Finance Capital, Slavery, and the Philosophy of History* (Durham, N.C., 2005). For the remaking of prison spaces, see Robin Evans, *The Fabrication of Virtue: English Prison Architecture, 1750–1840* (New York, 1982). The use of statistics and tables against the death penalty was widespread, but for one central example, see William Bradford *An Enquiry How Far the Punishment of Death Is Necessary in Pennsylvania* (Philadelphia, 1793).

44. For just some examples, see Karen Halttunen, *Murder Most Foul: The Killer and the American Gothic Imagination* (Cambridge, Mass., 1998); Charles Rosenberg, *The Trial of the Assassin Guiteau: Psychiatry and the Law in the Gilded Age* (Chicago, 1968); David Horn, *The Criminal Body: Lombroso and the Anatomy of Deviance* (New York, 2003).

45. This is not to say that they were totally successful. As William Novak demonstrates in his *The People's Welfare: Law and Regulation in Nineteenth-Century America* (Chicago, 1996), the police power continued, indeed became elaborated, on the local level throughout the nineteenth century. But the local nature of Novak's analysis reinforces the notion that this police power operated increasingly within a larger liberal or "security" context. The same might be said of the obvious persistence of police power in the American South, where first slave codes and then vagrancy laws attempted to maintain a police organization within a larger national framework based on liberalism and security.

46. The literature on these developments is huge, of course, but for two discussions see my *Laboratories of Virtue: Punishment, Revolution, and Authority, 1760–1835* (Chapel Hill, N.C., 1996); and Jacques Donzelot, *The Policing of Families* (New York, 1979).

47. On these developments, besides Foucault's *Discipline and Punish* and my *Laboratories of Virtue*, see the classic accounts of David J. Rothman, *The Discovery of the Asylum: Social Order and Disorder in the New Republic* (Boston, 1971); and Michael Iganiteff, *A Just Measure of Pain: The Penitentiary in the Industrial Revolution, 1750–1850* (New York, 1978). On the increasing diversity of penal institutions in the nineteenth century, see, among many, Estelle Freedman, *Their Sisters' Keepers: Women's Prison Reform in America,1830–1930* (Ann Arbor, Mich., 1981).

48. For discussions of these different developments, see David Garland, *Punishment and Welfare: A History of Penal Strategies* (Aldershot, U.K., 1985); Thomas A. Green, "Freedom and Criminal Responsibility in the Age of Pound: An Essay on Criminal Justice, *Michigan Law Review* 93 (1995): 1915–2053; Michael Willrich, *City of Courts: Socializing Justice in Progressive Era Chicago* (Chicago, 2003); Rebecca McLennan *The Crisis of Imprisonment: Protest, Politics, and the Making of the American Penal State, 1776–1941* (Chicago, 2008); Jonathan Simon, *Poor Discipline: Parole and the Social Control of the Underclass, 1890–1990* (Chicago, 1993).

49. For the general decline in the use of the death penalty in the United States starting in the 1930s, see *Sourcebook of Criminal Justice Statistics Online,* Table 6.85.2007, http://www.albany.edu/sourcebook/pdf/t6852007.pdf (accessed November 8, 2008); and Stuart Banner, *The Death Penalty: An American History* (Cambridge, Mass., 2002), 208–30.

50. I have discussed this characterization of Nazi Germany in my "Michel Foucault, the Death Penalty, and the Crisis of Historical Understanding," 205–7.

51. Foucault, *History of Sexuality,* 1:143. I should address two points here. First, I am not suggesting here another version of a strong state/weak state theory (where the United States is viewed as a generally weak state except in penal and military terms). One advantage of using Foucault's biopolitics as a notion is that as a series of rationalities and techniques it describes capabilities and ways of organizing reality. As a result, it points toward actual choices that are made rather than simply institutional developments. A second point concerns the Soviet Union—which also, after all, had the capacity to end the life of the globe. But in that case it did not possess the economic and technical power to bring life to the extent that the United States did. But the shared emphasis on national security and the assertion of sovereignty may help explain the Russian reluctance to eliminate the death penalty.

52. For this characterization of the dynamics of the Warren Court, I have relied on Lucas A. Powe Jr., *The Warren Court and American Politics* (Cambridge, Mass., 2000).

53. For the Legal Defense Fund, see Michael Meltsner's memoir, *Cruel and Unusual Punishment: The Supreme Court and the Death Penalty* (New York, 1973).

54. Simon, *Governing through Crime,* 89–94.

55. For an example of the argument that the Fourteenth Amendment demanded that the death penalty be understood in what I am calling biopolitical terms, see Reply Brief for Petitioner, November 6, 1970, *McGautha v. California* 402 U.S. 183 (1971).

56. *McGautha v. California* 402 U.S. 183 (1971); *Crampton v. Ohio* 402 U.S. 183 (1971).

57. *McGautha v. California,* 402 U.S. 196 (1971).

58. *McGautha v. California,* 402 U.S. 220. The reference to the "infant science of criminology" was mostly directed at the importance of the Model Penal Code.

59. *McGautha v. California,* 402 U.S. 197–204 (1971).

60. Of course, as both the appellants and the Court's dissenters could point out, because California provided no real way to judge the decision making of jurors it is hard to see how Harlan could be so certain of fairness.

61. *McGautha v. California,* 402 U.S. 220.

62. Ibid., 402 U.S. 204.

63. Ibid., 402 U.S. 217.

64. To be sure, Harlan did not speak for a unified Court. Brennan, Douglas, and Marshall all dissented. But of concern here is the controlling position on these issues.

65. See Petitioner's Brief, *Furman v. Georgia,* No. 71-5003, September 9, 1971; and Petitioner's Brief, *Aikens v. California,* No. 68-5027, September 10, 1971, "outcast" at 6. *Furman* was decided as part of a cluster of cases. *Aikens* was mooted because of a decision of the California Supreme Court, but its brief remained central to the presentation of the cases. I should note that these briefs (and, indeed, William Brennan in *Furman)* took the position that there was an inexorable moral movement against the death penalty, and in that way they anticipated the position of present-day critics of the immorality of capital punishment. But that that position took place as one side within the constitutional struggle over the death penalty should suggest another reason why it cannot act as a grid of intelligibility for understanding the historical shape and political rationality of capital punishment.

66. *Furman v. Georgia* 408 U.S. 305.

67. Ibid., 408 U.S. 315–72.

68. Ibid., 408 U.S. 310.

69. Ibid., 408 U.S. 309.

70. Ibid., 408 U.S. 310–11.

71. On the rapid and intense reestablishment of the death penalty, see Banner, *The Death Penalty*, 267–75.

72. *Gregg v. Georgia* 428 U.S. 153 (1976).

73. *Woodson v. North Carolina* 428 U.S. 280 (1976).

74. *Roper v. Simmons* 543 U.S. 551 (2005) (executing minors); *Atkins v. Virginia* 536 U.S. 304 (2002) (executing the mentally disabled). Note that in these cases international considerations and "evolving standards of decency" won a majority of the Court.

75. On the United States, see Andrew Bacevich, *The New American Militarism: How Americans Are Seduced by War* (New York, 2005).

76. "Opinion of Roberts, C.J., *Baze v. Rees*, 553 U.S. ___(2008), at 19.

77. *Furman v. Georgia*, 408 U.S. 270.

Through the Wrong End
of the Telescope

History, the Death Penalty, and
the American Experience

──────── R A N D A L L   M C G O W E N ────────

I begin this essay with a familiar image: an optical instrument meant
to help us investigate distant phenomena. Yet the telescope, if used inap-
propriately, can produce a fundamental misperception about the relationship of an object to the viewer. Similarly history has come to figure prominently in discussions of the place of capital punishment in the contemporary
world, especially when trying to explain the seeming gulf between America's
enthusiastic embrace of the death penalty and Europe's recent rejection of
the practice. Increasingly scholars have turned to the American past in an
effort to explain what appears to be a puzzling exception.[1] Their studies of
its culture and history have been powerful and suggestive. Nonetheless one
sometimes gets the sense that the perspective adopted in such work is wrong,
that the authors are looking too intently at their subject. They view America at a distance, as strange, exotic, and disturbing. In probing ever deeper
into the American psyche for the source of this conundrum, they sacrifice
what would be gained by taking a wider view of the problem. More particularly, these observers misread the recent history of capital punishment in
Europe, and they allow particular deep-seated assumptions about violence
and modernity to sway their accounts. The result is that they draw the wrong
lesson about the persistence of the question of death in the contemporary
political scene.

One problem with these investigations of the American experience is
that the institution of capital punishment comes to look opaque; it appears
mute, unchanging, a relic of some other historical period. It joins a long list
of practices safely exiled to the past. Thus its survival in America seems to
be an anomaly, a troubling return of the repressed, perhaps, but not one that

challenges the basic enlightened and humane identity of the modern age. This understanding of our present situation relies upon a historical narrative in which the steady progress of civilization is measured and proved by the overcoming of the past. The story is not a recent development. Since the eighteenth century the question of the death penalty has been intertwined with the issue of time. Setting aside for the moment the issue of its accuracy, eighteenth-century reformers proposed that a decisive break had occurred in their day between an earlier regime of penal measures marked by barbarism, and a more modern, usually called civilized, system based upon principles of humanity and rationality. Change, these writers contended, had been brought about less through individual effort than by the gradual operation of social, intellectual, and economic forces. As the most famous penal reformer, Cesare Beccaria, explained in 1764: "Anyone who knows how things were two or three centuries ago and how they are now, can see how, from luxury and ease of life, the most precious virtues have sprung up: humanity, charity and toleration of human error."[2] The decline of penalties that exploited pain was taken as a signal achievement of the age. History became a court of appeal because it seemed to offer self-evident testimony of the superiority of the present over the past.[3]

The tendency to look at the American present through the lens of a particular version of history casts the practice of capital punishment as a "survival" or a "throwback" to an earlier time. Its proponents appear as little more than defenders of an outmoded ritual. Once again the eighteenth century laid down the outlines of this argument. As Beccaria charged, "our current abuses, when their circumstances are fully understood, are a mockery and a reproof of past ages and not of the present day and its legislators."[4] Advocates of abolition see themselves as belonging to a different epoch, one in which human nature itself has changed. They are powerfully positioned with one foot in the future while their opponents stand in the past. These beliefs influence what the critics of capital punishment say and how they present their claims. Even in the most strongly presentist of accounts, we detect the shadow of these historical assumptions. Reformers have promoted a particular understanding of history, which has been of strategic value in the struggle against the death penalty, but they have also been possessed by this interpretation—regarding it not as rhetoric but as the truth about how things have changed—with sometimes unexpected consequences for their cause.

It is the contention of this essay that the question of American exceptionalism arises in large part from the particular historical assumptions at work in a rhetoric of reform that dates from the eighteenth century. The reformers offered a tale whose master theme claimed that the advance of what they called civilization would gradually eliminate the kinds of state violence that were best symbolized by the practice of the death penalty. This narrative implied that penal reform was a long-term process whose central causal engine was diffused throughout society and was identical with material improvement. The American experience seems to cast these assumptions into doubt. An undeniably modern nation continues to employ the death penalty with little apology for its practice. Scholars have scrambled to find in American history some way to explain the divergence between the United States and Europe. But this question is a false one. Instead we should be looking at the very assumptions that have for so long operated in the background to frame the debate over capital punishment. Indeed, the actual history of the controversy has not conformed to the expectations of humanitarian reformers. It is not enough, however, to say that the beliefs about the nature of change are in error. The challenge is to identify how these ideas could be both effective as well as wrong, and to see how they mislead one as to the primary source and character of penal change. This exercise may strip us of a source of confidence in the contest over capital punishment, but it may also help to refocus efforts at abolition in ways that promote more effective political action.[5]

The Promise of History

The Enlightenment made of penal practices a central cause in the campaign to promote the progress of society. The critics of the death penalty placed great emphasis upon treatment of the body as a measure of a civilization's character and an influence upon its destiny. At its simplest, reformers told themselves, and tried to convince others, that a range of punishments that inflicted suffering belonged to an earlier age, aroused more primitive emotions, and conflicted with the refined sensibility of their own age. They proposed a sharp dichotomy between older penalties, uniformly savage and irrational, and the more civilized, humane alternatives they advanced. Death, to them, crowned a horrendous assemblage of punishments that included torture, whipping, the pillory, and assorted other afflictions. These penalties seemed to demonstrate a delight in cruelty and a pleasure in exquisite torture. Such spectacles of suffering might appear overpowering, but they represented no more than a jumble of offensive sights and sounds. "The severity of our criminal laws," one Englishman wrote in 1777, "might perhaps be very proper in the days of Gothic tyranny and ferocity of manners; but at this period of civilization and refinement, a milder mode of punishment would be more adequate."[6] "How is it possible," a French judge asked in 1778, "that the most refined nation in Europe whose mores are the gentlest and the most accommodating, should still have laws . . . suited to a people plunged into the last degree of ignorance and barbarism?"[7]

These critics were sure of their footing. They mapped a new vision of society and a new moral economy upon a chronological terrain. The superiority of the present to the past was assumed, and there was no dispute about those features that most marked the difference between the two points in time. Their cause stood firmly anchored in an unfolding historical drama. Within their narrative of progress, the amelioration of penal arrangements appeared a self-evident good. This tale promised that the abolition of the death penalty would be delivered in the fullness of time. These beliefs were not mere arguments employed instrumentally against conservatives. They expressed how the reformers understood themselves, the kinds of appeals they made, and the expectations that guided them. As arguments, they had considerable polemical effect. Because these characterizations plugged into powerful beliefs about commercial and moral progress, the reformers secured an important rhetorical advantage over those defending traditional arrangements. By the late eighteenth century advocates of severe justice tried to expose what they saw as a language game. A London alderman, in a debate over policing and crime in 1785, complained that his opponents implied he was "a bloody-minded man, because he urged a rigorous execution of the laws." He denied that he was cruel. "It was," he charged, "the judge who reprieved enormous offenders, who committed cruelty," by weakening "protection of the innocent" and encouraging criminals. The necessity that these defenders of capital punishment felt to adopt the language employed by the reformers is powerful testimony to the rapidly changing terms for debating the purpose and forms of penal arrangements.[8]

Although the spread of these ideas alone cannot account for change, they cooperated in producing a significant transformation in the character of punishment. From the mid-eighteenth century European governments slowly retreated from the practice of physical inflictions. Prussia ended torture in 1754, Savoy in 1770, and France in the 1780s. Similarly these states discontinued the custom of displaying the bodies of the executed as a reminder of royal justice.[9] Continental legal reformers in the service of "enlightened" rulers applied the new principles as they undertook the revision of legal codes. Humanitarian concerns jostled with arguments about utility in the proposals that were put forward. In several territories, by the last quarter of the eighteenth century, the actual numbers of executions began to decline.[10] Although the pace of change varied considerably from place to place, the cumulative effect was striking. "It appeared to him," Sir James Mackintosh told Parliament in 1830, "as if he had lived, in the short compass of a life, through two different ages, opposite and contrasted in character."[11] By 1835 murder was virtually the only offense for which one suffered death. This development was as true of Britain and France as it was of Prussia. The political character of the regime seems scarcely to have mattered. Similarly the elaborate rituals of execution, including the measures taken to draw out the experience of suffering, disappeared. The execution became a simpler affair, the swift operation of the guillotine, the drop, or the sword. By mid-century it ceased in many places to be a public spectacle. Increasingly the execution was carried out behind prison walls before a small group of officially designated spectators.

As the number of crimes for which one could be executed declined, the battle over retaining the death penalty for murder sharpened. The cause clearly drew many adherents in Europe and America in the 1830s and 1840s. "Now, that general civilization had advanced," Stephen Lushington told the British Parliament in 1832, "the Legislature must finally yield to the general feeling against the severity of punishment."[12] When these participants looked at the various changes that had occurred over the previous fifty years, they expressed confidence that total abolition was within reach. "The antigallows movement [in America] won the support of prominent ministers, reformers, and men of letters and for over thirty years was a subject of heated controversy in the legislatures of many Northern states."[13] In Britain William Ewart, Daniel O'Connell, and Richard Cobden all looked forward with optimism to the eventual elimination of the gallows. Conservatives, on the other hand, despaired of halting the tide.[14] In Germany the Frankfurt Assembly, in 1848, took up the issue. One speaker confidently predicted that "in future times people will look back on the death penalty as a piece of barbarity just as we now look back on torture."[15] In some places a practical moratorium prevailed. Although the city of Hamburg did not formally abolish the death penalty, the town saw no executions between 1822 and 1856.[16] In the United States Michigan (1846), Rhode Island (1852), and Wisconsin (1853) ended capital punishment. Harriet Martineau wrote, in 1837, that "in a short time capital punishments will be abolished throughout the northern States."[17] To idealists and activists alike the machinery of death seemed doomed. From Italy to Scandinavia and the Low Countries, executions declined to a trickle, and the total elimination of death seemed years, rather than decades, away. French statistics testified to the trend; between 1826 and 1830 an average of seventy-two executions had taken place each year. After 1830 the number declined by half, and between 1896 and 1900 only an average of five a year died at the guillotine.[18] With so few being executed, it seemed the act of a moment to sweep the institution away.

When viewed at a certain distance, paying scant attention to the precise dating of debates or the specific issues under discussion, the period from 1750 to 1850 might seem to support the historical claims advanced by the opponents of capital punishment. Progress appeared to be taking place at a rapid pace across a wide area. "In Germany," one English author wrote, "there has been a gradual approximation to its entire cessation. In many of the American States it has been superseded by imprisonment for life. In England the number of crimes for the perpetration of which it is imposed has been largely reduced, and now it is practically abolished for every thing but murder. But its necessity, under any circumstances, and its justice are questioned not merely in England, but all over the world where men are in any degree removed from barbarism."[19] The various phases of the change seemed to point in one direction; a growing refinement, broader sympathy, and a rejection of brutality all contributed to make the death penalty appear inconsistent with the main currents in European culture. Few at mid-century could believe that their confidence was misplaced.

The Trouble with History

Yet history failed to deliver the much anticipated victory. The expected triumph over capital punishment, except in a few instances, did not occur in the nineteenth century. The discipline of history has been no kinder to the assumptions that framed the reformers' portrait of the past. In particular, a number of recent authors have pointed out that the reformers fundamentally misrepresented the character of traditional penal sanctions. The opposition between earlier and later forms of punishment was not as simple as abolitionists described. Humanity was not necessarily their privileged possession.

If recent studies have established anything, it is that early modern punishment was a complex phenomenon, with its distinctive blend of concern, inattention, and brutality. Punishment of the body took place within a symbolic universe suffused with particular religious beliefs. The authorities were more lavish in their infliction of pain and their taking of human life. Yet the goal of these inflictions was not exhausted by the tale of suffering. Within its own terms these measures allowed for the play of sympathy and identification, mercy and salvation. They accorded the condemned a significant role in a drama that spoke of forgiveness as well as intimidation.[20] The spectacle of death aroused powerful emotions, but characterizing it as "savage," as the reformers did, only obstructs the ability to understand what the goals and intentions of that penal regime were. As a consequence of this recent scholarship, it has become more difficult to assert a simple superiority of present penal measures over those employed in the past, especially when the goal of such claims is to establish the moral superiority of our culture in comparison with those of the past.[21] The idea of advancing civilization both overstates and misstates the character of the difference between past and present, and misleads us as to the kind of process that connects the two.

The actual history of the death penalty controversy after the mid-nineteenth century was not any kinder to the assumptions and expectations of the abolitionists. Far from exposing the steady march of progress, discontinuities and abrupt reversals of direction marked this history. The story of reform in Britain, for instance, is ambiguous, confounding many of the central beliefs advanced by critics of the gallows. Britain was the most economically advanced and wealthiest society in nineteenth-century Europe. It was the model looked to by many of how commerce altered the character of society, producing refinement and sensibility, order and comfort. It was admired for the character of its public culture, the influence of the press, and the free discussion it tolerated. English and Scottish authors could be said to be the chief proponents of the theory of progress that undergirded the perspective offered by legal reformers. Yet despite these many advantages, Britain was slow to follow the rest of Europe in reducing the number of offenses for which one could suffer death. A majority of those who perished on the gallows died for property offenses, and the numbers remained stubbornly high down to the 1820s. Contemporaries complained, with only slight exaggeration, that more people died on the gallows in England than in all the rest of Europe combined. Even a leading Tory politician, Robert Peel, could concede in Parliament, in 1830, that "it was impossible to conceal from ourselves, that capital punishments were more frequent, and the criminal code more severe, on the whole, in this country, than in any country in the world."[22] This confession did not inhibit his opposition to the removal of the death penalty from forgery and a number of other property crimes. Peel showed repeatedly that although he was ready to consolidate the criminal law, he was far from ready to embrace the position of the more radical reformers. Despite frequent parliamentary debate during the first three decades of the nineteenth century, the cause of criminal law reform made little legislative progress until the fourth decade of the century. The very decades that saw such remarkable progress for the Anti-Slavery campaign produced striking defeat for the cause of criminal law reform. The French case was little different. Penal reform had figured among the demands made at the time of the Revolution. Yet the Napoleonic criminal code of 1810 made the death penalty a bulwark for the support of law and order. Even the revision of the penal code in 1832 retained death for twenty-two offenses. Dogged resistance, rather than steady progress, marks the history of reform in these two countries in the early nineteenth century.[23]

In both England and France the sudden restriction of the penalty to murder was an unexpected triumph, though one that gave hope to individuals who demanded complete abolition. For several decades at mid-century this goal appeared to be attainable. Prominent writers lent their prestige to the cause. Victor Hugo contributed a blistering indictment of the death penalty to the campaign. In 1840 William Thackeray wrote a powerful essay on "Going to See a Man Hanged." Yet by the 1860s the prospect of total abolition began to recede. These years saw instead a renewed insistence on the necessity and value of the death penalty. Even the termination of public executions in Britain in 1868 came to seem an ambiguous victory.[24] The British movement for ending capital punishment gained little traction after this decade. A decisive moment occurred during the debate over the death penalty in 1868, when John Stuart Mill announced his opposition to further mitigation of the criminal code. He began by praising those whom he called "philanthropists" for their efforts to remove death from a vast array of property offenses. Their only mistake, he claimed, was "in not perceiving the right time and place for stopping in a career hitherto so eminently beneficial." His arguments for retention were scarcely original, though he added that society not only had the right to use the death penalty but that it might actually be more humane to do so.[25] Indeed, the late nineteenth century saw a significant hardening of attitudes toward offenders of all sorts and an increase in severity toward those perceived as the most dangerous to society. James Fitzjames Stephen announced the sterner line. "We are too soft and pitiful," he wrote. "The one great drawback to the advantages of civilization is, that an increase of comfort makes men look with indulgence on matters which ought to stir up the warmest indignation." "Is it healthier that they should excite nothing but regret for the occurrence and pity for the criminal, or ought they also to excite indignation and a desire for vengeance?" Nonetheless harsh measures did not mean that a society was savage; rather, he hastened to add, the penalty was only prudent. "Shamefully to expel a man from the world, to turn him out and have done with him, when he is clearly fit to live there no longer, may be a stern proceeding; but it is not the proceeding of people to whom the infliction of physical pain is a pleasure."[26]

There was more to the transformation of the issue of capital punishment than a mere shift in the political climate can explain. The greater scarcity of executions did not diminish the level of attention they generated. On the contrary, murder and the death penalty exerted an increased fascination, fanned by the attention of the popular press. Fictional works and press reporting fostered an undercurrent of unease with the threat that the murderer was supposed to represent.[27] Conservative regimes seized upon capital punishment as an issue they could use to check the spread of liberal sentiments and measures. Leading politicians exploited newspaper coverage that created an image of murderers as social aliens who represented a distinctive threat to middle-class life. Voters responded to these appeals. The decline in the actual incidence of murder did little to halt the advance of these notions.

With relatively little difficulty, politicians on the right appropriated central terms of the abolition program, turning the language to their own purposes. The idea of the sanctity of life, which had been proposed by abolitionists as the central justification for their measures, was now exploited by conservatives to justify the taking of the lives of those who murdered innocent citizens. Civilized society needed protection from the murderous individuals who haunted its borders. There was much that was novel about this defense of the death penalty; it certainly represented a potent political weapon. One bourgeois newspaper in Berlin demonstrated the flexibility and emotional force of this appeal, in the description it offered of a murderer. "The beast is put in prison," the paper said of one murderer, in 1880,

> but it gets fed there. The beast gets used to the cage, and, animal that it is, it does without freedom and enjoys the food. The humanitarians' premise is that they are dealing with human beings here. They forget that individuals who are human in form but equipped by nature with bestial instincts, without morality, without scruples of conscience, are not to be ranked any higher than the beasts one meets in the tropics or the wastes of the north. If humans come across such a beast, they strike it dead. And that's that.

Richard Evans characterizes such passages as employing "a new linguistic mode." It shared nothing with the terminology or appeals used to describe the goals of justice in early modern Europe.[28] These novel sentiments were widely shared on both sides of the Atlantic. They gained the support of leading academic authorities. In France the criminologist Dr. Emile Laurent argued that nature itself justified the extreme measures taken to deal with murderers. "One kills the ferocious beast," he wrote in 1908, "that one is unable to muzzle, the legitimacy of the death penalty lies in that truth . . . Kill them! says nature to society. Kill them, says the past of humanity to its present with a hundred historical voices."[29] The violence of this language is remarkable. It exploited to the full the rhetoric of war and retribution. At the same time it located the need for such measures in the nature of those who were to be subject to them. It also served to obscure the action of the state in executing the condemned; instead, it presented the government as the mere instrument of the will of the people.

A cliché of the capital punishment debates is that all the arguments over the question have been around for several centuries. In some sense this is true. Yet the precise terms employed at any particular moment have varied considerably. There has, perhaps, been greater consistency in the arguments deployed in favor of abolition, although even here there have been shades of difference in the claims advanced by humanitarians, liberals, and religiously inspired reformers. Over time, however, the arguments of the defenders of the death penalty have proved fluid and adaptable. Some themes, as we have seen, are replayed regularly, particularly the ideas of the justice of vengeance as a motive for punishment, the right of society to defend itself, and the demonizing of the murderer. But the specific formulation adopted, the peculiar accent employed, has varied considerably. To an extent unanticipated by the abolitionists, the notions of civilization and social progress provided resources for the retentionists as well.

Opponents of abolition never challenged the portrait the reformers drew of their own age. They never questioned the belief in civilization and its benefits. They accepted the narrative of social progress that emphasized the advance of civility and morality as bringing about a decline in violence and the spread of humane feeling. They, too, contended, they argued, for life. Where they differed from abolitionists was in how they described the threat society faced and the measures necessary to protect it. Whereas the reformers employed the language of barbarism to characterize the death penalty and, by implication, its defenders, the proponents of capital punishment seized upon the same terminology to describe those they threatened with death, whose very existence became the central argument for its retention. The ease with which this substitution occurred, as well as the success of the maneuver, points to a central structural feature of the debate that both sides share: the necessity to proclaim an absolute distinction and announce the superiority of one's own position in the present as a justification for action.[30]

The century between 1850 and 1950 is littered with moments when abolition seemed within reach and yet reformers failed to secure the final triumph. A vocal if not always numerous group on the left of the political spectrum championed the cause. The Progressive era in the United States saw a vigorous discussion of capital punishment, with ten states abolishing the penalty.[31] France experienced an extensive debate over the issue between July and December 1908, although it ended with a decisive failure for the abolitionists. In France newspapers led a fierce campaign on behalf of the death penalty. One conservative politician captured the popular mood when he asked his listeners to "think a little less about the criminal and a little more about honest folk."[32] The cause of abolition gained renewed attention in Britain in the aftermath of World War I, especially in Labour Party circles. Many members were sympathetic to the cause of abolition. Proponents even secured a couple of meaningless victories in votes in the House of Commons. The leadership, however, shared little of the passion for change and were more concerned about the unpopularity of the issue than they were with shepherding a measure through Parliament. Even more striking was the failure of the Labour government to advance the cause, despite their overwhelming electoral victory in 1945. Once again the real contest was between enthusiastic rank-and-file activists within the party, for whom the cause was popular, and a leadership that was politically timid, relatively uninterested in the question, and acutely aware that public opinion opposed abolition. In hopes of dodging what they believed was an unpopular question, the leaders permitted a free vote. Over the wishes of the cabinet, the Commons voted for abolition. The House of Lords, however, proved resistant to change. Without strong government support, the measure was doomed. Seeking to cover its embarrassment, the leadership turned to the time-honored expedient of creating a Royal Commission to investigate the issue.[33] The tabloid press continued to seize upon sensational murders to drum up support for the fierce justice of the gallows. Well into the twentieth century the death penalty regime in Britain and France seemed secure.

In terms of the argument of this essay, the German case is even more intriguing. Although Germany largely conformed to the general pattern we have charted in the cases of France and Britain, the swings have always been more extreme. It offers a fuller instance of the process by which the struggle over capital punishment became a key aspect of a wider and more profound struggle "for rival concepts of the state."[34] In Germany abolition of the death penalty occupied a prominent place in the liberal agenda, in contrast to the more marginal status it held in Britain and France. The North German Reichstag, in 1870, even voted to end capital punishment. This decision was almost immediately reversed, on a close vote, after an intense campaign by Bismarck, who appealed to national unity and the fear of outsiders in an effort to bring the legislature into line. Over the next two decades the Chancellor exploited the cause as a weapon for defeating liberals and dividing the middle classes from the expanding workers movement. "Once more," Evans notes, "the death penalty was being used more as a symbol of the state's political intentions than as an instrument of penal policy."[35] Ironically, so long as the conservative King Wilhelm I was on the throne, the rate of executions remained low. While not opposed to the death penalty in principle, this pious man was reluctant to sign death warrants. When Wilhelm II came to the throne, this check was removed, and there followed a dramatic surge in the numbers executed.[36]

Although the Social Democrats were divided over the issue of abolition at the conclusion of World War I, by the end of the 1920s political conditions seemed to favor a reexamination of the question. The party occupied a central place in a coalition government, and an avowed abolitionist became justice minister. The result was that in 1928 and 1929 there were no executions in Germany. One leftist paper proclaimed triumphantly "the death penalty [is] practically abolished!" The existence of a moratorium seemed promising, even if the committee charged with revising the criminal code deadlocked over the question. This brief opening, however, was firmly closed when political upheaval produced a transformation of the government, followed by a decisive shift in the political climate. The death penalty began to operate again in 1930. The National Socialists made the death penalty one of their principal concerns. They exploited the issue to distinguish between their respect for the healthy desire for revenge and retribution in contrast to the indulgence of sentimentality which they charged characterized parties of the left. "In these matters," one author wrote in 1931, "the people has a far surer judgement, and a far healthier instinct than politicians, men of letters, and theoreticians, who will always find in every murderer something to serve as an excuse for his deeds, no matter how much of a monster he might be." Not surprisingly, when the Nazis seized power they quickly expanded the number of offenses punishable by death and reduced the time between conviction and execution. The result was that the number of executed soared to heights not seen in more than two centuries.[37]

The Present and the Recent Past

At first glance the prospects for abolition looked unpromising at the end of World War II, not only in Germany but across much of Europe. The revelation of Nazi genocide produced shock and dismay, as well as much soul searching. Public debate around the issue of state-sponsored killing secured new footing. Yet in other respects little appeared to have changed, especially for the victorious states. The occupying powers in Germany employed the death penalty. They used death to settle accounts and to try to restore order to an unsettled country. Indeed, in most formerly occupied countries, a wave of vigilante justice saw swift and ferocious punishment meted out against collaborators. As many as ten thousand may have died in France alone. Perhaps fifteen thousand were killed in Italy. The number lynched in places like Belgium and the Netherlands was smaller, but few condemned these exercises in popular justice. There was, similarly, little opposition to the execution of collaborators that followed the return of normal government.[38]

Despite the unpromising start, the war experience produced a sober reassessment of the state's right to kill. Italy in 1947 and Austria in 1950 abolished the death penalty for ordinary crimes. In Germany itself few politicians in the years immediately after 1945 spoke out against the penalty. Yet, as the debate over the Basic Law developed in 1948–49, the older commitment of the left to abolition resurfaced. The Social Democrats pointed to the Nazi experience as justification for the urgency of the question. Many conservatives were unmoved by the appeal; indeed, some Christian Democrats employed the idea of society's right to defend itself in terms that echoed the language of the 1930s. Nonetheless, as the debate unfolded, it took a surprising turn, aided in part by some on the extreme right. Clearly for them the concern was less the merits of the abstract question than it was the desire to bring to an end the threat of the execution of former Nazis. Given divisions among Christian Democrats over the issue, the result was a decisive vote for abolition. The outcome was a "shock" to all observers. Almost as surprising was the unwillingness of the legislature to undo the act, despite strenuous efforts mounted by the Christian Democrats in the 1950s.[39]

Other European nations were slower to adopt abolition. In 1965 a Labour government carried a suspension of the death penalty that would become permanent a few years later. Similarly France under the Socialist Mitterrand would abolish the death penalty in 1981. Ireland, although it had not executed anyone since 1954, abolished capital punishment in 1990. In a number of countries abolition was a way of distinguishing the new political order from an older dictatorial regime. Portugal abolished the death penalty in 1976, and Spain ended the penalty for ordinary crimes in 1978. In much of Eastern Europe, abolition followed the fall of communist governments.[40]

This brief survey points up four conclusions about capital punishment in twentieth-century Europe. First, it is noteworthy how recent abolition has been for most countries. Prior to the 1970s the region presented a picture of great diversity both in terms of what their laws said and the actual practice of death. Second, it was usually parties of the left that brought about change, and it came through legislative action. Third, abolition, when it came, was often sudden and unexpected. The decisions of individual leaders frequently shaped the outcome. Roy Jenkins, the Home Secretary in the Labour government played an important role in pressing for suspension of the death penalty in Britain. It was Mitterand's choice of Robert Badinter that moved abolition to the top of the Socialist government's agenda.[41] Finally, local circumstances rather than any general trends influenced the timing of penal change. It is striking, for instance, how little the Scandinavian example, during the interwar period, mattered to the British. Only within the last decade or so, with the requirement for ratification of European Convention on Human Rights as a condition for membership in the Council of Europe, has international pressure come to play a decisive role in shaping the conduct of individual nations.

In the decades immediately after World War II, America presented a picture of death penalty practice fundamentally similar to that of Europe. Because criminal justice belonged to the individual states, the nation displayed a patchwork of different policies. Some states abolished capital punishment in the nineteenth century; others retained it but seldom, if ever, employed it. The South executed large numbers, but so did New York, California, Pennsylvania, and Ohio. Several states had eliminated death in the early years of the century, only to restore it in the interwar period. The 1950s, however, saw a gradual turning of popular opinion against the practice and an increase in public debate over its justice. The decade also saw a decline in the number of executions in all regions, in part as a result of changes in judicial practice, but also because juries proved more reluctant to return death sentences. Oregon abolished the death penalty in 1964, and New York, Iowa, Vermont, and West Virginia did so in 1965.[42] "As recently as the mid-1960s," Carol Steiker has written, "the U.S. looked like most of the rest of Europe (and Canada, and most of Australia) with regard to the use of capital punishment."[43] When the Supreme Court in 1972, in *Furman v. Georgia*, ruled the death penalty unconstitutional, it appeared to conform to the pattern of abolition that was gaining ground in Europe.

A particularly striking feature of judicial deliberations in the decade before *Furman* was the introduction into them of the historical understanding we have been tracking in this essay. Supreme Court Justice Arthur Goldberg, in 1963, proposed to the other justices that "evolving standards of decency" had transformed how society viewed the death penalty in such a way as to render the application of the penalty a violation of the Eighth Amendment prohibition on "cruel and unusual punishment." In shaping his argument Goldberg appealed beyond law and legislation to social practice. Society, he contended, had evolved in its morals. "Many, if not most, of the civilized nations of the western world" had abolished death, and the frequency of its use in the United States had sharply declined. This argument was soon seized upon by other opponents of death. A subsequent legal brief from the Legal Defense Fund of the NAACP expanded on this theme. "Capital punishment," it explained, "has largely gone the way of flogging and banishment, progressively excluded by this Nation and by civilized nations of men from the register of legitimate penal sanctions." "Capital punishment," it concluded triumphantly, "is condemned by history."[44] This language was quickly adopted by some state courts. When the California Supreme Court ruled, in 1972, that the death penalty was unconstitutional, the Chief Justice, in his opinion, appealed to "evolving standards of decency."[45] Although these ideas played only a modest role in the discussions on the Court surrounding *Furman*, they contributed to the confidence felt by advocates of abolition that they were on the brink of a historic victory. The Justices weighed issues of racial discrimination, procedural concerns, and the seeming randomness of outcomes along with the general argument that social mores had evolved in such a way as to render capital punishment no longer defensible. The Court was famously fractured in its conclusions. The outcome, however, seemed a decisive repudiation of the death penalty.

The subsequent history of the death penalty in the United States soon undercut this confident assertion. The entire episode spoke both of the force of the argument and yet also offered proof of the limits of its persuasive appeal. With startling speed the nation reversed directions with relation to the issue. The Court in *Furman* had left the door ajar for states to legislate on the penalty. The decision, in Stuart Banner's words, "touched off the biggest flurry of capital punishment legislation the nation had ever seen." Public support for the death penalty, which had briefly dipped below 50 percent in the mid-1960s, soared above 70 percent. Within four years of the case thirty-five states had moved to restore the punishment, and states began sentencing offenders to death once again, in numbers not seen since the 1930s. Executions resumed in 1977, and they grew in number by the 1980s. As Justice Potter Stewart noted, "in light of what 35 states have done since 1972," it was difficult to argue that "capital punishment is incompatible with evolving standards of decency." Many Americans argued that decency required the protection of the death penalty.[46]

Admittedly this was scarcely the last word in the debate over the moral standing of the death penalty. The nation presented no picture of unity over the question; most abolitionist states declined to introduce the penalty.[47] With increasing frequency judges at both the state and federal level appealed to the idea of "evolving standards" in cases that sought to restrict the application of the death penalty to juveniles or to the mentally retarded. In some cases the Supreme Court seemed open to the argument but in others a majority of the justices resisted the claim.[48] This ambivalence about the force of the principle points to the uncertain status of the notion. It is hard to argue that the last quarter of the twentieth century vindicated the optimistic assumptions of those who believed that capital punishment was inevitably doomed by the progress of history. The polemical effect of the belief in the evolution of civilized standards was clear, but its value as historical description seems more dubious.

It was only with the Court's reversal of direction in 1976 in *Gregg v. Georgia* that America seemed to set off on a path different from that in Europe. In one sense, the nation only returned to the situation prevailing before 1972, when the country was characterized by a variety of different state arrangements with respect to capital punishment. Older controversies such as those surrounding the means of execution and the danger of executing innocent people were reoriented or reinvigorated by the rise of lethal injection and DNA evidence. The South consolidated its position as the center of capital punishment practice. Yet, in other respects, the post-1976 period represents the rise of a number of new developments in the practice of capital justice. The decision of the Supreme Court nationalized the issue in a way in which it had never been before. It shifted the attention of opponents of death to the courts, leaving the political field open, for a time, to death penalty advocates. The result was an unparalleled outburst of capital punishment legislation. The accident of the timing of the Supreme Court's decision contributed to a radical shift in the nature of American penal policy. The foregrounding in the Court discussions of the issue of public opinion and changing moral standards had the inadvertent effect of validating an appeal to "popular sentiments and passions" in the controversy over punishment and its limits.[49] Conservatives seized upon the penalty as a way of condensing a host of popular misgivings about crime and the direction of the nation. It transformed a rhetoric that highlighted concern with the rights of the accused and the life of the condemned into a language that emphasized the rights and life of the victim. A host of novel strategies appeared for addressing public anxieties, such as victims' statements, lethal injection, and the pursuit of "closure" for the families of victims. As Franklin Zimring has noted, it "would be difficult to overstate" the novelty of the rhetoric surrounding the death penalty. The message arose at a time of disenchantment with the institutions of government, in a period of alienation from politics, and at a moment of loss of faith in civic life. Capital punishment did not stand in isolation; rather it formed part of a dense field of related issues around which a reorientation of American politics and social life occurred. Nowhere was this shift in the articulation of death so evident as in the rise of the discourse of victimhood. "I find," Zimring writes, "a degovernmentalization of the image of death penalties and executions in the United States, that is, an attempt to reimagine executions as a service that the government provides to the relatives of crime victims rather than as a manifestation of the power of the state."[50] Support for death became expressive at one and the same time of fear and anger, even as it expressed a language of community outrage and populist unity.[51] Even if various states adopt widely different practices of death, the extraordinary surge of incarceration across virtually every state suggests that the effect of the death penalty debate at the national level operated to heighten a general mood of retributiveness that swept the nation. The point to make about all these developments, once again, is how recent their appearance is and how much they seem a product of the political history of the last three decades. They speak less of continuity with the past or a relapse to an earlier stage than of a new configuration of forces operating within a peculiarly modern social context.

The Time in Which We Live

Suppose, for a moment, that we imagine a different history. Let us say that the 1972 Supreme Court decision in *Furman* had stood. The Court had been split in its determination; it did not contain an abolitionist majority. The decision was narrowly drawn. Still, it raised the bar high enough that it frustrated efforts to reintroduce the death penalty. The Justices that Hubert Humphrey chose after his narrow election victory displayed spine in refusing to surrender to the drumbeat of right-wing polemic. Thus an elite, crucially situated in a key institution, imposed its will upon a population opposed to abolition. Although inflammatory rhetoric guaranteed that the issue never entirely disappeared from view, polling over the subsequent decades suggested that support for the penalty was slowly declining. A constitutional amendment to restore it failed to secure the votes of enough state legislatures. However reluctantly, the public came to live with the outcome. Thus the history books recorded that 1967 saw the last execution in America. As several scholars noted, the American case conformed to the path taken by the French two decades later, in 1981, when an elite also bucked popular opinion to abolish the ultimate penalty. Both countries offered a remarkable contrast to the British experience, where a timid Labour government in the 1960s failed, as it had in 1945, to take the initiative in ending the punishment. The subsequent Thatcherite regime, exploiting fierce law-and-order rhetoric, sent an increasing number to the gallows. Scholars devoted many pages to the study of this new instance of the "peculiarities of the English."

This scenario may look like a glib exercise, but I propose this alternative history as a way of getting clear about the relationship between contingent events and longer-term trends when we talk about capital punishment. One might have posed the story differently, asking how the development of the issue would have gone had *Furman* not occurred. Perhaps capital punishment would not have gained such political potency had the question not been nationalized by the Supreme Court's decision. The purpose of these counterfactual speculations is the same. It is the claim of this essay that we must turn to history in order to break the grip of a particular theory of historical change that has for too long clouded the debate over the death penalty. History has been the unavoidable but also unreliable terrain in which we wrestle with this question. Overly simple notions of progress or improvement in society or human nature can operate to inspire reform, but these beliefs can also blind people to the role of political actions and choices in shaping events. This essay has tried to expose and interrogate the pivotal place of a particular interpretation of historical development in the debate over capital punishment, and it has done so by reexamining the tangled course of American and European involvement with capital punishment. In an important sense, the focus of concern here has been with the temporal horizon of the present. The argument has been that we suffer both from too little and too much historical perspective.[52] Most obviously this has been the case of scholars concluding that, because Europe and America currently have radically contrasting approaches to the death penalty, they must possess very different cultures with roots going deep into the past. But it has also permitted activists on both sides of the question to argue past each other, and it has led to an underestimation, at least in the United States, of the political nature of the controversy.

Ignored in such a conclusion about the importance of the past is that the split between Europe and America is of recent origin, and that political processes rather than cultural variations seem to play the largest role in explaining the divergence.[53] The notion of "Europe" is itself a recent development with a still uncertain future. Much of Europe displays the same social and political symptoms that in America have produced the politics of capital punishment. It is probably premature to announce that Europe will be spared the outbreak of some new episode of death penalty frenzy.[54] On the other hand, it would also be a mistake to exaggerate the grip of capital punishment in America. Twelve states refused to follow the rush to restore death after 1976. Many states that passed capital legislation have made little use of it. Powerful voices continue to be raised against the practice. If these considerations offer few grounds for optimism, they nonetheless should guard us against bleak despair. Rather than looking to cultural differences to explain the different paths, it probably makes sense to acknowledge the importance of political structures and the centrality of political contests over ideas and values. European abolitionism has no doubt gained from the emergence of the European Union and the principles enshrined in the Human Rights Convention. This declaration may serve as a bulwark against retreat in the face of calls for the return of the death penalty.[55] By contrast, the fragmentation that results from American federalism probably hinders progress toward reform. Particular states and even counties are free to pursue their own policies with respect to capital justice. Because America elects judges and prosecutors, issues like the death penalty get caught up in electoral politics. Varieties of populism can more easily make a battle cry of criminal justice.[56] Finally, it is worth noting that, in Europe, abolition came as a result of a political process. It may be futile, or at least unwise, to expect that the federal judiciary can deliver such an outcome in America. These structural considerations scarcely support the conclusion that America differs from Europe in some deep and fundamental way.[57] Rather, they reinforce the view that the American divergence from the recent European pattern is, for the most part, the product of particular contingent circumstances.

The argument of this essay, however, is not simply that more historical comparison will correct most of the misperceptions about American exceptionalism. Instead, I argue that a particular type of historical interpretation has led us to conceive of the problem in the wrong way. The reform narrative, from its earliest appearance, used a powerfully charged temporal rhetoric to justify its proposals. It established as a fundamental source of modern identity superiority to the past. In charging that earlier practices that targeted the body were barbaric, reformers sought to vindicate their own age even as they sought its improvement. For them the death penalty was a mere survival, a practice that spoke of the past rather than the present. They devoted much effort to demonstrating that it was inconsistent with the true spirit of their times. In so doing, they proved blind not only to the power of the institution to appeal to human emotions but its ability to cater to new political circumstances and take on new meanings. The retentionists saw more clearly that there was no necessary incompatibility between the present and the existence of capital punishment. They exploited the same images of barbaric survivals threatening civilized existence to demonstrate the even more urgent necessity of death. They used the death penalty in an effort to give a particular political cast to their society.

The theme of American exceptionalism, in other words, is infected with nostalgia for the idea that certain types of cruel practices belong to the past and not to the present. It expresses the hope that these activities can be overcome if we simply grasp our modernity. The metaphor of the telescope is imperfect. It too neatly suggests that a simple adjustment will offer us a true perspective. Nonetheless, it captures the operation of one of the central tropes that sustains the self-image of the age, namely, the assumption that unpleasant or morally suspect practices do not really belong to us but are survivals that do not endanger our moral condition. Americans express these ideas even as they countenance practices of capital punishment and torture that would seem to fly in the face of such confidence. They reconcile these contradictory positions by the story they tell themselves. In the past, suffering was inflicted by unthinking and unfeeling people. Now we are different (and better) than they were. Even in the midst of atrocity this notion comforts us. Adopting this viewpoint, we feel confident that we know what state killing is because we have defined its lineage. The danger is that one underestimates the extent to which the death penalty arises in and is sustained by our present circumstances. The current experience of Europe may suggest a different possibility, that the present is not a place haunted by the past so much as it is a moment struggling over what it wants to become.

NOTES

I thank David Garland and Michael Meranze for their helpful comments on this essay.

1. See, for instance, James Q. Whitman, *Harsh Justice* (Oxford, 2003); Franklin E. Zimring, *The Contradictions of American Capital Punishment* (Oxford, 2003); and, for a more general account, Michael Ignatieff, ed., *American Exceptionalism and Human Rights* (Princeton, N.J., 2005).

2. Cesare Beccaria, *On Crimes and Punishments and Other Writings*, ed. Richard Bellamy (Cambridge, 2000), 18.

3. For a recent exploration of these ideas, see Lynn Hunt, *Inventing Human Rights* (New York, 2007), esp. chap. 2.

4. Beccaria, *Crimes*, 3.

5. The fourth and most recent edition of Hood and Hoyle's *The Death Penalty* provides compelling testimony to the continuing hold that the argument for cultural change and its penal consequences has upon recent scholarship. The authors spend several pages summarizing arguments that challenge this theory. Yet they conclude with the hope that "it may not be many years" before the Court recognizes that "a majority of the states do not support the death penalty," and therefore rules that "the emerging standards of decency that mark the progress of a nation" will not permit the use of the penalty. Roger Hood & Carolyn Hoyle, *The Death Penalty: A Worldwide Perspective* (Oxford, 2008), 125–28.

6. William Smith, *Observations on the Laws Relative to Debtors and Felons* (London, 1777), 6.

7. Charles Dupaty, quoted in Gordon Wright, *Between the Guillotine and Liberty* (New York, 1983), 12–13.

8. *Parliamentary History* , xxv (1785–86), 907–8.

9. Pieter Spierenburg, *The Spectacle of Suffering* (Cambridge, 1984), 190.

10. Richard J. Evans, *Rituals of Retribution* (London, 1997), 121–27.

11. *Parliamentary Debates* 1830, new series, xiv, 1033.

12. *Parliamentary Debates* 1832, 3rd series, xi, 954.

13. David Brion Davis, "The Movement to Abolish Capital Punishment in America, 1787–1861," *American Historical Review* 63 (1957): 23.

14. Randall McGowen, "History, Culture, and the Death Penalty," *Historical Reflections* 29 (2003): 229–49.

15. Quoted in Evans, *Rituals*, 271, and, more generally, see 266–75.

16. Jürgen Martschukat, "Nineteenth-Century Executions as Performances of Law, Death, and Civilization," in *The Cultural Lives of Capital Punishment*, ed. Austin Sarat and Christian Boulanger (Stanford, Calif., 2005), 58–60.

17. Quoted in Stuart Banner, *The Death Penalty* (Oxford, 2002), 113.

18. Wright, *Between*, 168–70.

19. "Calcraft's Calling," *Temple Bar* 15 (1865): 144.

20. See, for instance, Mitchell Merback, *The Thief, the Cross, and the Wheel* (London, 1999); Lisa Silverman, *Tortured Subjects: Pain, Truth, and the Body in Early Modern France* (Chicago, 2001); Evans, *Rituals*, 65–108; Andrea McKenzie, *Tyburn's Martyrs: Execution in England, 1675–1775* (New York, 2007); Randall McGowen, "The Body and Punishment in Eighteenth-Century England," *The Journal of Modern History* 59 (1987): 651–79; Randall McGowen, "The Problem of Punishment in Eighteenth-Century England," in *Penal Practice and Culture, 1500–1900,* ed. Simon Devereaux and Paul Griffiths, 210–31 (London, 2004).

21. Of course, Michel Foucault in *Discipline and Punish* (New York, 1995) sought to raise such doubts.

22. *Parliamentary Debates* 1830, new series, xxiii, 1179; Randall McGowen, "Managing the Gallows: The Bank of England and the Death Penalty, 1797–1821," *Law and History Review* 25 (2007): 241–82.

23. Wright, *Between*, 167–68.

24. Randall McGowen, "Civilizing Punishment: The End of the Public Execution in England," *Journal of British Studies* 33 (1994): 257–82.

25. *Parliamentary Debates* 1868, vol. 191, 1648.

26. James Fitzjames Stephen, "Capital Punishments," *Fraser's Magazine* 69 (1864): 762–63.

27. Karen Halttunen, *Murder Most Foul* (Cambridge, Mass., 1998).

28. Evans, *Rituals*, 367.

29. Quoted in Robert Nye, "Two Capital Punishment Debates in France: 1908 and 1981," *Historical Reflections* 29 (2003): 218.

30. America offered another instance of this shifting of the question of barbaric and civilized from the debate over the death penalty to the means employed to cause death. "The present mode of executing criminals by hanging," a governor of New York announced in 1885, "has come down to us from the dark ages, and it may well be questioned whether the science of the present day cannot provide a means for taking the life of such as are condemned to die in a less barbarous manner." Cited in Timothy V. Kaufman-Osborn, *From Noose to Needle: Capital Punishment and the Late Liberal State* (Ann Arbor, Mich., 2002), 105.

31. Gottschalk, *The Prison and the Gallows* (Cambridge, 2006), 201–2.

32. Wright, *Between*, 171–74; Nye, "Two," 218–20.

33. Victor Bailey, "The Shadow of the Gallows: The Death Penalty and the British Labour Government, 1945–51," *Law and History Review* 18 (2000): 305–49.

34. Evans, *Rituals*, 484.

35. Ibid., 361, 322, 345–46.

36. Ibid., 429.

37. Quoted in ibid., 625, and, more generally, see 562–608.

38. Tony Judt, *Postwar: A History of Europe since 1945* (New York, 2005), 41–62; István Deák, Jan Gross, Tony Judt, eds., *The Politics of Retribution in Europe* (Princeton, N.J., 2000), pt. 1.

39. Evans, *Rituals*, 775–85.

40. For these dates, see Hugo Adam Bedau, ed., *The Death Penalty in America* (Oxford, 1997), 78-80; and Franklin Zimring, *The Contradictions of American Capital Punishment* (Oxford, 2003), 22–37.

41. Wright, *Between*, 215.

42. Banner, *Death Penalty*, 221–23, 227–30, 244–47.

43. Carol Steiker, "Capital Punishment and American Exceptionalism," *Oregon Law Review* 81 (2002): 99; and, more generally, see 97–130.

44. Cited in Stuart Banner, *The Death Penalty* (Oxford, 2002), 248–49, 258–59. Alan Dershowitz, at the time a clerk for Goldberg, drafted the memorandum that developed this argument. See also Marie Gottschalk, *Prison*, 206–22.

45. Gottschalk, *Prison*, 219–20.

46. Banner, *Death*, 267–71, 274.

47. Ibid., 267, and, more generally, see 254–84.

48. For evidence of the debate over "evolving standard," see Hood and Hoyle, *Death*, 187–214.

49. Gottschalk, *Prison*, 216–18.

50. Zimring, *Contradictions*, 52, 14.

51. This theme of the novelty of late-twentieth-century discourse about crime has been explored by David Garland, *The Culture of Control* (Chicago, 2001) and Jonathan Simon, *Governing through Crime* (Oxford, 2007).

52. Tony Judt has made a similar point about European memory of the war and what followed. "I shall argue that the special character of the wartime experience in continental Europe, and the ways in which the memory of that experience was distorted, sublimated, and appropriated, bequeathed to the postwar era an identity that was fundamentally false, dependent upon the erection of an unnatural and unsustainable frontier between past and present in European public memory." Judt, "The Past Is Another Country: Myth and Memory in Postwar Europe," in Deák, Gross, and Judt, *Politics,* 293.

53. David Garland, "Capital Punishment and American Culture," *Punishment and Society* 7 (2005): 347–76; Gottschalk, *Prison*, 216–30, 237–38.

54. The temptation to "govern through crime" is widespread throughout the world. It describes a possible response of late liberal society to a host of challenges. See Simon, *Governing through Crime.*

55. See Evi Girling, "European Identity and the Mission against the Death Penalty in the United States," in Sarat and Boulanger, *Cultural Lives*, 112–28.

56. For a very useful survey of these issues, see Carol Streiker, "Capital Punishment," 118–26.

57. For a discussion that parallels the one I offer here, see Andrew Moravcsik, "The Paradox of U.S. Human Rights Policy," in *American Exceptionalism and Human Rights*, ed. Michael Ignatieff (Princeton, N.J., 2005), 147–97.

———————————————————————————— 5 ——

Hanging and the English Judges

The Judicial Politics of Retention and Abolition

———— DOUGLAS HAY ————————————————————————————

The legislative history of capital punishment extends over centuries in England, colonial America, and the United States. We see great increases in the number of capital statutes in some periods, sharp reductions in others, and, ultimately, abolition in England and the other parts of the United Kingdom in the second half of the twentieth century. There were also significant shifts in the numbers and proportion of death sentences actually carried out. That the United States has for the most part retained capital punishment into the twenty-first century invites comparisons, and explanations, of the differences in that long history.

This chapter argues that the high judiciary were particularly important in England, first in upholding the death penalty in the face of criticism from the mid-1700s, then in acquiescing in its gradual removal from theft during a long parliamentary campaign for reform in the first half of the nineteenth century, and, finally, in effecting abolition for murder in 1965. The importance of the judges rested on the facts that there were so few of them (only twelve in the eighteenth century) and that there was no full separation of judicial, legislative, and executive power in England or elsewhere in the United Kingdom. Many of the chief justices of the courts of King's Bench, and sometimes those of Common Pleas and Exchequer, sat in the House of Lords, the most important legislative chamber until the early nineteenth century and where they exerted a continuing strong influence on legislation through the twentieth. The chief justice of King's Bench even sat in the cabinet, the heart of the executive, for some years in the mid-eighteenth and early nineteenth centuries, and the judges were constantly involved in drafting and reviewing drafts of statutes, including capital statutes, before their introduction as bills in Parliament. The Lord Chancellor was both the highest judge and the speaker of the House of Lords, as well as a leading member of the cabinet. The judges, always few in number, thus had great legislative influence in all matters of criminal law, in the most direct way, and their often close connections with executive government strengthened that influence. The obvious contrast with the separation of powers under the U.S. Constitution is striking. So, too, is the fact that, in the new republic after the revolution, abolitionist sentiment was strong, partly on the grounds that capital punishment was the mark of aristocratic and monarchical tyranny in Britain.

The more recent history of the death penalty in both countries also invites comparisons. My argument here is that between the time Parliament first accepted repeal of the death penalty for many property offenses, in the 1830s, and the suspension for effectively all crimes including murder in 1965, with final abolition in 1969, a parliamentary consensus gradually formed that could, and did, ignore retentionist public opinion. By the 1960s parliamentary resistance to capital punishment was stiffened by the new commitment to abolition of some of those judges who, by virtue of the peerages that accompanied their offices, sat in the Lords; the diehard oppositionists were increasingly isolated. This reversal took place because a new Labour government, committed to abolition, enjoyed the right to appoint the most influential judges.

Again, the contrast with the United States is telling. The popular election of judges (and prosecutors) in many states in individual electoral contests, in a Constitution in which capital punishment is largely based on state rather than federal laws, gives electoral enthusiasm about the death penalty strong regional support by legal elites, including some judges. There appears little possibility of an effective elite consensus such as that found in the legislature of the United Kingdom, a smaller and unitary state in a politically more homogeneous country. Strong party discipline (in spite of a free vote in Parliament) was also important in achieving abolition, another sharp institutional contrast with the United States. The ensuing British consensus for abolition was once again renewed in the late twentieth century, when Parliament repeatedly refused to reintroduce capital punishment, even for murder carried out by terrorist groups such as the Irish Republican Army. Indeed, it may be argued, the prospect of hanging terrorists actually helped deter British governments from reintroducing the death penalty, even for such murders, lest they be made martyrs.

My second argument is that the common law high judiciary had a very personal perspective on capital punishment, often quite distinct from that of the House of Commons. Through the centuries, the judges were primarily responsible for deciding which capital convicts were to suffer death in any given year, and how many went to the gallows. They often had personal views on particular offenses, and some judges were more likely to leave convicts to hang than were others. But two main issues throughout this long period concerned them above all: the security of the state, and the security of the properties and lives of citizens. The relative importance of each in their minds helps to explain the course of abolition at different periods, the nature of judicial support for the death penalty in England, and the reversal of that pattern in the last fifty years. But abolition of the death penalty is always provisional, contingent on other forces. I return to the American comparison in the conclusion.

Left for Execution

Occasionally we see an eighteenth-century judge confronting his personal responsibility for capital punishment for the first time:

> [I had] not hitherto had occasion to wear that Cap which is usually put on when sentence of death is passed. I remember when my Robes were brought Home, my Heart sunk within me when that part of the Dress was laid upon the Table.[1]

William Osgoode, the new chief justice of Upper Canada, was writing to a female friend, and doubtless wanted to show himself a man of compassion, troubled by his grave duties. Osgoode, like most judges, got over his squeamishness. When he was intent upon getting a man to the gallows (as in the 1797 case of the American spy Daniel M'Lane, who was working for the French revolutionary enemy) he spared no effort. He personally brokered a deal to pay the chief crown witnesses with large land grants; assigned as defense counsel his own young protégé, then living in his house; interpreted the law of treason as broadly as it could be stretched, and perhaps then some; and pronounced an impressive death sentence when the jury, not surprisingly, delivered a guilty verdict. An unhappy Irishman was eventually found to carry out the execution, including the partial disembowelment of M'Lane's warm corpse before a horrified crowd of Québecois.[2]

This was a treason trial and therefore unusual, but it was of exceptional importance to Osgoode—as such trials were to other judges, a point discussed below. Very few executions were carried out for ordinary property offenses, or even murder, in Osgoode's small jurisdictions in Canada, and in the new United States there was a movement to repeal most capital statutes as emblematic of monarchical government, bloody remnants of the past, unfit for the new republic or at least its free citizens. England's traditional attachment to the death penalty stood in stark contrast.[3] The number of death sentences pronounced in England between 1714 and 1830 was well over thirty-five thousand, probably closer to forty thousand. Murder, maiming, rape, riot, and arson together accounted for less than 10 percent: the vast majority of capital sentences, over 90 percent, were passed on men, women, and children who had stolen, sometimes using threats (robbery), or the possibility of violence (burglary), but often with no possible physical danger to the victim.[4] London's Old Bailey sessions generated hangings eight times a year in the capital, but it was outside the metropolis, on the six assize circuits, that the judges put on the black cap most often. There, twice a year in most counties, they sentenced to death over three times as many as were condemned in London, and left for execution almost three times as many as were hanged in the capital.[5]

In assessing their decisions and their attitudes to capital punishment, the incidence of pardons is a crucial piece of evidence. Much of the discussion of the death penalty in eighteenth-century England has centered on the pardon, and particularly on the kinds of extenuating and aggravating circumstances that the judges, ministers, hanging cabinet, and monarch took into account in "ordinary" capital cases when recommending that transportation to the colonies, or another lesser punishment, be substituted for hanging.[6] There were two main points at which such decisions were made on assize circuit cases outside London. The first was immediately after trial, when the judges decided whom "to leave for execution" and whom to recommend for pardon, a recommendation almost invariably followed. These have been termed "administrative pardons." The second point of decision was after petition by supporters of convicts who had been left for execution. Here the judge was asked to report to the government, and a pardon might follow: these I have termed "petition pardons." The distinction is not absolute: petitions usually arrived after the judges had left the assize towns, but sometimes before they had written the 'circuit letter' in which they recommended administrative pardons.[7]

In London Old Bailey cases this temporal distinction largely does not obtain, because the London recorder reported to the cabinet, sometimes shortly afterward, sometimes months later, making recommendations that formed the basis of decision. Those decisions to hang or not were thus influenced in unknown proportions by the opinions of the recorder, subsequent appeals, and petitions to the recorder before he reported, and the attitudes of the members of the "hanging cabinet" who were present at any given time.[8] Decisions subsequent to a petition to the government altered a decision of the hanging cabinet, but it was rare. Therefore it is possible to distinguish the

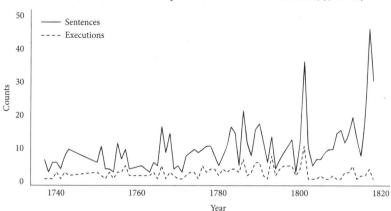

initial attitude to pardons of the judges on assize in a way that is not possible for Old Bailey cases. [9]

Capital cases were a significant part of ordinary criminal business: on average, about 40 percent of the cases in the Crown Court at assizes were capital charges during the period from 1740 to 1818, rising in some years to 60 percent. In the mid-sized county of Stafford, from which these figures come, the calendar of capital cases at each of the spring and summer assizes ranged from one to seventeen before 1766, then between five and thirty-four until 1815, before the huge postwar increase to fifty-four capital prosecutions in the spring of 1817, and sixty-three at the summer assizes that year.[10] After trials and convictions, the number of death sentences (before reprieves and subsequent petitions) similarly soared (see Figure 5.1).

The secular trend of death sentences in this county and the nation as a whole partly reflected population growth and partly new incentives to prosecute. The very large numbers in some crisis years were the product of the principal influences on crime and prosecution rates: economic conditions and whether or not the nation was at war or had just experienced demobilization of the forces. The peaks in the 1780s and 1801–2 and 1817 are such instances.[11] The critical significance of crisis years is discussed below, but the general secular trend first needs explanation.

Two general points need to be made about the increasing numbers of capital trials, particularly the enormous increase in the first three decades of the nineteenth century. First, they were more than balanced by an increasing number of administrative pardons, in which the judges reprieved after

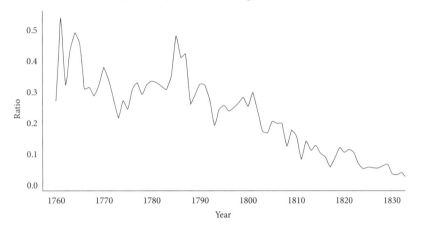

FIGURE 5.2. Ratio of convicts left for execution to death sentences, 1760 to 1830, all offenses, England and Wales.

trial, and recommended a pardon, which was granted conditional on a lesser punishment. This can be seen in Figure 5.1 and more clearly in the national statistics (see Figure 5.2). Thus a diminishing proportion of capital convicts were "left for execution," although not constantly diminishing.

Second, as an increasing proportion of capital convicts were reprieved, the profile of those left for execution changed. Since murderers were almost always executed (absent insanity), which continued to be the case, as the proportion of all capital convicts left for execution dropped, a greater percent of property offenders was reprieved and given a pardon conditional on another punishment. As a result, the proportion of all capital *sentences* that were for property offenses remained relatively constant, at about 90 percent of all sentences, but property offenders became a smaller proportion of the numbers *left to hang* from the 1790s, well before the parliamentary campaign to repeal capital punishment for theft. The profile of those "left to hang" by the judges did not change consistently over time—there was an increase in the proportion of property offenders hanged in the early nineteenth century, arising out of the Bank of England's determination to hang forgers but also out of the often desperate social conditions (attributable to dearth, demobilization, and political economy) endured by England's poor, and the judges' reaction to the riot and theft that resulted.[12] But the secular trend was for a smaller proportion of property offenders to be executed. Most executions were still for property offenses, but the death penalty was increasingly seen

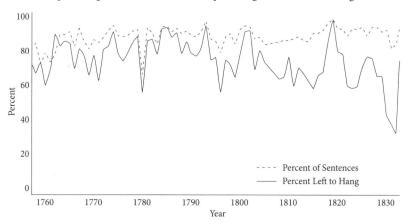

FIGURE 5.3. Property crimes:
percentage of death sentences and percentage of those left to hang.

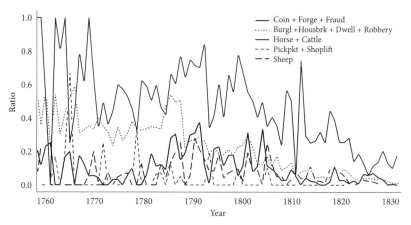

FIGURE 5.4. Ratio of convicts left for execution, property crimes. Note: the greater variation earlier in the century is owing to lower numbers in a smaller sample.

by the early nineteenth century as the punishment for murder (see Figures 5.3 and 5.6). The judges also made important distinctions between different property offenses. They did so collectively: for example, taking a more serious view of burglary than of animal theft before the 1780s (see Figure 5.4). And individual judges were particularly exercised by particular offenses.[13] More important for the argument in this chapter is that some judges clearly were more willing to leave convicts for hanging, a fact of some importance for their role in opposing legislative mitigation of capital punishment.

Hanging Judges

There is a very old anecdotal literature about the attitude of individual judges to capital offenders and their willingness to hang or to pardon. For the period after 1782 we now have easy access to the reports judges made on applications for mercy, following a petition to the monarch.[14] Some inferences about the attitudes of the judges in their day to day work with ordinary criminal offenders can be drawn from both the preceding sources, and sometimes from private correspondence between the judges. But it is also possible to compare the behavior of the judges through recently developed statistical techniques.

Although the only court in England with supreme criminal jurisdiction was King's Bench, where the chief justice (also chief justice of England) and his three puisnes interpreted and made much of the law, all twelve common law judges were involved. From time to time they were consulted as a group on matters of criminal law policy by government or Parliament, and they all participated when a case was reserved at trial on a difficult point of law.[15] But their ordinary criminal work as individuals was concentrated on the assize circuit and at the Old Bailey. In London the recorder usually had a High Court judge with him at the Old Bailey; they took the duty in rough rotation. Thus capital cases were also heard by the recorder in London, and some serjeants on the circuits, as a matter of course—in both cases, good preparation for possible promotion to the puisne bench of one of the three courts.[16] But the vast majority of capital trials and decisions about executions lay in the hands of the dozen judges of the three common law courts; from 1760 to 1820 only about sixty royal judges in all sat on capital cases on the circuits.[17] Compared to modern American practice, or contemporary French or even British colonial practice, the judicial influence on capital punishment was concentrated, at any one time, in the hands of a very few men.

How did they view their semiannual task in the Crown Courts on their assize circuits? This was not usually where their interests lay. Like the barristers, the judges tended to prefer the nisi prius courts, where a smaller number of civil suits (and misdemeanors being heard in the county after being removed into King's Bench on certiorari or on criminal information) were tried by special juries of gentlemen, with full and often leisurely argument. On circuit they shared the usually more onerous and less interesting work in the Crown Court. The custom on some circuits was for the junior judge to take the Crown Court in the more populous counties on that circuit, sometimes being spelled by the senior judge if there was a very heavy calendar. In periods like the 1750s, 1780s, and post-1815 when there were great increases in the level of prosecuted crime, the Crown calendar became a heavy burden, and the decision to reprieve with a recommendation for pardon, or to leave a convict to hang, probably was reached very quickly, after equally speedy trials. In short, most judicial decisions on the death penalty were reached quickly, as a matter of routine, immediately after the verdict.

Contemporaries identified some of these men as "hanging judges." Often the comment referred to a period of crisis, such as the 1750s and the 1780s, when it was explicit government policy, emphasized to the judges by the Lord Chancellor before they went on their circuits, not to yield to entreaties while on circuit by indulging in unwarranted administrative pardons.[18] Mr. Justice Buller (JKB 1778–1794) had a posthumous reputation as a harsh criminal judge, people remembering his charges in the 1780s to the effect that mercy too often "induced offenders to speculate upon the chances of life and death, like the gamester reckoning upon the chances of the die."[19] It is true that he can appear less than sympathetic when we listen to him responding to a request for a report. John Waltho was sentenced to death for stealing sheep in the spring of 1786 and left for execution, although the great majority of sheep stealers were usually pardoned and given a lesser penalty (see Figure 5.4). Buller refused to recommend mercy, commenting acidly on the petition which "appears to me to have been drawn by . . . [the prisoner's] Attorney, who has had recourse to fiction & invention more than to any facts which were proved, or consistent with the facts proved, on the trial. What is meant by 'the hurry and nice rules of an assize trial,' I cannot imagine."[20] For Buller, there was a calendar to get through. For Waltho, it was a matter of life and death. Waltho was convicted at what was, in fact, the busiest assize in that county between the years 1740 and 1800. Buller's efficiency looked different from the dock.[21]

On the other hand, Buller appears to have initiated the practice of distinguishing in his sentencing those whom he truly intended to hang from those for whom he intended to recommend an administrative pardon. If done in the name of administrative efficiency, it also had elements of humanity. In the latter cases he did not put on the black cap, and he abbreviated the formal death sentence to the simple words, "That you be hanged by the neck until dead."[22] He also took advice. One of the Bow Street Runners, John Townsend, commented on several judges to a parliamentary committee in 1816, noting that he had once successfully persuaded Buller to reprieve two men who had no previous convictions, and to hang the third, who had three. "And how are Judges or Justices to know how many times a man has been convicted but by the information of the officer in whose duty and department it is to keep a register of old offenders."[23] In his testimony to the parliamentary committee Townshend also remembered Mr. Justice Eyre (B 1772–87, CB 1787–93, CJCP 1793–99) going the Home circuit in a period of high crime rates, charging the grand jury at Hertford,

> Now, gentlemen of the jury, you have heard my opinion as to the enormity of the offences committed; be careful what bills you find, for whatever bills you find, if the parties are convicted before me, if they are convicted for a capital offence, I have made up my mind, as I go through the circuit, to execute every one.

On the other hand, Lord Chief Justice Kenyon (CJKB 1788–1802) enjoyed a reputation during his life and after as a humane man eager to reprieve, and especially not to cause distress to those whom he *intended* to reprieve.[24]

A bare comparison of the ratio of reprieves to death sentences for different judges cannot tell us whether these contemporary observations were accurate. Many factors determined the outcome of cases heard by a particular judge in a particular year. Analysis of the national figures shows that the hanging rate for different offenses, including different property offenses, varied greatly and hence the mix of offenses at an assize could result in more or fewer executions (see Figures 5.4 and 5.6). Other changing influences from year to year and place to place were government policy on pardons, the levels of prosecuted crime, and apparent threats to wider public order or the regime itself. Thus Buller tried many of his cases in years when the government discouraged pardons, and when prosecuted crime rates were very high. In contrast, William Blackstone, who was a justice of King's Bench then Common Pleas in the 1770s, heard a very different sample of cases. When I first presented an analysis of ratios of convicts left to hang (including Figures 5.2, 5.3, and 5.4) more than twenty years ago, there was no statistical technique suitable for the analysis of time series with varying and unevenly distributed data for different years.[25] Until recently, therefore, it was impossible to assess the relative harshness of any given judge after all other factors had been taken into account. In the last ten years multilevel longitudinal analysis has been developed, and it is ideally suited to this task.[26]

Figure 5.5 shows the predicted and actual trends in hanging scores of ten judges discussed in this chapter. As shown in the figure, Buller and Eyre, as contemporaries thought, were more punitive during most of their careers, and Kenyon was a relatively merciful judge. Different judges undoubtedly

FIGURE 5.5. Observed and predicted non-parametric trends for ten judges.

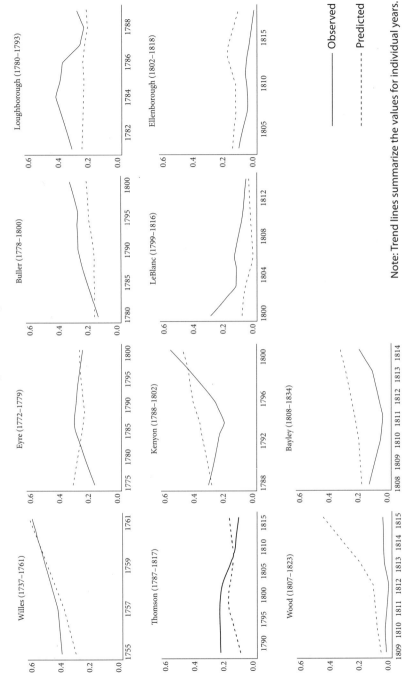

Note: Trend lines summarize the values for individual years.

——— Observed

- - - - Predicted

had different attitudes on the general desirability of capital punishment, as well as how often it needed to be used, and when, in the run-of-the mill cases. Their personal theories of crime, their political outlook, and their personal psychology all played a part. And particular offenses were apparently more deserving of execution in the eyes of particular judges.

McGowen's recent illuminating study of the conduct of forgery prosecutions by the Bank of England in late Georgian England provides a striking instance of how a particular offense could have special significance. The greatest corporation in the land controlled wholly not only the prosecution of its cases (on legislation it had a hand in drafting) but also controlled ensuing pardon decisions. Its lawyers and committee members in effect created a "private pardoning" apparatus dealing with capital sentences for forgery.[27] Until it was challenged by the Scottish Lord Advocate, Lord Sidmouth, and the Prince Regent in 1817–18, neither the government nor the judges contested the right of the Bank to decide not only whom to prosecute for forging its notes, and whether to do so on a capital charge, but also to determine whether condemned capital convicts should be spared, and which ones. By 1820 the constitutional objection that had been raised about the practice was dismissed: the Bank prevailed. The royal judges continued to be excluded from the discussion of Bank forgery pardons.

What are we to make of this episode, in terms of the larger system of capital sentences and pardons in which it was embedded? As McGowen points out, the issue of the death penalty was not settled by the first two decades of the nineteenth century but remained very much alive in political and social life, and, moreover, executions for forgery were accepted and defended with vigor at the highest commercial, judicial, and governmental levels. At the same time we must recognize that forgery cases were, as capital *property* offenses, always somewhat anomalous (see Figure 5.6), as were rates of those left for execution for other forgeries, and for coining and fraudulent bankrupts (see Figure 5.4), where the judges made the decisions. The high rates for such offenses were not confined to the early nineteenth century. What had changed was the zeal with which the Bank and Mint prosecuted in some years; the control that the Bank, as a private corporation, exerted; and the public criticism that now attended its punitive policies, as those convicted of other property crimes were almost invariably pardoned.

The distinctive nature of the Bank's campaign makes it unrepresentative, as well as unreliable, as a basis for generalizations about the capital sanction in general, as McGowen concedes. He also comments, "Scholars have frequently portrayed the gallows as a crude instrument, an extravagant

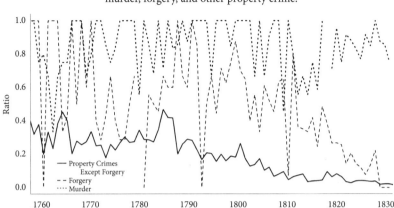

FIGURE 5.6. Ratio of convicts left for execution: murder, forgery, and other property crime.

and messy exercise of power. They have, sometimes, resorted to hyperbole to describe death as the last, most awful recourse of a state with few other defenses against an unruly population." He suggests that the Bank's forgery campaign was a "more subtle and flexible operation."[28]

I argued in 1975 (and in 1986) that the day-to-day operation of the criminal law "was not the illogical, capricious, inefficient, and messy *bricolage* portrayed by the parliamentary reformers of the early nineteenth century, and by historians like Radzinowicz." The pardon was indeed a "more subtle and flexible operation" than that earlier generation of historians realized, preoccupied as they were to explain progress (something in which we no longer believe) and hence prone to accept reformers' rhetoric as descriptive of reality.[29] But it is undoubtedly the case that the judges *were* much preoccupied with "an unruly population."

Capital Punishment in Times of Crisis

The semiannual rhythm of the assize circuit was punctuated by months and occasionally years in which the safety of the central and local state took precedence over routine crime. The recurring theme is political crisis, disruption with implications for the stability of the regime. The interruption of transportation to America during and after the revolutionary war (1776–87) constituted something of the kind, in the sense that there was a conjunction of weakness to punish at a period of political crisis.[30] We can understand the higher execution rates that resulted as justified by that sense of crisis, as well as the suspension of transportation, the usual condition of a capital pardon. But the judges were always sensitive to more specific, often brief, challenges to the stability of the regime. They considered hangings (or the calculated extension of mercy) to be indispensable at such junctures. In 1715 the exiled house of Stuart attempted an invasion and restoration; after its failure, many traitors (and rioters who supported them after the attempt failed) were hanged. Parliament had already passed the Riot Act to deal with Jacobite protesters, making the offense a capital felony. A second Jacobite rebellion and invasion in 1745 was punished in the bloodiest way possible at English criminal law. Mass trials were avoided by picking one out of each twenty capitally accused prisoners by lot (a technique used in army mutinies) and carefully staging exemplary executions, with full application of the horrific penalties of high treason. In 1746 Lord Chief Justice Lee polished his oratory for the death sentences and harried the administration for a proper gallery to be built in Westminster Hall, as at earlier great state trials, to accommodate important visitors. Other functionaries took care of the boiling of the severed heads and quartered bodies so that they would last as long as possible on Temple Bar and the English Gate at Carlisle. The executions of the Cato Street conspirators of 1820, who had plotted to murder the cabinet, were restrained in comparison.

Two Jacobite risings were alarming, and the judges sometimes thought they saw evidence—particularly through the 1740s to the 1760s, in 1780, and again between 1790 and 1832—that a conjunction of a riotous "unruly population" and regime change was far too likely. At times when the mob was active, they also took personal prudential measures. Lord Kenyon ordered for his domestic defense, during political agitation in London in 1799, "six huge blunderbusses"—"deadly instruments each capable of killing 50 men at a shot (more I believe than his Lordship's mouth ever sent from this world at one judgement)."[31] Mr. Justice Grose, on the other hand, refused the government's offer of protection during the Gordon riots in 1780, or perhaps he, too, had blunderbusses.

The mob held a dominant political as well as personal significance for the judges. The repeated outbreaks of widespread food riot in the eighteenth century, to take one instance among many other kinds of riot, involved the judges in a great deal of work, immediate strategic calculations, and deep inquiry into the purposes and doctrines of the common law. Again, capital punishment was central to all of these matters. From time to time judges sentenced food rioters to death, usually for housebreaking or robbery, and left them to hang in hopes of restoring order.

The chief justice of Common Pleas, Sir John Willes, was on the Midland summer assize circuit in 1756 and had just written to the Duke of Newcastle about the state of local opinion with respect to Admiral Byng (not a Jacobite but equally culpable) and how best to deal with him.[32] Willes arrived in Warwickshire in the middle of a massive food riot led by the colliers of Nuneaton. He wrote his brother judge, Sir John Eardley Wilmot, from Astrop in Northamptonshire on August 25, that there were few causes but so many criminals at Coventry that he and his fellow judges on the Midland circuit had not arrived at Warwick (the assize town) until noon on the 19th, where

I found every one in the greatest consternation. The sheriff and some of the justices came to me to acquaint me that the Monday and Tuesday before there had been a general insurrection of the mob from Nuneaton to the number of several hundreds, that they pulled down several houses and mills and two Quaker meeting houses. That their numbers increased every day, and that they were proceeding to commit other outrages, and threatened to kill anyone that opposed them. The proclamation [of the Riot Act] had been read, but with no effect, and I found the magistrates greatly intimidated, and they desired that soldiers might be immediately sent for to quell this insurrection. I told them I was against it for many reasons and made a [?] at last to dissuade them from it; and telling them that I would stand by them to the utmost, and not put an end to the assizes, till the disturbance was over. I at last gave them some courage, and succeeded so well, that four of the rioters were taken and brought to prison on Friday night, and five more of them on Saturday morning [the 21ˢᵗ], and amongst them the captain of the mob. Immediately I tried four of them, which were all against whom the evidence was ready; they were found guilty,[33] and I ordered the captain and another very infamous fellow to be executed the Wednesday following and then adjourned the assizes till next Monday,[34] when I assured them that I would come again, and declared publicly before I went, that if any more disturbances were committed, and the country was not quite quiet when I came again, I would immediately hang the others and proceed to try the rest, and if they were found guilty, I would execute them immediately, but if no more disturbances were made, I promised that I would apply to his Majesty, to pardon all but the two which I had ordered for execution. I desired the sheriff to send messages to me immediately if any further disturbances were committed; and having heard nothing from him since, I hope that I have put an end to this insurrection, which would probably have soon grown into a rebellion.

He added, as an afterthought, "in the main, it was a good circuit."

Willes ordered the sheriff to get as many constables as necessary to ensure control of the executions on Wednesday but specified that he should not ask for help from the military. The chief justice feared that asking for soldiers risked the confrontation being reported to France as a rebellion, thus encouraging a French invasion; this presumably also explains his earlier resistance to the magistrates' request for soldiers. Willes also reported that at least one rioter had declared that the Jacobite pretender would come to lead them. The lord chief justice clearly shared the belief that local economic insurrections could provoke external attempts at regime change, a fear of English rulers for centuries past.

Willes's judicial activism was immediately endorsed by the king, who expressed the view that his example of adjourning the assizes should be followed by the other judges when needed. His brother judges on their circuits followed events in Warwickshire closely by correspondence. The royal court and the government were delighted: "the general voice is, that these Insolent Rioters could not have fallen into better Hands."[35] Judges and other state actors knew that capital punishment had a very different role to play in cases threatening the security of the state. What was merely the "disagreeable business" of ordinary criminality in the Crown Court, enlivened occasionally by a knotty point to be reserved for consideration by all twelve judges or a ruling in King's Bench, was suddenly of central political importance. At issue was local "insurrection" threatening more general "rebellion."

Food rioting was important in the 1740s; erupted again in 1756 to 1757 (Willes warned his brethren that wheat prices remained high in his part of the country in April 1758 and that "the Poor murmur very much, and are I'm afraid ripe for any mischief," but disturbances were few); was almost countrywide in 1766–67; became serious in 1779, 1782 and 1783; emerged again in 1795 and 1796; was apparently national in scope in 1800 and 1801; and was threatening to occur again in 1812. The enormous riots of 1800–1801 led the judges into an attempt to reanimate the ancient criminal law against profiteering middlemen as common law, since Parliament had repealed the ancient statutes in 1772, convinced of the benefits of free markets.[36] The chief justice, Kenyon, believed that prosecuting profiteers might pacify rioters (and he thought Adam Smith's praise of free markets in food to be nonsense.) At the same time, a large number of rioters were indicted, convicted, and executed, usually for capital theft rather than under the Riot Act, and prosecution and execution rates soared.

By the first decades of the nineteenth century food riots became rarer, but industrial riot, sabotage, and quasi-insurrection did not. In earlier centuries the woolen and other textile trades had been closely regulated in an attempt to prevent trade cycles from causing popular uprisings, and both ordinary weavers and silk weavers had extorted protective legislation from Parliament through immensely large strikes and widespread riot.[37] At the same time, the authorities had relied at critical junctures on the death penalty, making it as visible as possible. The success of the Bank in having forgers executed in the middle of Birmingham rather than at the assize town of Warwick, described by McGowen, had many earlier parallels, including the execution, following massive riots by silk weavers in Spitalfields, of the weavers Doyle and Valline in front of Bethnall Green Church in 1769. That change of venue from Tyburn was contested on constitutional grounds. Mr. Justice Eyre probably owed his elevation to the bench in 1772 to his determination, as recorder of London, in ensuring that the executions took place there: bloody examples at the heart of the rebellious artisan community.[38]

As a justice of Exchequer, then of Common Pleas Eyre worked in the 1790s to expand the law of treason, haranguing jurors in 1794 that "men who assemble to procure a Reform in Parliament may involve themselves in the guilt of High Treason," by conspiring to overawe Parliament in a reform convention, thus effecting an overthrow of government, the destruction of the constitution, and hence the death of monarchy, "that glorious fabric, which it has been the work of ages to erect . . . cemented by the best blood of our ancestors."[39] He did his best to see that the prisoners' blood was added to the cement. And in the first decades of the nineteenth century, in the same years that the Bank was exercising its power to obtain executions and imposing its decisions on the judges (although probably few of them disagreed, and some probably had acted as counsel for the Bank when at the bar), the industrial sabotage of Luddism (1811–16) also seemed a danger requiring executions.

How did the judges react? Possibly more diversely than in the past, particularly since critics of capital punishment were scrutinizing the hanging scores of individual judges. But during Luddism, like earlier critical junctures, special commissions allowed the government to fine-tune repression by hand-picking judges for the purpose.

In the critical months following massive riot and machine-breaking in 1811 and 1812, the value of hand-picking judges for special commissions was exploited to the full. When machine-breaking began in the midlands and the north, some of the justices on the assize circuits had directed or encouraged acquittals in spite of the scale of disturbances. John Bayley, a puisne justice of King's Bench, did so at Nottingham in March and at York in August 1812, and would do so again at Nottingham in March 1815. George Wood, a baron of the Exchequer, sat on a trial at Lancaster in August 1812 where thirty-eight were acquitted. This was wholly unacceptable. The government was convinced exemplary executions were necessary, and when special commissions were issued for assizes at Chester and Lancaster in May 1812, and for York in January 1813, care was taken to select judges willing to see the convicts hang. Samuel Le Blanc, a puisne justice of King's Bench, sat with Baron Thomson at both Lancaster and York, at which a total of twenty-five prisoners were executed. At York Le Blanc tried the murderers of the mill owner William Horsfall, a notorious outrage. The judges privately advised prosecuting counsel J. A. Park and Henry Hobhouse, the government lawyer in charge of the prosecution strategy, against moving the executions of the three condemned men to Huddersfield, as the delay would raise hopes of mercy. They were hanged at York two days after trial. Before the next convictions were secured, Le Blanc conferred with Park on the advantages of speedy hangings, as had also been done at the Lancaster special commission. The judges said they would accept no applications for mercy but would leave the matter entirely to the discretion of the secretary of state. Le Blanc and Thomson recommended mercy for only one of the seventeen sentenced to death.[40]

A Long Tradition

The judges of Georgian England drafted much of the more penal legislation, conducted the capital trials, interviewed state prisoners before committing them for treason trials on which they sat, and in the early nineteenth century were among the most powerful voices insisting that any repeal of capital statutes was a danger to the state, property, and security. That opinion has been used to convict them of reactionary ignorance, suffering from the occupational hazard of lawyers—resistance to change. But that is to misunderstand their knowledge and experience, and their conviction that, as important as their role was in the ordinary administration of justice, in time of danger their responsibility as rulers was even greater. The fine-tuning of ordinary criminal punishment was part of their semiannual role in the assize courts and eight times a year in the Old Bailey, a routine and "disagreeable business." They adjusted the weight of the law accordingly, usually pardoning sheep stealers and cattle thieves, virtually always extending mercy to pickpockets, hanging coiners and deferring to the Bank's determination to hang forgers, and increasing the overall number of executions when high crime rates seemed to require more examples at the gallows. But they also believed that capital punishment in times of popular "insurrection" was the ultimate guarantee of the survival of the oligarchic, monarchical, aristocratic, and profoundly antidemocratic state they served, whether it was in little colonies like Lower Canada where Chief Justice William Osgoode trapped a spy, or in England itself, where the experience of treason and the fear of revolution profoundly shaped judicial attitudes and practice.

This nexus of judicial attitudes to the death penalty—differing by judge but showing common concerns about state security, social order, and the incidence of "ordinary" crime—persisted well into the nineteenth century, although ultimately was reshaped by Parliament's progressive repeal of capital punishment for property offenses. But even then, and even in the mid-twentieth century, the attachment of some leading judges to capital punishment had resonances with the past: some still claimed that social crisis was imminent, that only hangings held barbarism at bay. At the same time the enthusiasm of some judges for hanging was accompanied by ignorant or misleading self-congratulation about the supposed historical role of the Bench as a means of reform. Yet, in the end, it was judicial support at the highest level, ensured by careful Labour Party planning, that led to the abolition of capital punishment for murder in England in the 1960s. What follows is a brief account of the role of the judges in the nineteenth and twentieth centuries.

Judicial Opposition to Abolition

Although Blackstone and others called for repeal of some capital statutes in the mid-eighteenth century, legislative progress was slow. Apart from a few small exceptions hardly any of the hundred or so capital statutes were repealed. Pickpocketing in 1808, stealing linen from bleaching grounds in 1811, some excise crimes, and soldiers and sailors without a pass in 1812, all of which were hardly ever used. And others continued to be enacted, notably the 1812 frame breaking act to deal with Luddites. In this last case the death penalty was imposed in 1812, removed in 1813, and restored in 1817; the preceding year capital punishment had been enacted also for those riotously demolishing mine property.[41] And no matter how often the critics of the death penalty—led in the Commons by Sir Samuel Romilly from 1808 to 1817 and Sir James Mackintosh from then until 1832—told Parliament that the law was a disgrace to the nation and did not protect property, it was the deeper convictions, the usefulness of executions for maintaining order and for manipulating the powerful psychic symbols of terror and mercy that resonated for the House of Lords and the judges and government. The debate was a prolonged one, lasting from the first years of the nineteenth century until 1837, when Lord John Russell finally swept away almost all the last remaining capital statutes except for murder. The campaign for abolition in cases of murder took another century.

In this long resistance to change the judges were dominant. Governments and the upper house were convinced that bills significantly changing the criminal law before being introduced should be submitted for the judges' approval, a corollary of the probably ancient practice that, in fact, the most important criminal law bills originated with the judges or with the government after canvassing the judges. In 1786 Loughborough (then Lord Chancellor, formerly a judge and keen to hang [see Figure 5.5]) declared that "in all preceding time" any bill dealing with criminal law was first submitted to the judges, "the . . . men most likely to discover any defects in the execution of the criminal justice of the country, if any such defects there were; and in that case it might be presumed they were as competent to suggest a remedy as any other order of men who constituted a part of the mass of society." He insisted that "the judges were the persons with whom alterations of the conduct of criminal justice ought to originate." (He was speaking in opposition to Wilberforce's bill to widen the use of dissection beyond murder and to end the practice of burning women at the stake who were convicted of high and petty treason.) Lord Sydney, the Home Secretary, concurred: "all Bills affecting the criminal justice of the country ought to receive the approbation of the judges previous to their being proposed to Parliament."[42] Pitt, the prime minister, who had earlier shown an interest in reducing capital statutes, refused to support an inquiry to that end in 1787; he referred in his speech to the need to avoid the "smallest tendency to discredit the present existing system," insisting that before legislation was introduced it should be "fully weighed and settled by those learned and able men who filled the highest stations in the law department." The Member of Parliament (MP) who had moved for the inquiry retreated, explaining that his sole purpose had been to frame principles of reform that would be referred to the judges, who would, in effect, decide whether legislation should result.[43] Pitt's refusal to countenance the project may have arisen in part from the fact that Lord Mansfield was ailing but refusing to retire because he was attempting to ensure that Buller, rather than Kenyon, succeeded him as chief justice. But the fact that the principle of judicial preapproval was insisted on in the 1780s meant that it was also being questioned.

Who the judges were at any given time was undoubtedly important. As late as 1772 Lord Camden (who, as Charles Pratt, had been Chief Justice of Common Pleas from 1762 to 1766 and Lord Chancellor from 1766 to 1770) and Lord Mansfield (Chief Justice of King's Bench from 1756) apparently had not opposed a bill from the Commons that repealed six largely unused capital statutes.[44] And, in 1812, some of the judges assisted in effecting a repeal of a number of capital provisions in the excise laws that made it virtually impossible to get convictions.[45] But after Ellenborough became Lord Chief Justice of England in 1802, his resistance to repeal of any important capital statute was unremitting, right to the end of his long tenure in 1818.

Ellenborough was less punitive on the Bench than many other judges (see Figure 5.5). He himself was responsible for "Ellenborough's Act" (1803), which repealed a 1623 capital statute with a reverse onus for concealing the birth of a bastard child (a statute regularly nullified, in fact, by juries and judges), making it simple murder to kill a bastard child.[46] But his statute also provided the death penalty for the first time for inducing an early-term abortion through drugs, for a range of lesser arson offenses, and for shooting, stabbing, and cutting with intent to murder or even do "grievous bodily harm."[47] Ellenborough did not block Romilly's first successful bill of 1808, which repealed the virtually unused Elizabethan capital statute against pickpockets, but he argued in 1810 that it had been "a most dangerous innovation." In that year he utterly rejected the idea that there should be any further lessening of penalties: if the Lords enacted Romilly's bill of 1810 to repeal the death penalty for shoplifting (10&11 Wm III, c.23), he said, "we shall not know where to stand—we shall not know whether we are upon our heads or our feet."[48] Their Lordships heeded his words. He was prepared to accept the repeal of the death penalty for thefts of cloth from bleaching grounds the following year only because it was the proprietors (who had initially sponsored the death penalty) who now petitioned for the reduction in punishment.[49] But the Lords rejected further Commons bills repealing capital punishment for shoplifting in 1811, 1813, 1816, 1818, and 1820.

Ellenborough's endorsement of the traditional view, that a few judicious hangings was the only possible deterrent for any particular crime and a sure preserver of the social order, virtually blocked any legislative movement, because of the quasi-constitutional doctrine that criminal law bills had to originate with the judges or at least be endorsed by them. Speaking against Romilly's bills to end the death penalty for shoplifting and theft in dwellings to forty shillings, he argued that "they went to alter those laws, which a century had proved to be necessary, and which were now to be overturned by speculation and modern philosopy."[50] During his lifetime he was fully supported in this stance by Lord Eldon, Lord Chancellor for almost the entire period from 1801 to 1827, and the two of them frequently asserted that they spoke for all the judges.[51] After Ellenborough's death Eldon successfully opposed the repeal of the draconian Waltham Black Act of 1722 (9 Geo I c.22) by arguing that, "in the former instances in which these bills were discussed they [their Lordships] had the benefit of the experience and knowledge which distinguished that great man [Lord Ellenborough]. . . . Induced by his authority they had again and again rejected these bills."[52]

Romilly, the leading member of the Bar as well as an MP, had refused to submit his repeal bills to the judges in advance, not only because he knew their resolute opposition but also because he was convinced that the legislature, not the judiciary, should be the author of criminal legislation: the demand to submit bills first to the judges was "a most unconstitutional doctrine." But his attempt to insist on what most members probably considered a Frenchified or American constitutional principle was wholly rejected, as were almost all his bills.[53]

Romilly managed to get one further obsolete capital statute repealed: soldiers and sailors wandering without a pass.[54] There was some activity after his death in 1818. Petitions to Parliament in 1822, a Commons Select Committee on the Criminal Law,[55] and a shift in wider public opinion coincided with two critical changes in the politics of parliamentary opposition. Lord Ellenborough was succeeded by a younger and more flexible chief justice, Lord Tenterden (Charles Abbott, chief justice, 1818–1832). And in 1822 the government was significantly restructured to let in moderate Tories, some with an interest in criminal law reform, notably Robert Peel. Eldon himself seemed to be changing his attitude to the death penalty, at least with respect to its frequency of application, given shifts in wider public opinion and perhaps his own convictions. In October 1822 he wrote to Peel, the Home Secretary, regarding thirty-eight convicts then under sentence of death in London and Middlesex, that "I think, from the Recorder's communication to me, he is much more bloody minded than I am after three times reading all the cases." He added, "Times are gone by when so many persons can be executed at once as were so dealt with 20 years ago."[56]

Peel was convinced that only the restructuring of the police (which he effected in Ireland after 1816 and in London in 1829), coupled with prison reform and the recasting of much of the substantive criminal law, would help preserve aristocratic government, which was also a concern of the Whig administration after 1832.[57] He adopted very partial reform of the capital statutes as one of his aims. In this limited project he was able to secure the complete cooperation of the judges, whom he courted so assiduously that Tenterden congratulated Peel in the House of Lords for his zeal for reform.[58]

Peel repealed a few of the least used capital statutes between 1822 and 1827 in the course of a mass of other legislation dealing with substantive and adjectival criminal law.[59] But we should not exaggerate his enthusiasm nor suggest a volte-face by the judiciary. Peel set his face firmly against any more tampering—for example, with horse stealing, burglary (although he restricted the ambit of the offense), forgery, or many of the other most often used statutes. Tenterden and the other judges made it clear that they thought further repeal of the death penalty was unsafe: "We had, at present, in this country, no substitute for the punishment of death."[60] The biggest change came after the Whigs came into office in 1832. The reform government that came to power swept aside the capital statutes most frequently used for property offenses. Lord Russell's legislation—authorized by a Criminal Law Commission report— repealed most of the capital offenses that Peel had preserved. The judges continued to resist large changes, imposing modifications on the more far-reaching bills, but they were not wholly obstructionist regarding the government's main aims.[61] They were more willing to accept repeal with respect to thefts, because imprisonment was now much more widely available in a variety of prisons for convicts who were not transported; further, the principle of the police had been established in London from 1829 and in the rest of the country increasingly from the 1830s, providing a new means to deal with both crime and riot. Finally, public executions were now increasingly seen by both the Bench and the government as occasions of mischief rather than morality. Bigger and bigger crowds—sometimes fifty thousand strong—attended executions, and railway companies began running special trains to provincial hangings. From the mid-1830s the judiciary's opinion of capital punishment, and peers' views, more closely resembled opinion in the Commons. In fact, Russell agreed to a bill abolishing death for rape, in 1840, at the judges' suggestion.[62]

By the 1840s the only capital offenses remaining (apart from a few highly uncommon offenses against the state) were murder, sodomy, burglary with violence, robbery with wounding, and arson of houses with persons within. No further capital statutes were repealed until 1861. A Select Committee of 1847 that considered capital punishment, among other issues, consulted the judiciary and found that only four of thirty-one English, Irish, and Scots judges thought that capital punishment could be entirely dispensed with for these offenses; a third thought it could be restricted to murder only; and half thought it should be retained for all the offenses to which it currently applied. Of the thirteen English judges, two thought it could be abolished, nine were opposed, and three (including the Lord Chief Justice) gave no opinion. Baron Parke and Mr. Justice Patteson thought torture and mutilation might be more effective than fear of death but that such measures would not be tolerated by the public.[63] By the early 1860s, however, Parliament enacted consolidating legislation that in effect retained capital punishment only for murder.[64]

Thus the issue that would occupy the ensuing century was clear: whether or not capital punishment would be removed for murder. Supporters of that proposition encountered the judges again in the 1864 Royal Commission on Capital Punishment. All the English judges who were questioned opposed abolition, although a few thought an alternative should be provided or expressed serious reservations about the death penalty. The broad opinion was expressed by the Lord Chancellor, Lord Cranworth, who thought that the death penalty could not be dispensed with in cases of murder, as it was the best deterrent when witnessed by other would-be criminals and convicted felons; the occasional mistake could be justified, he believed, by the general benefit to society. Baron Bramwell thought that executions would deter persons of "low intellect" and were preferable to any alternative; he also deplored the growing use of the insanity defense. Baron Martin supported the death penalty because it deterred the lower classes, asserting that juries virtually never made mistakes. Lord Wensleydale (who sat until 1856 as Baron Parke) still believed that torture ("cutting off a man's members, depriving him of his eyesight, cutting off his limbs") would be more of a deterrent, but he again conceded, as in 1847, that this would be unacceptable to the public. The only judge supporting total abolition was an Irishman, Mr. Justice O'Hagan of the Irish court of Common Pleas, although he doubted that the public in England was ready for abolition. Another witness, later an Irish judge, thought that murderers should be punished with life imprisonment, and the former chief justice of Calcutta stated that the possibility of hanging an innocent person was a great disadvantage of the death penalty.[65] The English judges expressed various opinions with respect to infanticide, the possibility of defining degrees of murder, public versus private hangings,[66] and the insanity defense but were unanimous in supporting retention, and their language suggests concern about working-class militancy and crime; recent public panics about habitual and violent criminals probably helped determine their views.[67] An unabashed emphasis on vindictive retribution was celebrated by James Fitzjames Stephen, both in his many publications and then in statements during his tenure as a High Court judge (1879–91). For many late Victorians on the Bench, in Parliament, and in the wider public, revenge epitomized sound public policy.

Abolition

From 1860 until the early twentieth century the abolitionist case was rarely raised in Parliament. The scandal of more than three hundred military executions in the British army in the First World War, mainly for cowardice and desertion, and the horrors of the war itself, resuscitated arguments against the state deliberately putting citizens to death.[68] A successful campaign by Labour backbenchers (despite the hesitancy of the short-lived 1924 and 1929 Labour governments' leaders) led to the abolition of the death penalty for both cowardice and desertion in 1930.[69] Support in the Commons from members of other parties was important, but a basic divide was also evident. The main opposition was in the Lords—in this case, the army high command; in the Commons the parliamentary Labour Party was increasingly abolitionist, with no love for bloody-minded army officers nor, as would become evident, for Tory retentionists or judges. The Bench's long opposition to trade union rights and workers' claims in industrial accident cases undoubtedly weakened the influence conservative judges had with Labour governments and their backbench supporters.

The creation of the Labour party (1900 to 1906) and its increasing determination to abolish capital punishment (passed as a resolution by the 1923 annual conference, and committing the party at the 1934 conference) changed the terms of the debate. A 1929 Select Committee on Capital Punishment appointed under Labour refused to take evidence from the judges because their complete opposition to reform was assumed.[70] Support for capital punishment (and the number of executions) was lower in 1939 than it had been throughout the late nineteenth and early twentieth centuries. When Labour was returned to power with a large majority in 1945 the issue of abolition for murder was clearly on the table, but because of a division of opinion in the cabinet, poor parliamentary tactics, and the unremitting opposition of the high judiciary, the attempt to achieve abolition in the Criminal Justice Bill of 1948 failed. The only outcome was another Royal Commission (1948–53), which reported to what was now a Conservative government.[71]

In this postwar episode the judges, once again, were clearly a critical obstacle. Harold Laski noted, in 1945, "the painfully small part played by the judges in the reform of the Criminal Law," and warned of the danger of a Royal Commission with a judge in the chair. Those on the senior Bench were convinced that a postwar crime wave threatened the social order. The Lord Chief Justice, Lord Goddard, and some of his fellows opposed the abolition of corporal as well as capital punishment; even Lord Jowitt, the Labour

Lord Chancellor, was, at heart, a supporter of the death penalty. Goddard led the opposition in the Lords to abolition. In his maiden speech on Labour's Criminal Justice Bill of 1948, he made clear that he represented a Bench of law lords who favored hanging.[72] He insisted that capital punishment was in accord with public opinion, and that from his own experience and recent cases he knew that "there are many many cases where the murderer should be destroyed." Like his predecessor, Ellenborough, more than a hundred years before, he said that he had canvassed his brothers and found those that he asked to be unanimously in favor of retention: twenty King's Bench judges all favored retention. (He withdrew this claim a month later, after the vote, admitting that two now told him that they supported the proposal to suspend the death penalty for a trial period of five years.)[73] And he used a debating tactic that was one of his favorites for the next fifteen years: descriptions of horrifying cases of murder, including rape of elderly women (although rape was not capital), assault victims left to die in the streets, and gruesome disposal of victims' bodies. (He used the same approach in the last debates before abolition in the 1960s, describing horrific cases of murder to the House, deploring a breakdown in social discipline, arguing that, if repealed, capital punishment could never be reenacted, and that abolition therefore was a dangerous social experiment.)[74] In the debate in the Lords in 1948 Lord Oaksey, a Lord of appeal, argued for the retention of both corporal and capital punishment, citing the death sentences at Nuremberg in 1945, over which he had presided as president of the Tribunal, and the inconsistency of putting Germans to death but refusing to execute murderers in England.[75] Goddard, in his testimony to the Royal Commission of 1949–53, argued that reprieves had lately been far too common and that he wanted to retain the black cap while sentencing prisoners to death. He saw no reason not to hang women, and he was also against raising the age of execution for youths from eighteen to twenty-one. Mr. Justice Byrne concurred on most of these points. Lord Denning took the view that capital punishment should be preserved for the worst kinds of murder, for that was society's means of denouncing the worst of crimes. In Scotland the Lord Justice-General, Lord Cooper, told the commission that he would deplore abolition, as it was an indispensable safeguard.[76]

These, however, were the last gasps of judicial resistance. The execution of an innocent man in the Evans and Christie case, the controversy around Bentley's execution (as trial judge, Goddard overtly aided the prosecution),[77] new appointees to the bench, and a decisive shift in leading, and wider, public opinion made movement possible. A 1957 Homicide Act passed by a Conservative government that attempted to distinguish capital from noncapital murders pleased neither retentionists nor abolitionists and was considered unworkable by the judiciary. When Labour returned to power in 1964 executions were at a very low level, and the new prime minister, Harold Wilson, was determined on abolition, as were the overwhelming majority of Labour members of the House of Commons. The eventual bill was passed on a free vote rather than as a government party measure, but the government facilitated it in every way. Notably, they neutralized judicial opposition. Gerald Gardiner, the Lord Chancellor, was appointed by Wilson partly because Gardiner, when a barrister, had been the joint chairman of the National Campaign for the Abolition of Capital Punishment from the mid-1950s.[78] Lord Chief Justice Parker, Goddard's successor, was also a convinced abolitionist, and they both likely exerted great influence on more junior judges. The outcome was suspension of the death penalty for murder in 1965, now with the almost unanimous support of the English judiciary. A Conservative amendment required a confirmatory vote within five years, and several attempts at restoration were made in the interval, but in December 1969 final abolition of the death penalty for murder passed with large majorities in both houses. In the Lords an attempt by a former Conservative Lord Chancellor to extend the experimental period until 1973 was defeated, largely as the result of a "consummate" speech by Lord Chancellor Gardiner.

Conclusion

The longer British history has a certain consistency. Peel's initial inroads on capital punishment for theft in the 1820s were made with the assistance of Lord Tenterden, and Russell's in the 1830s were made with that of Denman. But the resistance to repeal had generally been led by the higher Bench, and the judges repeatedly set limits to how far Parliament was able to go. The reformer John Bright, arguing for the creation of the Royal Commission of 1864, deplored the fact that every improvement in the criminal law of England had been against the judges' advice.[79] Of course, the judges did not like to think that they were so bad. In the mid-twentieth century, as the pressure for repeal mounted, they began to rewrite history to cast their predecessors (and themselves) as reasonable reformers. In 1948, during the debate in the Lords on the Criminal Justice Bill, Goddard said, "It is a common reproach against Judges (though I believe it is absolutely groundless) that they are— the word generally used—reactionary, and are always on the side of severity. It is not so." And later in the debate, he stated: "Gibe as much as you will at Judges, who it is always said are opposed to alterations in the law. That is not true."[80] Between those two interventions the Labour Lord Chancellor Jowitt referred to Lord Goddard's main speech in opposition to abolition and equivocally praised him by invoking his predecessors:

> I think that he showed in that speech that the Judges are not the inhuman creatures they are sometimes supposed to be, not "stick in the muds," talking the language and thinking the thoughts of about 200 years ago. The old gibe about Lord Ellenborough[81] is really not sufficient ground on which to say for ever afterwards "You may completely disregard what the Judges think." After all, Lord Ellenborough was making the mistake of forgetting that juries were not convicting because the penalties of his time were so hopelessly out of proportion to the offenses. . . . When I recall some of the great Judges since Ellenborough's time, I think, for instance, of Sir Samuel Romilly—Who has done more to restrict and limit the death penalty than Romilly?—and of many other names which occur to any educated person. And I should like to think that our Judges today are in the same great line.[82]

Except, of course, that Romilly was never a judge: in fact, judges were his principal opponents.[83] Romilly was one of a "great line," never numerous, of critical lawyers, parliamentarians, and journalists who fought the death penalty in years when it was established, protected, and celebrated as part of the received wisdom of government. All those men and women knew that the tiny number of men sitting on the English Bench were their most formidable opponents, the most determined and effective defenders of the practice of ritual hanging of criminals, by the neck, until dead.

The Labour Party's increasing commitment to abolition, both at annual conferences and in Parliament, was, of course, crucial. Even though most of their constituents supported the death penalty, the parliamentary party held to the belief that executions were both barbaric and ineffective. But neutralizing the judiciary was also crucial: Goddard had shown just how effective a populist appeal by a hanging judge could be. By the time a parliamentary consensus against capital punishment was established in the seventh decade of the twentieth century, the judiciary's conservative influence, so long devoted to the cause of execution, had shifted to the side of abolition, even for murder, as it had earlier for theft. Attempts to reintroduce hanging for murder and terrorist offenses have been unsuccessful, partly because of the fear of governments in the late twentieth century that executions in Northern Ireland would have been wholly counterproductive, but largely because of the strength of the general parliamentary consensus.

The opponents of that consensus have increasingly appeared unsound, at least to their colleagues. Just before the attempt to restore the death penalty in Britain in May 1982, the somewhat eccentric Conservative Nicholas Fairbairn, former solicitor-general for Scotland, called for legislation to make it possible to prosecute *any* indictable offense as a capital crime, including, among many, rape, burglary, and robbery. The jury would decide whether a guilty verdict should be a capital one, an echo of the eighteenth-century practice in which juries were often presented with a capital charge but could find a noncapital verdict. In his opinion piece in *The Times,* on 27 April 1982, Fairbairn argued that not only was the death penalty a deterrent to particular crimes but it was especially praiseworthy for its symbolic importance: "When the death penalty existed the law had awe. In the most junior court in the land the juvenile tiptoed in before the justice of the peace for, while he could not be hanged for the petty offense with which he was charged, he knew he was in the chamber of life and death." His atavistic proposals strengthened, if anything, the existing parliamentary consensus. If any judges agreed with Fairbairn, they certainly did not say so publicly.

An increasing uneasiness in recent years with the ancient amalgam of judicial, legislative, and executive power in Britain may mean that the high judiciary's overt influence will be less important in future debates about capital punishment than at any time in the last three hundred years. Separation of powers on the American model has removed the direct legislative influence of the senior judges, who now sit on a Supreme Court rather than as law lords.

If that change suggests a convergence between American and British constitutional practice, other institutional and cultural differences suggest that capital punishment (and its absence) will continue to distinguish the two countries. My comments here are tentative, particularly with respect to the American experience. In the United States it appears that elected state judges (whether or not they have also been elected prosecutors earlier in their careers) remain deeply involved with the populist politics of the death penalty: in many states they cannot ignore widespread support for execution, whatever their personal views. The Supreme Court is, of course, important, but its importance can be exaggerated: the states without the death penalty are not free of it because of Supreme Court rulings but rather because of local politics. The politics of governance through crime and penal policy, of which Simon and Garland have given convincing accounts, remains deeply entrenched in some places, and, as is well known, particularly so (though by no means exclusively) in southern states. The role of local legacies of slavery and other ethnic enmities in that geographic pattern is suggestive but problematic; on the other hand, the general importance of racism, ethnic fear, and alarm about both state and personal security seems unequivocally clear, as is their deliberate exploitation in political controversy.

Clearly both Britain and the United States have long histories of cultural significance attaching to the death penalty, with numerous parallels but also distinctive differences. I have argued elsewhere that the long decline in murder rates in England, in the early modern period and then later, was perhaps owing to the gradual curtailment of capital punishment, which incrementally preceded the decline of interpersonal violence and threats to public order. The Whigs of the early nineteenth century were right: the death penalty made the mob more dangerous, and the safety of an undemocratic regime required that the elites not instruct the people in violence.[84] Whether or not declining state violence helped to reduce popular violence in Britain, it is clear that some unique characteristics of American democracy were important from the beginning. Although the new republic in the late eighteenth century partly repudiated capital punishment as the mark of British tyranny, aristocracy, and monarchy, it was considered an acceptable fate for American slaves. When that distinction was briefly repudiated during Reconstruction, it returned, reenergized, in the lynching of black Americans and less powerful whites in the late nineteenth and early twentieth centuries. In the late twentieth, the politics of fear (and generational changes in crime levels) proved increasingly useful to political platforms based on capital punishment.

Certainly the late twentieth and early twenty-first centuries have seen parallels to Goddard's hysteria about the imminent breakdown of British society in the face of postwar indiscipline, crime, and barbarity in both countries. In the immediate aftermath of the Second World War, many conservative British commentators attributed at least part of this alleged crisis to America's cultural example during the war. (How much of their rhetoric was, in fact, a reaction to national and imperial decline is a larger question.) However, the commitment of the victorious Labour Party in 1945 to ending fears—of unemployment, poverty, and sickness—through the construction of a welfare state, and the subsequent acceptance of that welfare state, and penal theories of rehabilitation, by both parties, left less room, except among a minority of conservatives, to play the politics of fear with the gallows. Still unknown is whether that postwar consensus is coming to an end, as British (as well as American and Canadian) politicians routinely use fear of crime for electoral ends, and as larger numbers of citizens face economic insecurity and a diminished welfare state.

NOTES

My thanks to Leila Mehkeri, Karen Tsang, and Chris Reed for research assistance.

1. William Osgoode, chief justice of Upper Canada and then Lower Canada, to Ellen Copley, 25 September 1793, Ontario Archives, MU3705.

2. F. Murray Greenwood, *Legacies of Fear: Law and Politics in Quebec in the Era of the French Revolution* (Toronto, 1993); Greenwood, "The Treason Trial and Execution of David McLane," *Manitoba Law Journal* 20 (1991): 3–14; *Dictionary of Canadian Biography*, vol. 4 (Toronto, 1979), 501–503, "David McLane."

3. For Upper and Lower Canada, see Peter Oliver, *Terror to Evil-doers: Prisons and Punishments in Nineteenth-Century Ontario* (Toronto, 1998); Douglas Hay, "The Meaning of the Criminal Law in Quebec, 1764–1774," in *Crime and Criminal Justice in Europe and Canada*, ed. L. Knafla (Waterloo, Ont., 1981): 77–110; J.-M. Fecteau, *La liberté du pauvre: Crime et pauvreté au XIXe siècle Québecois* (Montréal, 2004); Douglas Hay, "Civilians Tried in Military Courts: Quebec, 1759–1764," in *Canadian State Trials*, ed. M. Greenwood and B. Wright (Toronto, 1996), 114–28. For American revolutionary attitudes, see Louis P. Masur, *Rites of Execution: Capital Punishment and the Transformation of American Culture, 1776–1865* (New York, 1989); Adam Hirsch, T*he Rise of the Penitentiary: Prisons and Punishment in Early America* (New Haven, Conn., 1992); and Michael Meranze, *Laboratories of Virtue: Punishment, Revolution, and Authority in Philadelphia, 1760-1835* (Chapel Hill, N.C., 1996).

4. See below for sources.

5. Tracking how many death sentences were ultimately carried out is a surprisingly difficult task, as the sources are scattered through different state paper series and private collections at different periods, decisions to reverse initial decisions about executive pardons turn up in different places, and some (perhaps many) are undoubtedly lost.

6. For a discussion of the literature, and a reply to critics of some of my early work, see Douglas Hay, "Writing about the Death Penalty," in J. Beattie, J. Phillips, J. Muir, and D. Hay, "Symposium on [Douglas Hay's] "Property, Authority and the Criminal Law,'" *Legal History* 10/1–2 (2007): 13–52. I would only add here that a problem with assessing the nature of the post-petition pardon process on the basis of the Home Office registers (as Peter King has done) is that the regularized pardoning process embodied in that source after 1783 formalized the role of the judges; indeed, the very high execution rates of the 1780s (see Figures 5.1, 5.2, and 5.4) is one of the reasons it became more formal. Earlier in the century we can occasionally see how the judges themselves were the conduits through which pardon appeals were made, often before their formal circuit letter was written—in short, influencing by far the most common kinds of pardons, what Beattie has termed "administrative" pardons, decided upon by the judge himself. These can usually be found only in judges' personal papers. We find such evidence in scattered personal correspondence or diaries, a wide range of state and semiprivate papers, particularly before 1783. And quite often the basis of granting a pardon is as simple as this: someone who counted asked for it. Beattie's analysis of practice in London in the early eighteenth century agrees, in this respect, with mine: see Hay, "Writing about the Death Penalty," 14.

7. In April 1787, while still on the Lent circuit before the circuit letter had been written, Mr. Justice Grose replied to a request for a report by stating that he had sentenced a sheep stealer at Stafford (to death) "intending to recommend that he would be

transported for 7 years." In the event, he now recommended a free pardon (The National Archives (Kew), henceforth TNA, HO 47/6/25, 7 April 1787). For instances of other anomalies, see the introductions to *Pardons and Punishments: Judges' Reports on Criminals, 1783 to 1830: HO (Home Office) 47/ Calendared by The National Archives Local History Research Group, with an introduction by Paul Carter* (Kew, Surrey, 2004), 3 vols.; and Hay, "Writing about the Death Penalty."

8. The judge who sat with the recorder was rarely consulted, according to Mr. Justice Bayley, advising Wilberforce that he was unable to help him with a petition appeal for one Hugh Donaldson: "in the case of town offenders, the consideration of any thing which transpires after conviction belongs exclusively to the secretary of state for the Home Department, &, I believe, the judges never interfere" (Oxford University, Bodleian Library, MSS Wilberforce d.17 fol.233 n.d.).

9. Such administrative pardons followed reprieves, which were noted at the time of the assize by the clerk. The assize clerks in the early nineteenth century were asked by Parliament to tally death sentences and reprieves for as much of the past century as they could, and the following analysis depends largely, although not entirely, on their work. The source for the following figures and statistics is an edited and corrected data base of thirty thousand death sentences in varying periods between 1689 and 1817 in London and Middlesex; on the Home, Norfolk, Western, and Oxford circuits; for the counties of Lancashire, Durham, and Staffordshire; and for the whole country for the period from 1820 to 1837. For brevity, this data set is referred to as "England and Wales"; in this chapter I have used the figures only from 1760 to 1832. The sources are several: briefly, the 1819 statistical returns in the appendices to *Parliamentary Papers* 1819 (585) "Select Committee on Criminal Laws," corroborative counts in assize minute books in TNA record group ASSI, comparison with the published Old Bailey sessions, and soundings for several counties in the main SP and Home Office series recording pardons. I am grateful to Simon Devereaux for sharing some of his corrected figures for the Old Bailey, allowing me to assess the accuracy of my own for London and Middlesex (his corrected figures do not significantly change relative ratios or incidence), and to Randall McGowen for directing me many years ago to the sources for the early nineteenth century. I am also grateful to Paul Carter and other staff at The National Archives, Kew, for making available to me unpublished material from their pardon project. I shall publish a fuller description of the data set in the future.

10. All felonies without benefit of clergy at assizes, death sentences TNA ASSI 2 and ASSI 5, execution data from a wide range of sources. The execution data are for actual executions, not just those "left for execution." Staffordshire's population (and rank among thirty-nine English counties, excluding Monmouth) was about 125,000 in 1701 (14th), 250,000 in 1801 (10th), and 415,000 in 1831 (7th). P. Deane and W. A. Cole, *British Economic Growth 1688–1959: Trends and Structure* (Cambridge, 1964), 103; E. A. Wrigley, "English county populations in the later eighteenth century," *Economic History Review*, 60/1 (February 2007): 35–69.

11. See D. Hay, "War, Dearth and Theft in the Eighteenth Century: The Record of the English Courts," *Past and Present,* no. 9 (May 1982): 117–60; John Beattie, *Crime and the Courts in England, 1660–1800* (Princeton, N.J., 1979), 226–34; Peter King, "War as a Judicial Resource: Press Gangs and Prosecution Rates, 1740–1830," in *Law, Crime and English Society, 1660–1840,* ed. Norma Landau (Cambridge, 2002).

12. On the Bank and forgery, see below.

13. See Figure 5.5 for the overall scores of individual judges. I plan to publish a detailed account of their attitudes, including emphasis on particular crimes, in the future.

14. *Pardons and Punishments.*

15. D. R. Bentley, ed., *Select Cases from the Twelve Judges' Notebooks* (London, 1997). See also forthcoming work on these cases by Jim Oldham and Randall McGowen, presented at the American Society for Legal History Conference, Ottawa, 14 November 2008.

16. In a few places in England lay municipal justices acting under city charters tried capital cases with juries and supplied the reports respecting capital and other pardons throughout the eighteenth and well into the nineteenth century. I discuss this in forthcoming work on Lichfield City.

17. The judges went, in pairs, on most of the six assize circuits twice a year (only once in some northern counties for part of the period). In each county one sat in the nisi prius court to try civil cases, one in the Crown Court to clear the jails and hear other criminal cases, which early in the century often included minor felonies and even petty misdemeanors. They were sometimes assisted by one or more serjeants, who were given the commissions of assize, oyer and terminer, and general jail delivery when through illness, age, or other pressing matters not all the judges were available to ride the circuit. It was understood that the chief justice might often excuse himself: Mansfield (CJKB 1756-1788), for example, apparently never took the Lent assizes on his circuit, which was, in theory, the Home: Essex, Hertford, Sussex, Kent, and Surrey (James Oldham, *The Mansfield Manuscripts and the Growth of English Law in the Eighteenth Century* [Chapel Hill, N.C., 1992], 2:1313 n.10).

18. Hay, "Writing about the Death Penalty," 9.

19. W. D. Evans, witness before the 1819 Commons Select Committee on Criminal Laws, added that Buller had mentioned the difficulty of finding a new destination for transportees (*Parliamentary Papers* 1819 (585) 8:34).

20. TNA, HO 47/4/22, 3 April 1786.

21. Waltho's execution broadsheet (William Salt Library, Stafford) mentions a respite, but I have not found any further reprieve or pardon in the Home Office papers. Buller's "usual dispatch" was sometimes noted in the press (*Aris's Birmingham Gazette,* 1 August 1796).

22. Ibid., same witness, 36. The practice was established and extended thirty years later by the *Judgment of Death Act,* 4 Geo IV c.48 (1823), which allowed the judge to order the sentence to be recorded and not pronounced at all in open court, except in cases of murder.

23. Townshend, before the 1816 Select Committee on the Police of the Metropolis, *Parliamentary Papers* 1816 (510), 5: 143–45.

24. Hay, *ODNB,* "Lloyd Kenyon."

25. "Capital Punishment in England, 1750–1832: A Quantitative Analysis," Annual Conference, American Society for Legal History, Toronto, 25 October 1986. Available on SSRN.

26. My thanks to Heather Krause and Professor Georges Monette, Department of Mathematics and Statistics, York University, for their great assistance in this analysis. The source data are the proportion of those left for execution and the names of the judge(s) sitting on the Home, Midland, Northern, Norfolk, and Western circuits, at assizes in

Durham, Stafford, and Lancaster, and in London and Middlesex, in each year with surviving data for different periods between 1718 and 1818. An individual annual score was calculated for each of 20 types of capital crime, for 48 judges, resulting in 5,512 judge/crime/year combinations (reflecting that some crimes were not tried in certain years). This analysis controls for variations in hanging rates from year to year, for variations in each year between different judges, and for the fact that for many years we do not know which of two assize judges sat in the Crown Court. Using a mixed model, with both fixed effects for each year and place (circuit, circuit population, crime levels, distribution of different crimes, government policy, the number of men in the armed forces, and perceptions of threat to the regime) and random effects (who sat on the bench at any given time and place), the procedure generates predicted scores for each year for each judge for each crime, based on the fixed effects, together with actual scores, in a semi-parametric analysis that shows change over time. The graphs shown in Figure 5.5 for each judge are their consolidated scores, predicted and actual, for all the crimes they tried in each year. I shall publish a fuller account in the future.

27. Randall McGowen, "Managing the Gallows: The Bank of England and the Death Penalty, 1797–1821," *Law and History Review*, 25 (2007): 241–82.

28. McGowen, text at note 97.

29. Hay, "Writing about the Death Penalty."

30. Simon Devereaux, "Imposing the Royal Pardon: Execution, Transportation, and Convict Resistance in London, 1789" *Law and History Review*, 25(2007): 101–38; D. Hay, "The Laws of God and the Laws of Man: Lord George Gordon and the Death Penalty," in *Protest and Survival: The Historical Experience. Essays in Honour of E. P. Thompson*, ed. John Rule and Robert Malcolmson (London, 1993), 60–111.

31. Matthew Robinson Boulton to James Watt, 4 February 1799, Birmingham City Archives, Boulton and Watt Collection, parcel B. *ODNB*, "Lloyd Kenyon."

32. BL Add Mss 32867 fol.1 Willes to Newcastle, Warwick 21 August 1756. Byng, who had been arrested after his arrival back in England in July, after the defeat in Minorca, was court-martialed for neglect of duty and sentenced to death in January 1757; he was executed by firing squad in Portsmouth on 14 March 1757. The most recent account is Steve Moore, "Losing Minorca: An Event in British Political History," (Ph.D. diss., York University, 2008).

33. On the Riot Act, 1 Geo I st.2 c.5.

34. "Monday s[eve]n night."

35. Willes was more prepared than many to leave convicts for hanging; see Figure 5.5.

36. I have described this crisis in "The State and the Market: Lord Kenyon and Mr Waddington," *Past and Present*, no. 162 (February 1999).

37. For an overview of food riots and policy with respect to industrial disputes, see D. Hay and N. Rogers, *Eighteenth-Century English Society: Shuttles and Swords* (Oxford, 1997), chaps. 5 and 6.

38. See my article "James Eyre," *ODNB*.

39. *The Times*, 3 October 1979.

40. See my article "Simon LeBlanc," *ODNB*; and Figure 5.5 for his hanging score in ordinary cases.

41. 52 Geo III, c.16; 54 Geo III, c.42; 57 Geo III, c.126.

42. *Parliamentary Debates*, Lords, 5 July 1786, vol. 23 (1786), 87–99.

43. *Parliamentary Debates*, Commons, 27 April 1787, vol. 11 (1787), 350–54. Leon Radzinowicz and Roger Hood, in *A History of English Criminal Law and Its Administration*, 5 vols. (London, 1948–86), 1:447, tentatively attributes this outcome to the fact that Parliament had rejected the London Police Bill of 1785, and also to fears aroused by the revolution in France. The latter seems unlikely, since the revolution would not begin for two years.

44. Radzinowicz and Hood, *A History of English Criminal Law*, 1:445–46, citing a speech of Mackintosh in 1819. Mackintosh thought that it had been lost because of the opposition of other members. Romilly's memory was that "the leading authorities" in the Lords agreed on the repeal of five of the statutes but that the bill was lost by the prorogation of Parliament.

45. *Parliamentary Papers* 1819 (585), "Select Committee on Criminal Laws," 56–59.

46. 21 James I c.27; Edward Hyde East, *A Treatise of Pleas of the Crown* (London, 1803), 1:228.

47. 43 Geo III c.58 (1803).

48. *Parliamentary Debates*, Lords, 30 May 1810, vol. 27 (1810), 197–200.

49. 18 Geo II c.27 and 3 Geo III c.34; *Hansard*, 1st ser., vol. 20 (1811), col. 299.

50. Quoted in Radzinowicz and Hood, *A History of English Criminal Law*, 1:517.

51. Ibid., 1:587–89.

52. *Hansard*, 2nd ser., vol. 2 (1820), cols. 492–93. See E. P. Thompson, *Whigs and Hunters: The Origin of the Black Act* (Harmondsworth, 1977).

53. Samuel Romilly, *Memoirs of the Life of Sir Samuel Romilly*, 2nd ed. (London, 1840), 2:177–78. See also K. J. M. Smith, *Lawyers, Legislators and Theorists: Developments in English Criminal Jurisprudence 1800–1957* (Oxford, 1998), 56ff.

54. 39 Eliz. c. 17.

55. As a matter of policy it sought no evidence from sitting judges, although it requested the opinion of several retired ones; only Sir Archibald Macdonald (CB 1793–1813) cooperated. The committee believed that it would be "unbecoming and inconvenient" for judges who might have to hear cases under existing law to give opinions about that law.

56. BL, Add Mss 40315 fols. 63–64, Eldon to Peel, attributed in a penciled note to October 1822. However, he did not therefore believe in statutory reform. In debates in 1832 on abolition for sheep stealing and horse theft, Eldon rejected the proposal, partly on the grounds that he had "employed his thoughts for twenty-five years and could never find what he considered a proper secondary punishment," nor did he think any lawyer could (*Hansard*, 3rd ser., vol. 13 (1832), cols. 987, 989).

57. Randall McGowen, "The Image of Justice and Reform of the Criminal Law in Early Nineteenth-Century England," *Buffalo Law Review* 35 (1983): 89–125.

58. Radzinowicz and Hood, *A History of English Criminal Law*, 1:589 n. 83; *Hansard*, 2nd ser., vol. 17 (1827), col. 1261.

59. See Radzinowicz and Hood, *A History of English Criminal Law*, 1:580–84.

60. Ibid., 1:590–91, 594; 4:332 n. 90. Quoted words are Tenterden speaking in 1832 on the sheep and horse legislation (*Hansard*, 3rd ser., vol. 13 [1832], col. 985).

61. Radzinowicz and Hood, *A History of English Criminal Law*, 1:603–4; 4:332 n. 91.

62. Ibid., 4:322, 332; Brian P. Block and John Hostettler, *Hanging in the Balance: A History of the Abolition of Capital Punishment in Britain* (Winchester, 1997), 57.

63. Their answers are given in 1866 [3590] Royal Commission on Capital Punishment, *Report and Minutes of Evidence*, Appendix, 640–43.

64. The other exceptions were treason, piracy, and arson in dockyards and arsenals. Radzinowicz and Hood iv 330–33, 341–42.

65. 1866 [3590] Royal Commission on Capital Punishment, *Report and Minutes of Evidence*, 55–71, 72–88, 88–100, 100–108.

66. In 1868 the Capital Punishment Amendment Act removed executions from public view. On its genesis, see David D. Cooper, *The Lesson of the Scaffold: The Public Execution Controversy in Victorian England* (London, 1974).

67. Randall McGowen, "History, Culture and the Death Penalty: The British Debates, 1840–70," *Historical Reflections/Réflexions historiques* 29/2 (2003): 241–42.

68. On the attachment to harsh punishments in the British military establishment, see Gerard Oram, "'The administration of discipline by the English is very rigid': British Military Law and the Death Penalty (1868–1918)," *Crime, Histoire & Sociétés/Crime, History & Societies* 5/1 (2001): 93–110.

69. John McHugh, "The Labour Party and the Parliamentary Campaign to Abolish the Military Death Penalty, 1919–1930," *Historical Journal* 42/1 (1999): 233–49.

70. James B. Christoph, *Capital Punishment and British Politics: The British Movement to Abolish the Death Penalty 1945–57* (Chicago, 1962), 35; Victor Bailey, "The Shadow of the Gallows: The Death Penalty and the British Labour Government, 1945–51," *Law and History Review* 18/2 (summer 2000): 313, 315–17.

71. See the thorough analysis by Bailey, "Shadow of the Gallows," 305–49, the source for the following paragraphs except where noted.

72. Christoph, *Capital Punishment and British Politics*, 58.

73. Gerald Gardiner and Nigel Curtis-Raleigh, "The Judicial Attitude to Penal Reform," *Law Quarterly Review* 65 (April 1949): 197; Bailey, "The Shadow of the Gallows," 339. Gardiner and Curtis-Raleigh argued that the Bench had always been opposed to virtually any reform in criminal law. On Gardiner's important role in final abolition, when he was Lord Chancellor, see below.

74. Block and Hostettler, *Hanging in the Balance*, 117–19.

75. Bailey, "The Shadow of the Gallows," 339.

76. Block and Hostettler, *Hanging in the Balance*, 129–30.

77. Evans hanged in 1949 for murders committed by Christie; Bentley hanged in 1953, but his conviction was quashed in 1998, Lord Bingham observing that "the language used [by Goddard, the trial judge] was not that of a judge but of an advocate" (*Oxford Dictionary of National Biography*, "John Reginald Halliday Christie," "Rayner Goddard").

78. See Neville Twitchell, "Abolition of the Death Penalty," in *The Labour Governments, 1964-1970*, ed. Peter Dorey (London, 2006), chap. 18, 332–37, on which this paragraph is based.

79. Block and Hostettler, *Hanging in the Balance*, 63.

80. *Hansard*, 5th ser., vol.155 (1948), 492; vol. 157 (1948), 4035, cited in Gardiner and Curtis-Raleigh, 196.

81. Lord Ellenborough had been quoted in the debate.

82. *Hansard*, 5th ser., vol. 155 (1948), 546–47, cited incorrectly in Gardiner and Curtis-Raleigh, 196.

83. Gardiner and Curtis-Raleigh point out that the Lord Chancellor, introducing the Right Honourable Mr. Justice Birkett at the 1948 Clarke Hall Lecture, similarly invoked "judge" Romilly, as well as judges Erskine and Brougham, for opposing capital punishment in 1810. They note that Erskine was Lord Chancellor for one year but held no other judicial office and that at the time of the debates Brougham was still a junior at the bar.

84. D. Hay, "Time, Inequality, and Law's Violence," in *Law's Violence,* ed. Austin Sarat (Ann Arbor, Mich., 1992), 141–73.

6

Interposition

Segregation, Capital Punishment, and the
Forging of the Post–New Deal Political Leader

JONATHAN SIMON

Introduction: From the New Deal to the "Crime Deal" via the Politics of Race

Historians and political scientists have long viewed Franklin Roosevelt's "New Deal," as a watershed period in American political development that created a fundamental new political order, one that dominated politics and transformed American governance for at least forty years from roughly 1936 to 1976.[1] More recently sociologists of punishment have suggested that the roots of America's turn toward hyper-punitive mass incarceration policies since 1980 mark the emergence of a post–New Deal political order, formed in large part around fear of crime.[2] Crime, or fear of crime, became a key construct, and the crime victim, a key figure, around which the fragmenting political contradictions of the New Deal order could be realigned and reframed.

Perhaps the most famous of these contradictions was race. The New Deal coalition had held together in the Democratic Party by subordinating the issue of racial inequality to the issues of economic opportunity. Once the Civil Rights movement pushed the national government for effective action on civil rights, first through the courts and then through Congress and the presidency, this coalition began to come apart. At the national level President Lyndon Johnson understood that signing the Civil Rights Act of 1964 probably lost the South for the Democratic Party for a generation, whereas Republican politicians like Richard Nixon and Ronald Reagan saw these opportunities to pick up votes by signaling a willingness to soften civil rights enforcement. At the same time leading supporters of Jim Crow segregation policies in the South saw in fear of crime, and demands for tough "law and order" policies, a way to recast their opposition to federal policies, from a southern-only defense of segregation to a national defense of citizens against crime.[3]

As political scientist Vesla Weaver[4] suggests, a full understanding of these sea changes in American political order requires attention below the national level to state-level politicians. The creation of a post–New Deal political order around fear of crime required the transformation of state-level political organizations. Political leaders, shaped to govern through New Deal mechanisms, needed to find new political footing. For crime to be that footing required more than simply rising public concern about crime (even assuming it preceded political initiatives). It also required that those leaders find a way to interpolate themselves into an issue, long dominated by local political figures (prosecutors and judges).

This chapter explores the path of the governor from a little "New Deal" executive derivative of the national government in Washington to a dominant executive in a post–New Deal order based on fear of crime and in which the governors have regularly dominated over Washington. Key to the story is the proximity of both segregation and capital punishment as important legal challenges to state authority during the pivotal decade from 1954 to 1964. Entering this decade, promising New Deal–style governors focused on building up a new political power base around welfarist New Deal policies were emerging both in the North and South. Beginning first with segregation, but soon thereafter with capital punishment, constitutional attacks to state authority on social issues with strong populist appeals across traditional economic boundaries posed a powerful political challenge to these little New Deal leaders. In the South governors like Faubus (Arkansas) and Wallace (Alabama) abandoned their appeal based on welfarist social policies to one based on an unapologetic defense of segregation. Although their association with segregation prevented them from rising to national power (although Wallace tried), their ability to cast their mission as one of defending citizens against the unconstitutional excesses of courts, a legal theory loosely known as "interposition," gave them a new logic of appeal distinct from racism itself (and one readily transferable). In the North governors like Mike DiSalle (Ohio) and Edmund "Pat" Brown (California), who as yet faced no problem with segregation (those lawsuits come later), and who were well posed to push the limits of a welfarist governance (think of Brown's investment in the University of California system), found themselves tangled in a formally unrelated (but culturally and politically probably quite related) issue, that of capital punishment. Unable to convince divided publics to embrace abolition, both governors ended up damaging their political standing and ultimately lost elections before promising national political careers could begin. A few years later, however, when California's Supreme Court struck down the state's death penalty, Ronald Reagan, the man who defeated Brown, would borrow the populism of Faubus and Wallace to turn defense of capital punishment (asserted as a defense of the lives of citizens) into a powerful political cause that would lock his hold on California and help propel him to a national political career that would help define the end of the New Deal political order.

The doctrine of "interposition," though a constitutional failure, provided a model for a populist politics of the governor that has arguably been more effectively realized around the issue of capital punishment where governors have often succeeded in positioning themselves as defenders of the people's right to the death penalty against the assertion of courts. This success, as I have argued elsewhere,[5] has made governors the odds-on favorites to become the chief executive in the post–New Deal era.

Interposition: Segregation, Southern Governors, and the Defense of the People

In his meticulous study of the causal relationship between the *Brown* decision and the triumph of civil rights legislation in the 1960s, historian Michael Klarman[6] focuses on a set of southern politicians, mostly governors, who saw strategic value in creating dramatic confrontations between white citizens and federal authorities, and between state law enforcement and civil rights activists. In his words, these were "southern politicians who had been elected to office on the strength of the post-*Brown* backlash, and who fully appreciated the political gains to be had from fostering violent clashes with federal authorities and brutally suppressing civil rights demonstrations."[7]

For Klarman, the success of these southern politicians at the state level led to a victory for the Civil Rights movement at the national level (through the dialectical reaction of northern voters to the violent images those confrontations produced on national television). Here I suggest that they also modeled a new kind of populist relationship between governors and the citizens of a state that would become a successful national model by the end of the 1960s. While that model came too late to save southern school segregation, it would lead to a political crippling of civil rights that has seen northern segregation largely preserved, and much of the force of the major civil rights acts of the 1960s diminished.

The governors' role in massive resistance would help model a path for executives to govern through crime and seek to maximize their political advantage in an emerging culture of control. Several elements of the interposition strategy anticipated the reformation of politics around the problem of violent crime after 1968. First, massive resistance was justified as necessary to protect citizens of both races from violence, and especially white citizens from the potential threat of violence posed by proximity to blacks (rape being a major implied vulnerability that required only a hint to invoke). Second, the threat of criminality was intertwined with the threat of an overreaching federal government, and especially an overreaching judiciary, seeking to achieve abstract goals while being heedless of the cost to local citizens.[8] This, of course, was a fear with a very old pedigree, but massive resistance gave it a new meaning, one now associated with the threat of violence. Third, and this is the key place that interposition played in the story, the legal implementation of *Brown v. Board of Education*[9] created opportunities for southern governors (and other executive officials like sheriffs and police chiefs) and legislatures to place themselves between the citizenry and the danger to social order posed by federal court orders implementing *Brown* and other civil rights mandates. It is this gesture, rather than an ideology of racism, that I believe southern governors contributed to the formation of the culture of control and the regime of governing through crime that began to arise in the wake of *Jim Crow*.

Massive Resistance and Interposition

Brown v. Board of Education was announced on May 17, 1954. *Brown II*, decided the next spring, gave federal district courts responsibility for coordinating actual desegregation with "all deliberate speed." By late 1955 five southern states—Alabama, Virginia, Georgia, Mississippi, and South Carolina—had enacted so-called interposition resolutions, declaring *Brown* a usurpation of states' rights and empowering their governments to protect their citizens from the implementation of the decision. It would be years in most cases before actual desegregation orders were prepared by district courts and orders to reorganize schools materialized, but in a rapid and coordinated movement, the core of the old Confederacy had constructed an odd act of what looked like a novel assertion of sovereignty even though its legality was very much in doubt from the start.

The most (in)famous piece of this configuration was a legal theory known as "interposition," in which states claimed authority to (at least temporarily) prevent the implementation of a federal court order (such as a school desegregation order) when that order was both a radical departure from settled constitutional law and a matter in which the basic security of the citizenry was at stake. Five southern states asserted this claim in seeking to prevent the implementation of desegregation orders. The theory traced its origins to South Carolina U.S. Senator and Vice President John C. Calhoun (1782–1850), but the post-*Brown* claim was really the unique creation of James J. Kilpatrick (1920–2010), a legendary print and later television editorialist, whose fiercely anti-*Brown* editorials in the *Richmond News-Leader* developed the claim in its modern form.[10] Realizing that white supremacy was rapidly becoming an untenable basis for defending segregation, Kilpatrick argued that it was better to resist on the twin grounds of constitutional integrity (allegedly violated by *Brown*) and the personal security of state citizens (the classic basis for the state's police power).

Liberally construing Calhoun's antebellum constitutional theories to fit the dilemma of post-*Brown* southern political leaders, Kilpatrick fashioned a bold argument based on a long history of state resistance to federal courts (including, nicely, northern states resisting fugitive slave law orders). Recognizing that the conclusion of the Civil War and the Reconstruction Amendments had undeniably altered the original foundations of Calhoun's position, Kilpatrick fashioned a rough if ready legal compromise. States should be able to suspend implementation of a radical and dangerous court decision, at least until the American people could consider their objections in the form of a constitutional amendment that would, if enacted, reverse the Supreme Court's decision. Kilpatrick's editorials, which he had published interlaced with various historical sources supporting his position, was widely read when repackaged as a pamphlet. He later published two more books elaborating the case.

Courts quickly and decisively rejected the rejuvenated interposition doctrine, but as Kilpatrick and the leading governors recognized, it provided a successful political and rhetorical posture for governors seeking to reframe their authority around citizens' insecurities. Although many of the governors who seized upon interposition were solid New Dealers, with interposition they were able to begin creating a distinctive political capital with citizens, one based not on replicating the New Deal but on hedging against its potentially unpopular social reform agenda that was a growing feature of federal power beginning with Harry Truman.

Whatever the merits of nullification before the Civil War and the ratification of several "Reconstruction Amendments" intended to rework the relationship between the states and federal rights, interposition was clearly recognized to be a doctrinal loser, and no one was surprised when the Supreme Court, in one of the last unanimous decisions they were to hand down on desegregation, declared the argument completely invalid in *Cooper v. Aaron*.[11] Kilpatrick was a journalist without legal training, but he appears to have fully understood that the argument was certain to be rejected by the Court that had decided *Brown*. Historian John Thorndike, the author of the leading historical study of Kilpatrick's interposition strategy, argues that the strategy was a rhetorical and political one, designed to maximize the unity of the South and the capacity to attract some northern opinion.

> To understand the full significance of Kilpatrick's interposition crusade, it must be treated as a fundamentally political event. Such an approach reveals a fluid and dynamic rhetorical campaign, consistent in some of its ideological essentials but flexible in its application. In particular, the intended audience for the interposition argument shifted between 1955 and 1957. Originally conceived as a means by which to rally the South, interposition later became a tool to persuade the North. . . . Kilpatrick believed that the likelihood of northern persuasion depended, at least in part, on the appearance of southern unity.[12]

Kilpatrick appreciated that interposition as a legal argument, allowed him to link southern massive resistance to a long tradition of states seeking to protect their citizens against violent denial of their rights by federal law, including the antebellum question of enforcement actions under the fugitive slave law. The other ingredient, indelibly linked to the race question for Kilpatrick—but, he feared, not understood by northerners—was the triple "social" threat to whites of "illegitimacy, sexually transmitted disease and violent crime."[13] Of the three it was violent crime that would turn out to be easiest to invoke both symbolically and through state-encouraged violence. The violence attending to implementation of school decrees was the frontline argument for massive resistance between 1957 and 1961. Although it was roundly rejected by the courts, circumstances in the nation were about to make it a far from dead political argument.

Southern Governors and the Post–New Deal Situation

The governors who would become nationally famous and infamous by leading their states in the campaign of official and private defiance of civil rights law—a campaign that came to be known as "massive resistance"— included a number who started out as progressives on both race and economic policy, governors who sought to modernize their states and adopted in many respects a New Deal model of leadership. Two of them, Orville Faubus of Arkansas (1910–1994; governor of Arkansas 1955–1967) and George Wallace of Alabama (1919-1998; governor of Alabama 1963–67, 1971–79, 1983–87) stand out as leaders with national potential. Most important for our story, each achieved the longevity in office they sought, and in Wallace's case two surprisingly credible runs for the White House, once as an Independent (1968), when he won 2.4 percent of the national vote but nearly 23 percent of the southern electorate, and once as a Democrat, when he won a number of primaries prior to an assassination attempt in 1972.

Faubus was an economic populist from a part of Arkansas with the least white animus toward blacks. Elected shortly following the *Brown* decision, Faubus recognized that the segregation issue could transform his role from an ordinary governor to a regional or even national leader. At first Faubus remained on the fence about massive resistance, rejecting calls from the legislature for special sessions to consider a response.[14] But by the time the Little Rock lawsuit was filed, Faubus had decided to seek a third term as governor, very rare in Arkansas, and saw in leading massive resistance a chance to supercharge his political power among the virtually all-white voting population. The infamous confrontation between Faubus and the Eisenhower administration over the integration of Little Rock High School gave Faubus an exceptional opportunity to play out interposition, not as a legal tactic but as a gesture in a piece of political theater witnessed by the whole nation. As Klarman concludes:

> By manufacturing a racial crisis that in turn led to a confrontation with the federal military, Faubus transformed himself into a nearly invincible state politician as well as something of a regional folk hero. While Faubus tolerated, rather than perpetrated, violence against blacks asserting their constitutional rights, the lesson for other southern politicians was clear: the more extreme a politician's resistance to the objectives of the civil rights movement, the greater the political rewards he might reasonably expect at the polls.[15]

George Wallace followed an even clearer path from New Dealer to segregationist. Wallace was also a progressive on economic policy and, more quietly, on race, where he was among the half of the Alabama delegation that chose not to walk out of the 1948 Democratic National Convention following Hubert Humphrey's speech in favor of civil rights as human rights. According to Klarman, he was even known as a "liberal" and to some a "dangerous left-winger."[16] He began moving to the right on race after *Brown*.

After losing the 1958 Democratic primary for governor, Wallace happened upon a wonderful opportunity to interpose himself between "the people" and the federal courts when legendary federal district court judge Frank Johnson ordered Wallace in his capacity as circuit judge for Barbour County to turn over the county registrar of voter records for a voting rights case. Wallace responded that he would arrest any federal officer who attempted to collect the records, but privately he backed down in the face of a contempt order. Once in the governor's mansion, Wallace sought out a dramatic confrontation with the federal courts over school desegregation. Klarman's vivid account provides a palpable sense of interposition as a subject position for governors.

> Wallace endeavored to entrap the Kennedy administration into using federal troops in Alabama, as it had at Ole Miss, fully appreciating the political gains that would accrue from his playing to the southern tradition of "foreseeable defeat before overwhelming odds." Resistance to federal authority at Tuscaloosa gave Wallace the opportunity "of becoming the apotheosis of the will of his people." In the now-famous charade, Wallace first physically blocked the entrance to the university and then, as planned in advance, stepped aside before a show of superior federal force. From the moment of his stand in the schoolhouse door, Wallace entered a new political dimension, both at the state and national levels.[17]

The politics of resistance to *Brown v. Board of Education* produced a new/old narrative of the relevance of governors as "interposing" themselves between the allegedly unlawful decisions of the Supreme Court and the personal safety of their citizens. While politicians would receive little traction on the specific issue of segregation, the image of a personal relationship between the governor and the security of the citizen, one threatened by the operation of unaccountable federal courts was one that would lend itself ever so well to the crime issue as it emerged in the 1960s. For Klarman the political logic here was ironic. Governors like Faubus and Wallace enhanced their own political power, but as methods of resisting civil rights their tactics backfired, leading to inflamed northern opinion and, eventually, powerful civil rights laws from Congress. But there was another lesson here as well. The more a governor could identify himself with the physical insecurity of the voters, and especially against the power of the courts, the more he or she could obtain a form of political support largely invulnerable to disappointing results on the ground. This was a lesson open to governors outside the South.

Abolition: Northern New Deal Governors and the Death Penalty

Reviewing the presidential field in early 1959, pollster Lou Harris identified two democratic governors as the most likely state chief executives to emerge as contenders in the Democratic nomination fight, expected to be dominated by senators: Pat Brown of California and Mike DiSalle of Ohio.[18] Both represented large delegate-rich states with major industries and large Democratic voting blocks. Both Brown and DiSalle were Catholic liberals eager to build on the social justice tradition of Roosevelt's New Deal. Both had agendas focused on education, labor, and health care, rather than penal issues, but both ran into considerable political resistance around the growing controversy over capital punishment and their own abolitionist sympathies. Each would be defeated seeking reelection to their respective state houses (Brown after two terms, DiSalle after one) and disappear from state and national politics. The death penalty seems to have played a significant role in both defeats, as suggested by the fact that each eventually wrote a political memoir focused specifically on the capital punishment problem of governors. In the following sections I draw on books published by both former governors, specifically on their handling of the death penalty. DiSalle published his account first in 1965; Brown published his in 1989. Both had assistance from professional writers.

When the Political Is Personal

As clemency scholar Austin Sarat notes, both books rely heavily on "the trope of anguish, the agony of the person forced by circumstances to exercise godlike power on the basis of fallible human judgment."[19] For both Brown and DiSalle, capital punishment and the problem of clemency took on a highly personal quality of responsibility and threat. Indeed, both men seemed motivated to write their memoirs at least in part to further explain and justify these uniquely personal judgments. But if we read both books as windows into the distinct historical problems of state leadership in the late 1950s and early 1960s, we can observe distinctive features of the political organization of this most existential of political decisions.

Capital punishment and clemency, in particular, opened a clear gulf between local and state politicians. Those most motivated to see or prevent a killer being executed—friends and family of the victim and the condemned—

were likely to be highly concentrated locally and to accord great weight to this issue, whereas those concerned with the death penalty as a political issue were probably fairly dispersed. Local politicians were likely to feel intense pressure from families and friends of both sides, and a statewide leader was uniquely likely to confront an ambiguous situation.[20] Governor DiSalle observed that on clemency cases local politicians would shrilly attack him in public while privately agreeing with his decision.

> The same type of political shyness worked the other way, too. One member of the legislature would write or call me on behalf of some inmate seeking clemency and would then rush to Columbus to tell me to pay no attention to the request which he had made only to impress the convict's relatives who were politically potent in his county." [21]

Capital punishment also produced a highly personal kind of politics in which those affronted by the abolitionist preferences of both Brown and DiSalle felt free to express anger and condemnation of the politicians in highly personal terms and against members of the governors' own families. Brown described a very direct and personal sense of vulnerability after intervening (temporarily as it turned out) in the execution of famed death row inmate Caryl Chessman.

> The violence and anger of the anti-Chessman movement . . . now had a new target—Pat Brown. The volume of mail pouring into my office increased, with attacks on me as common as abuse of Chessman and the legal system. Dummies of me were hung in effigy in Modesto, Long Beach and West Los Angeles. Members of my own party accused me of weakness, cowardice and passing the buck to the state legislature. Even newspapers like the *Sacramento Bee*, which had always been a strong and loyal supporter, turned against me on this issue. At the opening of the Hollywood Park racetrack a few days after the stay was announced, Bernice [Brown, his wife] went down to put the wreath on the winning horse while I stayed in the stands. When the name "Mrs. Pat Brown" was announced, there was a loud chorus of booing; rage and shame almost made me run for the door. I was booed again at Squaw Valley when the [1960] Winter Olympics ended, and at the opening of Candlestick Park in San Francisco while Vice President Nixon looked on. One state assemblyman announced that he was starting a recall movement to remove me from office.[22]

For Brown, the Chessman case seemed to have been particularly painful since Brown's own children became involved in the movement to spare Chessman's life. Brown would ultimately go to the legislature seeking abolition as an alternative to the execution of Chessman, a move that narrowly failed.[23]

Opponents

Both Brown and DiSalle saw capital punishment, at least in retrospect, as giving a mortal weapon to their campaign opponents and their accomplices in the media. Brown has little doubt that this was the most effective issue for both Richard Nixon, who lost to Brown in 1962, and Ronald Reagan, who defeated Brown in 1966.

> During my two terms as governor, because of my high percentage of commutations, I became known as an outspoken foe of capital punishment. It wasn't an image I consciously tried to create; in fact, the evidence is strong that it seriously damaged my political future. Richard Nixon made it such a major issue during the 1962 gubernatorial campaign that at one point I was sure I'd lose and seriously considered dropping out. In 1966, the death-penalty issue did help Ronald Reagan defeat me for governor, thus launching one political career and effectively terminating another.[24]

Brown blamed himself, among others, for creating a political climate around Chessman that made his execution a populist cause (despite or because of his international celebrity and status as a victim of cruelty).

> By the time I became the someone with that power, other people—myself included as attorney general—had successfully stoked the fires of public indignation so high against him for "heckling his keeper" that such action was virtually impossible, especially for an elected official with a responsibility to his constituency and the programs he hoped to implement for the common good. I firmly believe all of that. I also believe that I should have found a way to spare Chessman's life.[25]

DiSalle also viewed his clemency decisions as exposing himself to easy point scoring by his political enemies and by newspaper editorialists.

Whenever I extended mercy to a prisoner, the sensational press and my political enemies, knowing I had long been opposed to capital punishment, would accuse me of encouraging crime by coddling criminals. The slanted news stories and vituperative editorials invariably brought down an avalanche of venomous letters, telegrams, and anonymous postcards. Their message—with the scabrous shrillness removed in paraphrase—was the same: the Governor is a sentimentalist whose heart is bigger than, though not as soft as, his brain, who weeps for the poor murderer but is cold-bloodedly unconcerned about the murderer's victim.[26]

Clemency and Political Capital

In his classic article on crime and society in eighteenth-century England, Douglas Hay argued that the broad power to reprieve a capital sentence, officially exercised by the sovereign but mediated by the wider gentry and judiciary, offered a tremendous tool for gaining popular consent to the highly unequal social order being forged by English capital with the cooperation of the aristocracy.[27] Without the great expense and considerable political resistance likely to be generated by a standing army or armed executive force, the extension and refusal of pardons allowed power to project majesty as well as terror, to win sympathy and gratitude as well as fear. For New Deal–era governors, however, the power to grant clemency was a kind of kryptonite, weakening them politically with every exercise. Both Brown and DiSalle tried hard to provide individual consideration despite having broad moral objections to the death penalty, and allowed more condemned prisoners to die than they saved, but each also perceived himself as paying a heavy and specific political price for each act of clemency.

Brown found that clemency decisions often pitted him directly against police chiefs and county sheriffs prepared to compete with the governor over representing the security interests of the public.

"The two top police officers in Los Angeles, Chief Parker and Sheriff Peter Pitchess, held a press conference to denounce my decision, saying that 'law-enforcement officers and the people they protect have suffered a major defeat'" (Brown 1989:69). To this, Brown "lashed out at Parker and Pitchess, telling reporters that 'if the Sheriff and the Chief of Police were doing their jobs as well as I'm doing mine, perhaps Los Angeles wouldn't have the highest crime rate in the country.' This didn't win me any new fans in the LAPD" (Pitchess and Brown later "became good friends").[28]

"In the case of Richard Lindsey, . . . if I spared this man's life, I would almost certainly be dooming an important farm labor minimum-wage bill that we had worked hard to promote."[29]

Brown viewed the authorization of the execution as a way to secure progressive legislation. He "was fighting a conservative legislature to spend more money on a growing state, to improve its schools and its mental health facilities and its working conditions. Should I risk, did I even have the *right* to risk, destroying any of that because of one demented criminal? By letting Richard Lindsey go to the gas chamber, I was giving her [Rose Marie Riddle, the murdered little girl] parents [who were farm laborers] and people like them a chance at a living wage."[30]

The Empirical Sovereign: Governor as Investigator

Both Brown and DiSalle were able orators who could and did appeal to their respective state legislatures to abolish the death penalty. But as innovative New Deal leaders, they also sought to develop a style of acting on the death penalty consistent with the New Deal model of the executive. Key to that model, as figured by Roosevelt himself, was a close concern with the empirical facts and a direct proximity to those personally involved in wielding science and experimentation to solve social problems. Brown "inaugurated the practice of personally conducting executive clemency hearings in every death case" and "insisted on conducting the hearings personally," sometimes sending his own investigators out to collect further information.[31]

DiSalle was even more driven to intervene personally. The strangest case involved one of the few women on America's death rows, Edythe Klumpp, who had confessed to and was convicted of the murder of her lover's wife. Klumpp afterward changed her story, prompting the governor and another man to give her "truth serum," by means of which they found out that her lover (the victim's husband) had actually committed the crime and she only helped him destroy the body.[32] The tactic of using Sodium Amytal, and personally interrogating the prisoner, was certain to draw massive media attention (another facet of the New Deal chief), but in this case the results were largely negative.

The flood of invective, criticism, and abuse that inundated my office swept away the considerable numbers of letters and telegrams praising my stand. Editorial writers made unscientific fun of "truth serum" as a means of learning the truth, particularly in a case that had already been decided by the courts. Some excoriated me for having set myself above the conclusions of the courts and jurors, ignoring the fact that my conclusions were based on evidence that had not been considered by any judge or jury. There were many letters to the editor like this one: "We no longer need police, courts, juries or judges. The Great DiSalle will see that justice is served. He will simply give the accused a spoonful of truth serum. . . ." City editors deployed reporters to interview judges, lawyers, and public officials who would condemn me for having "dismayed law enforcement throughout Ohio," as well as for having "insulted . . . the whole modern system of criminology."[33]

In a second clemency case, that of Frank Poindexter, DiSalle traveled to Hamilton, Ohio, to personally reinvestigate a case in which three men had been involved in planning a robbery that resulted in murder and only the most mentally marginal of them had been sentenced to death. DiSalle issued a temporary stay four days prior to the execution and then traveled to Hamilton, the scene of the crime, to "understand what really took place."

> The press let me know that my trip was regarded with hostility by Hamiltonians. [The husband of the victim] told a reporter for the Cincinnati *Enquirer*: "It's ridiculous what the man is doing, or maybe I should put it, what he is trying to do." To the Associated Press he declared: "It stinks!" A group of neighbors were waiting outside Hires's [the name of the husband and murdered wife] home when I arrived. One man shouted, "You cheap politician, why don't you go back to Columbus where you can do some good?"[34]

The most curious tactic in DiSalle's repertoire was apparently a practice in Ohio for some time prior to DiSalle's term. Although it did not directly involve capital punishment, it clearly did so indirectly and DiSalle devotes a whole chapter of his clemency memoir to the topic. In Ohio, governors had to personally approve of parole for murderers under sentence of life. Prisoners with especially good records of behavior and specific talents were recommended by prison officials "for service at the Executive Mansion." Thus the cooks, drivers, and other staff (one would assume security excluded) of the governor's household were life-sentenced murderers all. In his memoir, DiSalle sets up the issue through the lens of his wife whom he depicts as apprehensive about sleeping in the same house with a number of killers:

> Although she shared my belief in rehabilitation, she had never been called upon to put the theory to a practical test. And I was aware that living under the same roof with convicted killers could be an ordeal for her.[35]

The relevance to the death penalty is obvious and stated by DiSalle in the very next paragraph. His wife, "never convinced that the death penalty might not be justified in certain cases," could not contemplate the state killing any of the very nice men whom she had come to know in the mansion.[36] And, indeed, this lengthiest chapter of the book is filled with rich life histories of several of the most memorable of the men that Governor DiSalle came to know during his single term. But if the governor calculated that knowledge leads to forgiveness, he was also rehearsing a kind of empiricism toward crime that captures well one of the chief attributes of the New Deal chief, as embodied by Franklin Roosevelt himself who, as "Dr. New Deal," touted himself as someone willing to try any remedy that would address the dire needs of the people.

The Case for Abolition

Governor Brown appealed directly to the legislature to abolish the death penalty in a speech delivered on March 2, 1960. Specifically the speech articulated all the major themes of modern abolitionism, including that the death penalty cannot be proven to deter and that the death penalty demonstrably fails to be concentrated on the most irretrievable criminals.

> These are all hard cases to review and consider. There have been 19 of them these past 14 months. They present a dreary procession of sordid, senseless violence, perpetrated by the wandering outcasts of the state. Not a single one of these 19 accomplished a pittance of material gain. Nine of the 19 suffered obvious and deep mental imbalance. In the only three cases where actual murder was entertained by conscious design, sickness of mind was clinically established to have existed for many years. All of them were products of the hinterlands of social, economic, and educational disadvantage.[37]

Brown also pointed to the shocking possibility of executing the innocent, again exemplified in a case where he had to use his pardon power to spare a clearly innocent man. Brown emphasized his own experience in prosecution and law enforcement.

> I have reached this momentous resolution after 16 years of careful, intimate and personal experience with the application of the death penalty in this State. This experience embraces seven years as District Attorney of

San Francisco, eight years as Attorney General of this State, and now 14 months as Governor. I have had a day-to-day, first-hand familiarity with crime and punishment surpassed by very few.[38]

Brown's speech also focused on the taint of racism on the death penalty and sought to cast California against a very specific alternative, that of the South as a region that lagged in the formation of a progressive public sector and whose race policies had inflamed much opinion in the state, especially on its college campuses.

> As shocking as may be the statistics in our deep South where the most extensive use of the death penalty is made and against the most defenseless and downtrodden of the population, the Negroes, let it be remembered too that in California, in the 15-year period ending in 1953, covering 110 executions, 30% were of Mexicans and Negroes, more than double the combined population percentages of these two groups at the time. Indeed, only last year, 1959, out of 48 executions in the United States, 21 only were whites, while 27 were of Negroes. These figures are not mine. I tender them to you for critical examination and comparison. But I believe you will find them compelling evidence of the gross unfairness and social injustice which has characterized the application of the death penalty.[39]

He even presented the legislature with a chart showing the execution rates of the southern states (compared to California) and their contrastingly higher murder rates.

Recovering Elements of a New Deal Model of Leadership on the Death Penalty

Both Brown and DiSalle clearly believe that they lost reelection bids (and possibly national political careers) because of the death penalty. This is not uncontested. At least one master's thesis blames DiSalle's loss on the structural advantage of Republican candidates in a solidly GOP state (at this time) combined with his support for an unpopular tax increase.[40] Historian Theodore Hamm's study of Brown's handling of the Caryl Chessman death sentence suggests that other factors contributed to his defeat by Ronald Reagan in 1966, including the Watts riot and the rarity of third terms in California (even though there was no term limit at the time).[41] Both governors clearly faced major disadvantages on the death penalty. While national opinion was moving toward abolition (it would peak with a slight majority for abolition a few years later), voters in both California and Ohio remained solidly in favor of the death penalty. The strength of the national movement meant that each faced major pressure from his liberal base to make progress on this issue, but the residual pro–death penalty majority made it a difficult choice for an elected legislature.

Both Brown and DiSalle embraced the challenge to use clemency as a tool to reduce the injustice of the death penalty while seeking to win legislative support for abolition. Failing at the latter, they paid all the political costs of opposing the death penalty while failing to mobilize their liberal base through actual victory on the death penalty.

Reading back from today's era of governing through crime in which governors have openly adopted a prosecutorial stance, it is notable that both governors sought to confront the issue of capital punishment in ways that seemed consistent with the New Deal style of governing. This led to a focus on empirical investigation both of the effects of capital punishment and of particular cases. Both governors sought to embrace the model of individualized judgment about individual offenders that the reigning treatment ideal presupposed.

Both also were prescient in seeing the personal security of the individual citizen as an emerging vulnerability of the New Deal state which had done so much to provide mechanisms of collective security. DiSalle's personal exposure to murderers in the governor's mansion is particularly salient in this regard. The chief executive of a culture of control fully embraces the mandate to protect the family through an unrelenting toughness on crime. In sleeping among murderers, the governor and his wife were relating their confidence in rehabilitation and in individualized judgment in a startlingly clear way. (Compare this to the emphasis on exposing others to crime risk that has surrounded issues of contemporary governors granting furloughs or paroles).

Both Brown and DiSalle might have done better to either ignore the death penalty (as their advisers and many supporters clearly hoped) or to have committed themselves to a de facto abolition by the grand gesture of a collective clemency (like Governor Ryan of Illinois in 2002).[42] As Sarat shows, they both felt that the nature of clemency required an individualized consideration of each case. Governors in the era of governing through crime have not felt the burden of the individual anguish: George W. Bush estimated that he spent around fifteen minutes being briefed on Texas clemency petitions for each of the more than 130 persons executed on his watch.

Brown seized upon the issue that might have provided the strongest foundation for a de facto abolition: the racial bias of the death penalty and the comparison with the segregationist South whose capital punishment practices seemed just as tainted as its school systems at a time when national political opinion had swung dramatically against the South. By linking California's death penalty to the South's segregationist state, Brown offered a compelling reason to risk his leadership on a direct confrontation with the prospect. He would have been saying, in effect, that "since the Supreme Court will not lift this racist institution from the nation, I will do so for my state." This gesture, hinted at (above) but never completed, would have formed a near mirror image "interposition," the failed legal but successful political strategy deployed by a number of southern governors to avoid being (politically) crushed between the Supreme Court's *Brown v. Board of Education* decision and the overwhelming opposition to desegregation from the almost completely white voting population in their states.

Reagan, Capital Punishment, and the Second Coming of Interposition

While southern governors enjoyed enormous political returns in their states for expounding extreme positions in defense of segregation, the northern reaction against the segregation prevented those southern politicians directly linked to its defense, from capturing a major party nomination (Wallace being a possible exception although his candidacy for the Democratic nomination in 1972 never got beyond the level of serious protest candidacy before an assassin's bullet ended his campaign.)[43] Ongoing national antipathy toward segregation, cemented in those infamous images of the mid-1960s, assured that only a southern liberal, like Jimmy Carter or Bill Clinton, was likely to win national approval for at least a generation.

This, and the fact that segregation proved impossible to defend as state policy, have led most historians to treat interposition as a curiosity that pointed to the complexities of white supremacy politics in states like Virginia. I suggest that interposition was yet to yield its strongest political effects. Freed of its association with segregation, it was reframed as the role of governors and state law in protecting citizens against the intertwined dangers of rising violent crime and an elitist judiciary's criminal procedure revolution which expanded the rights of criminal suspects and defendants. Now it would no longer need to carry the burden of its previous legal defeats. The essence of interposition from here on would be the relationship between state executive actors, courts, and the linked fates of criminal suspects and the citizenry.

Although the Warren Court's criminal procedure decisions would provide significant targets for this law enforcement–based reassertion of state sovereignty, no single issue would act as a better "conductor" for this energy than capital punishment and the Supreme Court's 1972 decision in *Furman v. Georgia*, striking down all existing capital statutes.[44] The response to *Furman* was less furious but far more generalized nationally than *Brown*. Five states adopted new capital punishment statutes in the first months after *Furman*, and by the time that *Gregg v. Georgia*[45] was argued thirty-five states had restored the death penalty.[46]

Among the politicians that led these state crusades to save the death penalty and citizens from the Supreme Court and murderers there would be many who would rise to prominence in statewide and federal offices. None captured the opportunities of the moment better than California's popular conservative governor, Ronald Reagan. As discussed above, Reagan defeated the liberal Democrat Brown in the 1966 election in a campaign focused heavily on crime fear and race in the aftermath of the Watts riots. Reagan made Brown's waffling on executions a symbol for his leadership. In his first year in office, Reagan fulfilled a campaign promise and denied clemency to Aaron Mitchell, an African American man convicted of murdering two police officers. Mitchell's execution was the first in California in five years and the last for nearly thirty-five.

But when the California Supreme Court found capital punishment unconstitutional under the state constitution in February 1972, a few months before *Furman*, Reagan immediately attacked the court for having "set itself above the people."[47] Reagan, whose talents as an actor made him highly effective at crafting the right mix of anger, buffered by humor, and pathos in his public personality that came across far less partisan and mean sounding than politicians like Richard Nixon, deftly made the Court, not liberals or Democrats, the focus of his attack.[48] The Court was not just wrong in its insistence that "society is responsible for each and every wrongdoer," but its solicitude came at the expense of the state's power to protect the citizenry. In his first quoted remarks on the decision, Reagan tied the theme of rising crime—a theme he had raised in the 1966 campaign—to the death penalty on the grounds of deterrence, and to a contrast between elitist expert knowledge and popular belief: "In a time of increasing crime and increasing violence in types of crime . . . [c]apital punishment is needed, the death penalty is a deterrent to murder and I think the majority of people believe the same thing.[49]

The decision in *People v. Anderson*[50]—shocking at the time to many, including Governor Reagan because he had appointed a number of the justices in the majority—was in fact an unparalleled opportunity, giving Reagan a several months head start on other governors and politicians waiting for the Supreme Court's decision in *Furman*, months that Reagan used to put his face on the national reaction against the sudden judicial abolition of capital punishment. A popular referendum in 1972 voted overwhelmingly for the return of the California death penalty, and by 1973 the state had enacted a new capital statute. Reagan, as governor, had a natural leadership role in both campaigns.

Reagan's framing of this reaction skirted perilously close, at times, to invoking the kind of explicitly racialized narrative about crime that had proven so self-defeating with segregation: "With all our science and sophistication, our culture and our pride in intellectual accomplishment, the jungle is still waiting to take over. The man with the badge holds it back."[51] Much more often Reagan used crime and capital punishment to define a new civic duty unmarred by racial discrimination. In a speech to business and civic leaders, about a year and half after *Anderson*, and during debate in the legislature over whether to enact a new capital statute (the voters had already amended the state constitution to permit capital punishment). Although the speech traditionally focused on the economy, Reagan instead concentrated on "law and order."

> "For a number of years, we have had a moratorium on capital punishment . . . Unfortunately, it has not been a total moratorium. Last year alone, there were 1789 executions in California. The executions to[o]k place in our streets, in the victims' homes and in places of business. One thousand, seven hundred and eighty-nine innocent people in our state were executed with no recognition of their constitutional rights or of the moratorium that only gave shelter to their executioners."[52]

Reagan went on in the address to discuss the exclusionary rule (another example of the Supreme Court's due process protections) as handcuffing the police. Although the vast majority of such cases deal with drugs, Reagan went right to murder: "If a policeman stops a car for speeding and finds a dead body in the trunk, I don't think our legal system should ignore the fact that someone has been killed."[53] If it was important for Ronald Reagan's political future to be the national face of reaction against judicial elites who were seemingly indifferent to popular fears of violence, it was arguably even more important for the political future of capital punishment to have a non-southern governor as the national face of a resurgent death penalty. In citing the reality of elevated homicide rates in the early 1970s (they would not level off in California until 1980, lagging behind much of the nation), Reagan offered a defense of capital punishment apparently freed from the stigma of its clearly racist application (not only in the South but in much of the nation). Like his predecessor, Brown, Reagan cited his own study of capital cases in the clemency process (although he had faced far fewer during his years, as a moratorium was in place for most of his two terms) to support his conclusions about the effectiveness of the death penalty as a deterrent. The alternative, life or even life without parole, left the people unprotected largely because of the power of authorities to release murderers back into society.

> Life imprisonment without parole won't work, Reagan told newsmen, because "people a few years from now are not bound by what someone said at this time." Current California law, he said, "makes anyone eligible for parole after seven years of a life sentence has been served—and this is something to think about with this decision [the *Anderson* case] that's been handed down."[54]

Indeed, Reagan combined his trademark friendly and happy demeanor with a guilt-free embrace of capital punishment that could both acknowledge the cruelty of capital punishment while shrugging it off: "I think there is cruelty when you execute a chicken to have a Sunday afternoon dinner," he said. But he insisted that is not the same as "cruel or unusual punishment," which the state constitution bans and which the court used as a basis for its decision.[55]

The death penalty did not figure largely in the campaign between former governor Reagan and (southern liberal governor) President Jimmy Carter in 1980. But Reagan would make solid support for capital punishment a consistent feature of his conservative populism for the rest of his life. His vice president, George H. W. Bush, the last non-governor to serve in the White House until Barack Obama, would make restoring and using a federal death penalty a premier policy issue and, to a lesser degree, so would southern liberal Bill Clinton.

Conclusion

Capital punishment and school segregation were two forms of state power under attack in the 1950s. To their critics, each institution was deeply tainted by racism and both were increasingly seen as out of step with America's posture as the leading democracy in the world. Both capital punishment and segregation posed dilemmas for governors struggling to redefine the role of state executives after the New Deal had enormously expanded the role of the federal government in the lives of the American people. These challenges were deeply sectional. Strong opposition to capital punishment was growing in many states outside the South, while segregation at this point was being problematized only in the South. Here the stories diverge in time. The Supreme Court, in 1954, found school segregation unconstitutional, setting off an immediate challenge to southern leaders, and especially New Deal–type governors who had generally built their support from the progressive wing of white voters in their states. It would be almost twenty years before a more divided Court temporarily ended capital punishment.

In this chapter I have tried to suggest that the approaches New Deal governors took to each challenge were fateful in their political survival, and ultimately in shaping the political posture of governors in the post–New Deal national political landscape. It may have been that liberal governors like Pat Brown and Mike DiSalle would have failed to achieve reelection, let alone national leadership, even without the pressure of capital punishment. As Lou Harris observed at the time, 1960 was a year for senators on the Democratic side. But their inability to frame a political and legal discourse with which to express their opposition to capital punishment clearly wounded them, and would come in many ways to anticipate the difficulties liberals would face on the death penalty and other crime issues in the decades ahead.

Southern progressives faced an even more dramatic challenge in 1954. The growing strength of the New Deal in the South seemed to presage a gradual weakening of Jim Crow politics and a slow softening of segregation. When the Supreme Court unanimously struck down segregation in 1954, leaders like Orville Faubus and George Wallace, who had built their base on this progressive tendency while hoping to avoid direct confrontation on race, now found that they had to decide in a very short time how to respond to the reactive surge in support for segregation among southern whites. Had either openly supported *Brown* or even sought compromise, he would certainly have been wiped out in the next Democratic primary for governor.

Their vigorous embrace of segregation was an act of opportunism that has been widely appreciated by historians. Fewer have appreciated the importance of how they opposed it.

I have tried to suggest that, although interposition may have failed to protect de jure segregation, it contained the germ of a powerful political logic that would ultimately prove highly productive for governors as they reclaimed the national political stage after 1976. Others have argued that the roots of the politics of crime emerged from the political failures faced by defenders of segregation.[56] I have sought to advance that argument by identifying a specific discursive link. If I am correct, this shows how the crime issue could emerge from the South, but ultimately not through generalization of racist ideologies about African Americans. Instead, it was the schema of governors as defenders of vulnerable citizens against the threat of lawlessness posed by activist courts that political leaders outside the South would adopt successfully.[57] As the crime problem came to dominate American governance after 1968, this logic would yield enormous dividends for governors. The emerging culture of control was one in which segregation (now in de facto form) and capital punishment would both find new strength as American institutions.

NOTES

The research for this chapter was greatly assisted by Omari French, Berkeley Law, JD, Class of 2010.

1. Bruce Ackermann, *We the People,* Vol. 1, *Foundations* (Cambridge, Mass., 1993); Steve Fraser and Gary Gerstle, *The Rise and Fall of the New Deal Political Order, 1960–1980* (Princeton, N.J., 1989).

2. David Garland, *The Culture of Control: Crime and Social Order in a Contemporary Society* (Chicago, 2001); Jonathan Simon, *Governing through Crime: How the War on Crime Transformed American Democracy and Created a Culture of Fear* (New York, 2007).

3. Katherine Beckett, *Making Crime Pay: Law and Order in Contemporary American Politics* (New York, 1997).

4. Vesla Weaver, "Frontlash: Race and the Development of Punitive Crime Policy," *Studies in American Political Development* 21 (2008): 23–265.

5. Simon, *Governing through Crime.*

6. Michael Klarman, "Brown, Racial-Change, and the Civil Rights Movement," 80 *Virginia Law Review* (1994): 7–150.

7. Ibid., 118.

8. Naomi Murakawa, "The Racial Antecedents of the Federal Sentencing Guidelines: How Congress Judged the Judges from *Brown* to *Booker,*" *Roger Williams University Law Review* 11 (2008): 473–94.

9. 347 U.S. 483 (1954).

10. Joseph J. Thorndike, "The Sometime Sordid Level of Race and Segregation: James J. Kilpatrick and the Virginia Campaign against *Brown*," in *Massive Resistance to School Desegregation in Virginia,* ed. Matthew D. Lassiter and Andrew Lewis (Charlottesville, 1998).

11. 358 U.S. 1 (1958).

12. Thorndike, "The Sometime Sordid Level of Race and Segregation," at 57.

13. Ibid., 66.

14. A. Stephen Stephan, "The Status of Integration and Segregation in Arkansas." *Journal of Negro Education* 25, no. 3 (summer 1956): 212–20.

15. Klarman, "Brown, Racial-Change, and the Civil Rights Movement," 118–19.

16. Ibid., 125.

17. Ibid., 127.

18. Louis Harris, "Why a Governor Will Not Be President." *Political Science Quarterly* 23 (1959): 361–70.

19. Austin Sarat, *Mercy on Trial: What It Means to Stop an Execution* (Princeton, N.J., 2004), 153.

20. Richard G. Zimmerman, *Call Me Mike: A Political Biography of Michael V. DiSalle.* (Kent, Ohio, 2003).

21. Michael V. DiSalle and Lawrence G. Blochman, *The Power of Life and Death* (New York, 1965).

22. Edmund G. Brown, with Dick Adler, *Public Justice, Private Mercy: A Governor's Education on Death Row* (New York, 1989).

23. Theodore Hamm, *Rebel and a Cause: Caryl Chessman and the Politics of the Death Penalty in Postwar California, 1948-1974* (Berkeley, 2001).

24. Brown, *Public Justice, Private Mercy,* at viii.

25. Ibid., 52.

26. DiSalle and Blochman, *The Power of Life and Death,* 3–4.

27. Douglas Hay, "Property, Authority, and the Criminal Law," in Douglas Hay, Peter Linebaugh, and E. P. Thompson, *Albion's Fatal Tree: Crime and Society in Eighteenth-Century England* (New York, 1975).

28. Brown, *Public Justice, Private Mercy,* 69.

29. Ibid., 72.

30. Ibid., 83. Brown did not intervene in the case and Lindsey was executed; the bill passed and became law. Brown writes of the Lindsey case, "It was the kind of crime which seemed to cry out for vengeance, for ritual punishment as swift and terrible as the act itself."

31. Ibid., 45. Quoted in Sarat, *Mercy on Trial,* 148.

32. DiSalle and Blochman, *The Power of Life and Death,* 28–39.

33. Ibid., 39–40.

34. Ibid., 53.

35. Ibid., 135–36.

36. Ibid.

37. Brown, *Public Justice, Private Mercy,* 45.

38. Ibid., 43.

39. Ibid., 45.

40. Diana Draur, "Michael V. DiSalle in Ohio Politics: 1950–1962," master's thesis (1986), University of Nebraska at Omaha.

41. Hamm, *Rebel and a Cause.*

42. Sarat, *Mercy on Trial.*

43. Earl Black, "Southern Governors and Political Change: Campaign Stances on Racial Segregation and Economic Development, 1950–69," *Journal of Politics* 33, no. 3 (August 1971): 703–34.

44. 408 U.S. 238 (1972).

45. 428 U.S. 153 (1976).

46. Stuart Banner, *The Death Penalty: An American History* (Cambridge, Mass., 2003).

47. Ed Meagher, "Court Setting Itself above the People, Governor Charges," *Los Angeles Times*, February 19, 1972, 1.

48. Lou Cannon, *Governor Reagan: His Rise to Power* (New York, 2003).

49. Ibid.

50. 493 P.2d 880 (California Supreme Court 1972).

51. Cannon, *Governor Reagan*, 216.

52. Jerry Gilliam, "Reagan Defends Capital Punishment Backers," *Los Angeles Times,* September 8, 1973, 23.

53. Ibid.

54. Tom Goff, "Reagan Wants Death Penalty Vote," *Los Angeles Times*, March 1, 1972, A3.

55. Ibid.

56. Beckett, *Making Crime Pay;* Murakawa, "The Racial Antecedents of the Federal Sentencing Guidelines"; Weaver, "Frontlash."

57. My intention here is not to overstate the case. There is no discursive equivalent of a "DNA fingerprint" that can link Faubus's and Wallace's stands on segregation to Reagan's stand on capital punishment.

7

The Convict's Two Lives

Civil and Natural Death in the American Prison

REBECCA MCLENNAN

There is a death in deede, and there is a civill death, or a death
in law, mors civilis and mors naturalis.
> —Edward Coke, *The First Part of the*
> *Institutes of the Laws of England,* 1628

In 1870 the warden and agent of the Virginia State Penitentiary at Richmond dispatched several dozen male prisoners to forced labor camps owned and operated by the Chesapeake and Ohio Railroad Company in Bath County, some miles from Richmond.[1] That summer, while toiling on the railroad tracks beneath the hot Virginia sun, several of these prison laborers—including twenty-year-old Woody Ruffin, a former slave from Petersburg—made a break for freedom. The railroad company's overseers thwarted their escape but not before one of the guards, Lewis F. Swats, had been killed.[2] Upon recapture, the prisoners were immediately returned to the state penitentiary at Richmond. Ruffin was shortly thereafter tried before the city's Circuit Court for the murder of guard Swats. The jury found him guilty as charged, and the judge sentenced him to the gallows.

Fighting now for his natural life, not just his freedom, Ruffin appealed his case to the Virginia Supreme Court. Counsel argued that the state's Bill of Rights guaranteed "a man" prosecuted for a capital or other crime the right to a trial by an "impartial jury of his vicinage" and that Ruffin's vicinage at the time of the alleged murder had been Bath County, where the crime occurred, and not the city of Richmond. The court ought, therefore, to overturn the Richmond court's verdict and order a new trial by impartial jury in Bath County.[3] (Presumably the defense attorney hoped that a Bath County jury would find Ruffin "not guilty." Although Virginia had been "Redeemed" the previous year, black men still served on juries, and the majority of Bath County's population was black).

The court denied Ruffin's appeal. Writing for the bench, Justice Christian ruled that the state's 1860 penal code clearly directed that the Richmond Circuit Court "shall have full jurisdiction of all criminal proceedings against convicts in the penitentiary."[4] That Ruffin had been in the custody of a private railroad company operating in another county at the time of the alleged murder was immaterial:

> If [a state prisoner] can be said to have a vicinage at all," wrote Justice Christian, "that vicinage as to him is within the walls of the penitentiary, which (if not literally and actually) yet in the eye of the law surround him wherever he may go, until he is lawfully discharged. . . . He is for the time being a slave, in a condition of penal servitude to the State.[5]

Christian went on to refute the very presupposition on which the substance of Ruffin's appeal depended: the presumption that Ruffin, as a man undergoing criminal prosecution, was protected by the state Bill of Rights. "The bill of rights is a declaration of general principles to govern a society of freemen, and not of convicted felons and men civilly dead," the justice objected. As a "consequence of his [original] crime"—the one that had supposedly landed Ruffin in the state penitentiary in the first place—Ruffin had "not only forfeited his liberty, but all his personal rights except those that the law in its humanity accords to him. He is for the time being the slave of the State. He is *civiliter mortuus*; and his estate, if he has any, is administered like that of a dead man."[6] Having put Ruffin in his supposed legal and moral place—the extra-constitutional graveyard of the civilly dead—Justice Christian upheld Ruffin's conviction for the murder of guard Swats. He ordered Ruffin conveyed to the gallows and hanged by the neck until dead.

Civil death had indeed put Woody Ruffin on a slippery slope. Barred from availing himself of the full protections of the Virginia Bill of Rights, his legal capacity to avert natural death at the hands of the state was significantly compromised; his last remaining chance to defend himself in a court of law against a charge of capital crime had been extinguished. Barring a reprieve, commutation, or pardon by the governor of Virginia, the state's hangman would substitute a cold, lifeless, body for a living, civilly dead one.

Ruffin's brush with court-ordered death (close to hanging day, for reasons that remain obscure, the governor commuted his sentence to life imprisonment)[7] opens an illuminating window onto the history of capital punishment and of a new modality of death that emerged through and in support of the prison-based penal system of the nineteenth century. Although Ruffin's 1871 appeal is seemingly remote from our own time and place, Justice Christian's reasoning and the larger body of civil death jurisprudence on which he drew also present a clue to the puzzle of why the resurgence of legal executions in America after 1975 and the almost coterminous rush toward mass incarceration occurred so seamlessly and, as Marie Gottschalt and others have remarked, with surprisingly little resistance.[8] Political and cultural forces rooted firmly in the 1960s and 1970s provided the motive power for the founding of our own violent, unforgiving penal regime, but historic structures deep within the social force field of legal punishment eased their advance. Among these were the laws, jurisprudence, institutional practices, and affective structures that came, in the course of the nineteenth century, to comprise an elaborate machinery of civil death.

As I shall argue here, coterminous with the rise of the penitentiary house and cellular prison in the United States, this machinery constituted convicts as a juridical class separate and unequal to other citizens (thereby breaking decisively from older, American communitarian ideas about the moral and legal status of transgressors and the proper methods and objectives of punishment as rituals of cleansing and reconciliation).[9] The original character of American prisons as enforcers of a novel species of involuntary servitude generated and sustained a jurisprudence of civil death that ultimately fixed the legal status not only of prisoners but of convicts as well. In the course of the nineteenth century convicts' separate status was constituted and elaborated in voting, administrative, employment, constitutional, and educational laws that, together, ensnared the convict in a dense thicket of civil penalties for crime. Later, as state and federal government built out the welfare and education state, laws limiting convicts' entitlements further extended the collateral consequences of criminal conviction and more deeply inscribed convicts as a separate and unequal class.[10]

The American way of civil death (to innovate Jessica's Mitford's well-known book title) outlasted the system of forced labor to which it was originally addressed and survived the welfarist turn of Progressive and New Deal penology. Once assembled, the machinery of civil death functioned largely unattended and, until very recently, all but invisibly;[11] the disabilities it imposed were an automatic consequence of conviction, provided for by statute rather than ordered by courts. In 1970, despite six decades' of progressive penal reform and the Warren court's groundbreaking recognition of the prisoner's right to rights, the "convict" everywhere remained a distinct, exceptional category of the less-than-fully civilly alive citizen.[12] As such, convicts proved to be a soft *legal* target for neoconservatives who sought to dismantle the welfare state in general and penal welfarism—with its rehabilitative orientation—in particular. As I shall argue here, civil death helped lay the wide, straight road along which advocates of capital punishment, minimum mandatory sentencing, and three strikes laws were able to advance quickly and to lethal effect a century later. This essay is a first pass at excavating the lineages of the convict's civil death, and a tentative contribution to a more sustained exploration of some of the buried structures of legal thought and practice that distinguished and delimited (sometimes with mortal consequence) the convict's two lives.[13]

Lineages of Civil Death

The history of nineteenth-century civil death jurisprudence and the prison-based penal system to which it gave legal expression and force troubles a long-standing and commonplace narrative of American penal history. As the story goes, by 1850 most states had adopted a new, carceral mode of punishment that, for most crimes, substituted life behind bars for death or dismemberment; to the extent that execution and bodily chastisements continued to play a role in the new regime, they were merely the vestigial remains of the older, sanguinary one.[14] Although it is indisputable that nineteenth-century legislatures rejected capital and public bodily chastisements for almost all crimes, and that both the number of capital crimes and rates of execution declined precipitously in the United States after 1790, neither the practice nor specter of capital punishment was as cleanly disarticulated from the new apparatus of punishment as historians tend to assume. The rights upon which the state, since at least the age of Hobbes, had staked and continued to stake its authority to punish at all—that is, its supposed sovereign rights to regulate life and death and exercise a monopoly of the legitimate use of violence—assumed new symbolic and practical force through the very system of carceral punishment that was putatively predicated upon a reasoned rejection of the state's constitutive right of death. Death as a consequence of conviction did not disappear with the rise of carceral punishment but instead assumed a new modality. It did so largely through the revival and embodiment in institutional structures, practices, and penal culture of the obscure Anglo-Saxon legal doctrine of *civiliter mortuus*—the principle upon which Justice Christian had declared Woody Ruffin civilly dead. By the time Christian heard Ruffin's appeal, American penal jurisprudence had for some years distinguished different degrees and qualities of civil death—and, by implication, different degrees of civil life as well.

In invoking *civiliter mortuus*, Justice Christian drew on a body of law, ideology, and practice that had become foundational not just to southern but to American penal law between 1799 (the year New York enacted its civil death statute) and the beginning of the Civil War. The precise medieval and early modern lineages of the doctrine of civil death remain obscure. But, notwithstanding the comments of an exasperated New York judge who, in 1888, cautioned that anyone inclined to trace its roots "will find that he has to grope his way along paths marked by obscure, flickering and sometimes misleading lights,"[15] legal scholars seem to agree that, in late medieval and early modern England, attainder, abjuration, and banishment by Parliament on grounds of treason all resulted in civil death in the strict sense—that is, a complete loss of civil rights. (Civil death also occurred as a matter of course when a man entered a religious order—and hence an autonomous juridical order—and became a monk professed).[16] In these four cases, the law treated the man as though he were naturally dead. A fifth category of persons—convicted felons—was placed in a state of attainder, and subject to forfeiture of estates, corruption of blood, and civil death. The civilly dead convict-felon could not bring actions or serve as a witness, but, unlike the four other kinds of civilly dead persons, he was fully vulnerable to the punitive force of law. He could be sued, and he was legally capable of committing crimes and being prosecuted for them. He was also still under protection of law (which meant that he was capable not only of murder but of being murdered in the legal sense of the term).[17] Civil death, then, had degrees: some of the "dead" were deader than others.

Civil death's entry into American law after 1799 and its subsequent elaboration left far clearer, if long since forgotten, tracks. As is well known, in the early republic forfeiture and corruption of blood were prohibited by state and federal constitutions. Civil death, however, survived (though not, ironically, in its native England, where it was all but obsolete by 1850).[18] Significantly it was those states that experimented with the novel institution of the so-called penitentiary-house (1796–ca.1820) that codified a version of civil death. Following New York's lead in 1799, a full one-third of states enacted laws, known as civil death statutes, which provided that "a person sentenced for imprisonment for life is thereafter deemed civilly dead." Another seventeen enacted variations of the principle and, in most states with penitentiary-houses, prisoners serving terms less than life were deemed civilly dead for the duration of the sentence. In New York the courts appear to have initially read the statute as exacting full civil death. But, by 1822, courts typically interpreted civil death statutes as imposing upon prisoners the same kind of civil half-death that felony convicts had been dealt by common law.[19] In other words, convicts were unable to bring suit, but they were legally responsible.

In early interpretations, these early statutes narrowed the breadth of the common law doctrine, both by reserving perpetual civil death only for that minority of persons serving life terms in a penitentiary, and by restricting temporary civil death to imprisoned convicts rather than imposing it on all convicts, free or incarcerated. (Civil death here underscored and illuminated the fact that the life term was a direct and open substitute for execution proper.) The prisoner's civil death ended upon release from the penitentiary. Moreover, as Michael Meranze and W. David Lewis have shown, a robust, rights-conscious culture of the early republic enabled convicts under sentence to push back against efforts to limit their rights. Early republican prisoners quite successfully pressed a range of customary laboring rights, including that of Blue Monday, customary rights relating to the length of the workday and immunity to the (slavish) lash.[20]

Here it is important to recall that, despite the commonplace elision today between "convict" and "prisoner," they were and are distinct categories: Then, as now, all convicted prisoners were convicts, but not all convicts were prisoners; the convict served time as a prisoner, but upon release neither the conviction nor the legal status of convict disappeared.[21] ("Felon" also suffers similar vagaries in common usage. A felon is a person who has committed a felony and not merely a person undergoing imprisonment as punishment for a crime. Unless a felon's record is expunged, he or she remains a felon and is not, in the strict meaning of the term, an "ex-felon"). Today, ex-prisoners are not automatically "ex-cons," as common parlance would have it; depending on the offense and state laws, ex-prisoners only cease to be ex-convicts or ex-felons through successful application to a state or federal court for their record to be expunged from the public record, a process restricted to certain crimes and categories of felons—and usually unavailable to repeat offenders. Most ex-prisoners remain permanent convicts, and the minority of convicts whose application for court-ordered expunging of their criminal record are usually still debarred from a handful of professions and remain in the federal government's record.[22]

In the early republic, civil death—even in its limited form—did not apply to convicts who had completed their prison sentence. But beginning in 1818, civil death's reach and function began to change. Its metamorphosis began in the penitentiary-house, with the reversal, after 1818, of early republican limits on the corporal punishment of prisoners. Courts and legislatures gradually granted the state the right to suspend (or even entirely extinguish) many of the natural and common rights that penitentiary inmates had quite successfully defended, and which civil death statutes had not, in the first twenty years of the century, seemed to affect in any palpable way. Courts also gradually excluded prisoners from the most obvious body of law to which they might (and did in fact) turn for protection of their common and natural rights—the law of master-servant. Beginning with New York in 1821, the states also disfranchised not just prisoners but all felon-convicts and prohibited them from holding office and serving on juries. Significantly—and contrary to what most commentators on contemporary felon disfranchisement have argued or assumed—criminal disfranchisement occurred first in northern states, where there were significant prison populations and where the overwhelming majority of prisoners were white.[23] Some states made it possible for voting rights to be restored, but in the course of the century, most toughened the conditions under which re-enfranchisement could occur, requiring in some cases not only a full pardon from the governor (which erased the conviction) but, in addition, an explicit restoration of the full rights of citizenship.[24] Pardoning rates fell in most states from over 50 percent in some states, before 1830, to 13 percent or less of the prison population after 1830, which further limited re-enfranchisement.[25] (Notably, in the antebellum period, the two states that did not disfranchise felons were Pennsylvania and South Carolina—two of the few states that did not adopt the otherwise ubiquitous contract prison labor system until well after the Civil War). Whereas, in 1800, explicit statutory limitations on convicts serving on juries were very "rare" (although most states required that jurors be judicious or of fair character), by 1850 states much more vigorously legislated jury service: a significant minority of states now specified that the juror not be "a criminal" or a person convicted of felony, infamous crime, moral turpitude, or a combination of these illegalities.[26]

Soon colonial and early republican conceptions of the typical offender as a temporarily wayward soul who could be reclaimed to the community gave way to an exclusionary, alienating conception. Unlike in Europe, observed Alexis de Tocqueville in 1835, the lawbreaker in America was an "enemy of the human race" and "every human being is against him."[27] So accepted was the principle of the convict's exclusion by 1865 that the framers of the Thirteenth Amendment un-controversially exempted convicts from the otherwise universal prohibition on slavery and involuntary servitude. Significantly that amendment did not refer to the exempted class as "prisoners"; it referred to them as the "party . . . duly convicted of crime." Between disfranchisement and the Thirteenth Amendment, the principle of exclusion at the core of civil death was extended beyond the imprisoned convict to convicts per se; by 1865, to be a convict was to occupy a different, unchanging legal status to which certain disabilities and exclusions were attached in perpetuity.

Prisons and Servitude

The transformation of civil death after 1818—both the seepage of its exclusionary logic beyond the prison and the de jure and de facto abridgement of many of the prisoner's common and natural rights—coincided with the collapse and abandonment of the house of repentance (or penitentiary-house) and the forging of a new mode of punishment. This new mode of punishment was the distinctive species of involuntary servitude that flourished in most northern states before the Civil War (and across the entire country in the post-bellum period) and which consisted in cellular incarceration by night, forced labor for a private contractor or lessee during the day, and a strict regimen backed up by routine corporal punishment.[28] Civil death law facilitated the emergence of this system of servitude and gave it legal expression. In order to make sense of civil death, therefore, we must examine how prisons operated—not just as human warehouses (Mauer), or social laboratories in which elite clergy and other reformers tried to actualize their conceptions of republican virtue and enlightened social order (Rothman), or the concrete expression of elaborate fantasies of a novel, disciplinary power (Foucault); we need (also) an account of the very particular species of involuntary servitude of which they were the principal site of enforcement.

Contrary to popular and scholarly orthodoxy, the large-scale practice of hiring out prisoners as forced labor for private contractors was not unique to the post–Civil War south. Indeed, the southern variant of prison labor and its companion legal doctrines found ample precedent and legal force north of the Mason-Dixon Line. Both the everyday practices of penal servitude, to which Woody Ruffin and other southern prisoners were subjected after the Civil War (and particularly after the defeat of Reconstruction), and the extensive body of legal and moral norms that arose around and in service of those practices, were elaborated earliest and most systematically in northern states such as New York, Rhode Island, and Massachusetts.

The foundation of contractual penal servitude was the sale of prisoners' labor power to private interests. The systematic contracting out of prison labor was first developed at New York's state prison at Auburn, in the late 1820s, and in the course of the 1830s and 1840s that prison's labor-based system of incarceration became the basic model of prison management in almost all other northern, and a handful of southern, states. An 1825 law directing New York's prison agents "to cause all the expense . . . of any kind, to be supported wholly, or as nearly as shall be practicable, by the labor of the prisoners," prompted Auburn's warden and agent to bring private contractors into the prison and to put the prisoners to work for them.[29] After initial reluctance on the part of local manufacturers (who feared that the prisoners would wreck their equipment and materials), Auburn soon became a humming factory engaged in the production of tools, rifles, shoes, clothing, combs, furniture, and barrels.[30]

Private manufacturers brought machinery and materials into the prison, paid a fixed, daily rate for the labor of prisoners (or, sometimes, a piece rate), and distributed and sold the products of their labor.[31] Under new legislation that repealed the early republican prohibition on the whipping of prisoners, and licensed keepers to mete out summary corporal punishment, the new labor regime was enforced, by day, by the lash. By night the new disciplinary architecture of cellular isolation broke the easy communicative bonds that prisoners had enjoyed in the (non-cellular) early republican penitentiaries, making it far more difficult (though not impossible) for prisoners to successfully collude in resisting or otherwise challenging their subjection to the new regime.

The basic Auburn model of hard, silent, congregate labor for a contractor by day (enforced at the end of a whip), and cellular lockdown by night, was quite quickly replicated both in New York and in most other northern states. Once the construction of Sing Sing was completed in 1831, that prison's force of six-hundred-odd penal laborers were put to work as stonecutters in the prison's sizable marble and granite quarries. (Much of the Sing Sing stone was shipped south to Manhattan, where it was used in the construction of New York University, among a number of prominent institutions).[32] Increasingly New York's prison contractors maintained large-scale operations in the prisons, making use of quite advanced forms of mechanized production. Many contractors maintained factories on the outside as well, dividing the production process into skilled and unskilled stages. From the contractors' point of view, many of the operations were very lucrative; some reaped profits as high as 150 percent over three years; from the state's point of view, contract labor was a vital source of revenue for the penal system, approaching and sometimes significantly exceeding the annual cost incurred in running the prisons.[33]

Most other northern and a handful of southern states soon followed suit. Relative to Pennsylvania's rival "solitary" model of perpetual cellular incarceration (at Eastern State Penitentiary), Auburn's congregate prison was cheaper to build and to administrate, and, at a time in which handicraft was giving way to industrial modes of production, its workshop labor system was much better adapted (than the voluntary, individual handicraft labor system in use at Eastern) to the political imperative of making prisoners pay for as much of the cost of incarceration as possible. Between 1825 and 1850 prisons of the Auburn type were built and operated in Maine, New Hampshire, Vermont, Massachusetts, Connecticut, New York, the District of Columbia, Virginia, Tennessee, Louisiana, Missouri, Illinois, and Ohio. (Rhode Island and New Jersey built Pennsylvania-style prisons; Georgia and Kentucky fused contract penal labor with the non-cellular prison design of Walnut Street).[34]

As the Auburn system became ubiquitous in the 1830s and 1840s, imprisonment increasingly became an experience of hard labor for private contractors and lessees. Shortly after Connecticut opened the state prison at Wethersfield in 1827, prison administrators phased in the contract system. Wethersfield's agent, like most northern prison agents, gradually decreased the number of industries at the prison and increased the scale of production: by the 1860s, just three large industries operated at Wethersfield.[35] New Hampshire and Vermont followed similar trajectories, as did most of the western states in the 1840s: Michigan, for example, put almost all its state prisoners to work for contractors;[36] in Illinois, after 1839, private contractors ran the state prison at Alton; after 1845 one contractor leased the entire prison for eight years (at a cost of $5,000), putting the prisoners to work manufacturing ropes, wagons, barrels, and other items.[37] In the South, too, a similar pattern prevailed, albeit on a much smaller scale. Although the antebellum southern prison population was as little as one-tenth the size of the North's, and the penal arm of state government was considerably weaker, many southern states (where the overwhelming majority of prisoners were both freeborn and white)[38] followed the Auburn model, complete with its contract labor system.[39]

By the end of the 1840s, in most states of the union, a free man convicted of a felony crime could expect to spend several years imprisoned and at productive labor for the benefit of private contractors or, in some instances, a state-owned business. The great majority of men undergoing legal punishment found themselves sequestered in great cellular fortresses, "let out in the morning and barr'd at night," in the words of Walt Whitman.[40] In the North, Pennsylvania alone continued to reject outright both the congregate labor system and the contracting out of prisoners as laborers. Below the Mason-Dixon Line, only the South Carolina and the Florida legislatures failed to adopt the "Yankee invention" of imprisonment at hard labor—preferring instead older, biblically sanctioned punishments such as public flogging and executions.[41]

After a brief (and as yet under-studied) period of reform and experimentation in both the North and South during the era of Reconstruction,[42] the contractual prison labor system resumed its aggressive expansion and process of rationalization. By 1887, the year in which the U.S. Commissioner of Labor, Carroll Wright, completed his exhaustive 605-page study of the nation's prison labor system, the contracting out of prison labor had become a highly profitable and monopolistic business:[43] on any one day, as many as forty-five thousand prisoners—70 percent of the nation's incarcerated men, women, and youths—were being put to hard, productive labor in the service of profit-making enterprises of one sort or another.

Although one in five of these convict laborers toiled within the southern lease system, most of the rest labored in the great prison factories and prison work camps of the Northeast, the Midwest, and the Far West. Their labor was not simply make-work in character, as was the oakum-picking, ditch-digging, and treadmilling of the British prison system. Nor were the prison goods of states such as New York, Illinois, and Ohio lacking in market value. In the fiscal year 1885–86, for example, American prisoners made goods or performed work worth almost $29 million—a sum equivalent, as a relative share of the GDP, to more than $34 *billion* in 2009 dollars.[44] Notably prisoners put to labor under the South's ubiquitous convict lease produced less than 15 percent of the total value of all goods made by American prison labor: prisoners laboring under the contract, piece-price, and public-account systems (almost all outside the South) generated a full 85 percent of the value of all goods made, mined, or extracted by the country's prison labor force.[45]

Penal Servitude in American Law

The advent and widespread adoption of Auburn's contract prison labor system signaled an important departure not only in the field of penology, but in the realms of labor relations and law as well. The novelty of the state prison system lay partly in its substitution of continuous, institutionalized penal discipline for the short, sharp act of public chastisement, and in the keepers' relatively successful subjection of hitherto rowdy and rights-conscious prisoners to labor discipline; but it also lay in the legal elaboration of a fairly robust and well-defined species of involuntary servitude—a system that is usefully described as one of contractual penal servitude. Although we still do not have a complete picture of the emergence of penal jurisprudence in the early and mid-nineteenth century, what is clear is that law had to grapple with the forced labor relation at the heart of the new penal regimes.

While various species of voluntary and involuntary servitude had long flourished on North American soil,[46] the fusion of legal punishment and forced labor engendered the creation of a new, hybrid variant of involuntary servitude; a new kind of involuntary servant (the prisoner); and a new type of master (nominally the state, but often in practice the all-powerful contractor). The penal codes implicitly authorized the state to make of any person, freeborn or otherwise, convicted of a crime an imprisoned, involuntary servant. In time, this distinctive species of servitude engendered the articulation, in law and legal discourse, of a new kind of legal relation (that between prisoner and imprisoning power) and a body of rules and regulations designed both to reinforce and to make (juridical) sense of the workaday practices of penal servitude. What appears to have emerged after 1818 was a distinctive body of laws and regulations through which legislators and jurists sought to express, fix, and justify the prisoner-laborer's legal and moral status.

Among its many legacies, nineteenth-century America's great experiment with criminal imprisonment and forced productive labor spawned a juridical puzzle: What was the appropriate legal status of persons undergoing criminal incarceration? Prior to the time that punishment involved the routine sequestration of offenders, and hence an extension of the duration of punishment (from a few hours in the town square to months, years, or decades in a prison), the legal status of the person undergoing punishment was not a pressing concern. But in a revolutionary world in which the most basic natural and common law right was widely held to be the freeborn man's freedom from slavery,[47] that question proved vexing indeed.

In this regard, imprisonment encountered similar challenges to chattel slavery. Just as English Common Law had no readily available body of doctrines on the status of slaves, it had no obvious and single reservoir of doctrine and customary law upon which to draw in the endeavor to fix the prisoner's legal status.[48] Like slaves, prisoners assumed a troubled double status at law. As persons subjected to involuntary servitude became, in echoes of Plato, both human subjects and objects of regulation.[49] In North American law, as Thomas Morris and Ariela Gross have most recently shown, slaves' double status as subject and object was specified as that of human subjects who were also objects, specifically of property relations: that is, they were human property that could be conveyed, regulated, and disposed of (exactly what kind of property, real or personal, took several decades' worth of jurisprudence to determine). Similarly the prisoner's double status also became one of subject and object, but the prisoner's objective status was not that of property, at least not in the same sense that slaves were deemed property: prisoners were not (and legally could not) be bought, sold, owned, or disowned.[50] But, to a degree that we have yet to recognize, the objective quality of the nineteenth-century prisoner nonetheless involved a species of possession (in which the state seizes and holds the convict's person); a right of force over the prisoner's body (in a modern variation of the Anglo-Norman concept of *prise*—that is, a thing that is seized for the sovereign's use [a term from which the word "prisoner" directly descends]); and a right of property in the labor power of the prisoner. Although prisoners' persons could not be sold, the state sold their labor power to private interests. At the beginning of the new, carceral era it was unclear what would become of the prisoner's natural and positive rights—including those that the revolutionary era had declared "inalienable"—and whether the prisoner was a servant, slave, or ward, or occupied some other, as yet undetermined status.

The prisoner's vexed, double status in the nineteenth century was, among other things, an attempt to grapple with a concrete, flesh-and-blood fact: that people held against their will and subjected to the will of others asserted themselves in myriad ways against (and, in some times and places, for) those who held them. As a consequence of prisoners' irreducible humanity, a formal body of rules designed to secure and regulate punishment, penal law found itself in the contradictory position of both recognizing and denying prisoners' subjectivity.[51]

Law soon tied itself in knots wrestling with the prisoner's double status as human and regulated object. Woody Ruffin's infamous case illustrates the point well: on the one hand, Justice Christian claims that, in the eyes of the law, Ruffin is for all intents and purposes legally "dead." He construes this, in obiter, as the grounds upon which Ruffin is disqualified as a rights-bearing subject under the Virginia Bill of Rights: "The bill of rights is a declaration of general principles to govern a society of freemen, and not of convicted felons and men civilly dead." And yet Ruffin stands in a court of law, as no person lacking legal standing could, and his case is heard. Ruffin is also, under the same law that declares him legally dead, assumed legally capable of the crime of murder. He is culpable and capable. And although denied standing as a full constitutional subject, and declared dead in the eyes of the law, the judge nonetheless construes him as fully subject to the statute of 1860 that gave the Richmond Circuit Court full jurisdiction over criminal proceedings against convicts held in the penitentiary and that implicitly guarantees him a trial.

In this light, Ruffin's legal standing (and that of convicts in general) is revealed to be more complicated than either Judge Christian or historians and criminal justice reformers have acknowledged.[52] The statute law regulates Ruffin, as only humans can be regulated, and in ways that acknowledge and confirm some degree of legal subjectivity (he is entitled to a trial, after all, as only humans were under nineteenth-century—if not classical Roman—law). Much like the felon-convict, his civil death was a half-death.

Much as the interests of chattel slavery—particularly in the antebellum period, during which time the institution was "domesticated"—required the law to recognize, under certain circumstances, slaves as potential informants and witnesses (something of which only human and not other forms of property are potentially capable), law could not give up on prisoners and convicts as observers and sources of testimony. And just as the advances of abolitionism after 1820 prompted a slew of reforms within southern law relating to the limits of a master's rights over his slaves and extending his responsibilities to them, the social movement that coalesced in the 1870s and 1880s to call for the abolition of the prison labor contracting system (on the grounds that it was unjust and inherently cruel) brought pressure to bear on the states to defend their practices—and try to render them more "humane." Unwilling to abandon the practice that had become the fiscal, disciplinary, and ideological basis of their prison systems, states instead enacted laws that conferred certain formal entitlements (if not rights) on prisoners, such as protection from whipping by a cat-o'-nine tails and a set number of gills of water when locked-down in a punishment cell. They also made guards and wardens liable to prosecution for abridging these protections—and then pointed to these laws (just as John C. Calhoun and his fellow pro-slavery ideologues had pointed to these slave "welfare" laws) to defend the contract prison system as humane and subject to active regulation.

Yet those few former prisoners who went to court and pressed claims to basic protections for prisoners against excessive exploitation on the prison factory floor and willful negligence of the sort that resulted in the injury or death of prisoners met with little success. One possible avenue of legal redress for prisoners lay in the protections afforded a servant under the law of master and servant. But until the 1890s (when prison law began to change) most state courts denied that such a relation existed between the prisoner and either the state or the contractor. In 1881, for example, the New York State Supreme Court ruled that the relation between contractor and prisoner was not one of master and servant, and that the prisoner, therefore, was not protected at law as a "servant" would be in relation to his "master."[53] The New

York Supreme Court elaborated upon this principle, three years later, when a former prisoner, Warren E. Lewis, sued New York State for damages for serious injuries he had sustained while performing hard labor as a prisoner at the Elmira Reformatory for Boys in 1879.[54] A ladle that Lewis's overseer knew to be defective had broken, causing molten iron to course down the prisoner's legs and across his feet, severely burning him. "The claimant was not a voluntary servant for hire and reward," Justice Danforth ruled, finding for the state, "nor was the State his master in any ordinary sense. [Lewis] was compelled to labor as a means of reformation, and to endure imprisonment as a punishment and for the protection of the community."

Justice Danforth went on to argue that the "cause" of the prisoner's injuries lay not with the state or the irresponsible overseer or the manufacturer of the defective ladle but with the prisoner himself, and, in particular, with the crime he had committed and for which he was sentenced to imprisonment at hard labor in the first place: "While employed, [Lewis] was subject to such regulations as the keeper charged with his custody might, from time to time, prescribe, and if in the course of service he sustained injury, *it must be attributed to the cause which placed him in confinement.* He acquires thereby no claim against the State" (my emphasis).[55] The prisoner, having committed a crime that was punishable by a prison term, was responsible for any accidents and injuries that might befall him in the course of his forced labor in prison: in effect, Justice Danforth claimed that Lewis had brought his devastating injuries upon himself. In fact the contractor, in his conduct of prison industries, was free of even the (admittedly rather limited) legal constraints imposed by the master-servant relation, while the convict lost the benefit of that relation's protections. (The federal courts also refused to protect prisoners at this time, although on different grounds: the handful of state prisoners who filed civil rights suits in federal court found their cases dismissed on the grounds that federal courts lacked jurisdiction over state prisons.)[56]

The Deathly Prison

It is clear that a sentence to imprisonment at hard labor probably saved the life and limb of many a felon who, before the early republican era, would likely have been executed, banished, branded, or mutilated as punishment for his crimes. But in light of what we now know about imprisonment's relation to involuntary servitude, and some of the formal and informal rules that buttressed that regime, to characterize the penitentiary as simply a life-preserving alternative to the gallows and other forms of corporeal violence is to miss the critical role that death continued to play in legal punishment, if in new and different forms. Situated in a liminal space between law and no law, prisons were deathly institutions. (In this regard, the nineteenth-century prison can be seen as a precursor to the juridical "black hole" of the various camps holding that questionable category of persons known as "unlawful enemy combatants." It also touches upon questions of the sort with which Giorgio Agamben and his readers are concerned regarding the constitution of sovereignty through and by a state of exception.)

Although civil death pertained only to the convict's legal "life," because it deprived convicts undergoing imprisonment of certain key protections (most conspicuously the right of freedom from involuntary servitude and the status of servant under master-servant law), it had certain very real consequences for flesh-and-blood prisoners. Neither the brute fact nor the specter of corporal death was ever very far from the nineteenth-century American prison. The ever present *threat* of untimely, violent, or acciden-tal death in prisons and prison work camps—and the event and relatively high frequency of actual death within the prisons and prison work camps—worked to establish the prison, both conceptually and materially, as a lim-inal and potentially deadly space. The authority, sometimes de facto and other times de jure, of the state and its agents to mortally wound any pris-oner attempting to liberate himself from prison—and, hence, his condition of servitude—effectively made the prisoner's life conditional upon at least an outward show of consent to his incarceration. (Here was a fairly straightfor-ward transposition of the military's law of desertion onto the penal arm of the state.)

Prisoners also contended with the ever present threat of an untimely "nat-ural" death in the prison (whether at the hands of the state's guards, private overseers, or fellow prisoners, or through negligence, industrial accident, or overwork), which was augmented by the relative leeway given prison offi-cials in matters of corporal discipline. The free hand that most contractors enjoyed in the prison, though usually de facto and in contravention of state laws reserving the exercise of authority in the prisons to agents of the state, made prison industries particularly deadly. The terms and conditions of the contracts for prison labor were highly conducive to life-threatening forms of overwork and correctional discipline: the highly "flexible" character of the contractor's labor market (wherein the state was typically bound to replace any and all convict laborers who were not capable or who, through overwork became incapable, of working at the pace desired by the contractor) incited contractors to work "their" laborers to the bone. Official annual mortality rates, which were relatively high in free American industry by world standards, were substantially higher for prison workers, ranging from a routine 5 percent in northern prison factories to more than 15 percent in the most violent and exploitative of the southern mining and railroad convict camps. Occasionally the death rate in some camps approached 40 percent; the official figure subsequently settled around the 8 percent mark in most southern states. There is also evidence to suggest that official figures underestimated work-related mortality in the prisons: in the 1870s prison wardens in at least one northern state (New York) routinely transferred near-mortally injured or sickened prison laborers out of the prison factory and to the hospital of another prison. The prisoner's subsequent death was then recorded as "natural" rather than "industrial" or work-related.[57]

Novel rituals of degradation—which had been almost entirely absent from the penitentiary-houses of the early republican era—reinforced the fact of the convict's civil death. In the early years of the contractual prison labor system Elam Lynds, a former army major and principal keeper at Auburn, invented the elaborate rituals of commitment to prison that every other state in the union would eventually adopt. For the first time commitment, hitherto a rather informal and haphazard affair, became a carefully choreographed ritual in which the convict's entrance to prison and departure from the free world was consciously staged as a form of social burial. Upon transfer from the police to the prison keepers, the state's agents took hold of the convict's body, stripped him, took away his freemen's clothing and all his belongings, dressed him in stripes, and shaved his head. At Auburn this effort to reduce the convict to prisoner, and subjugate him, was concluded with a speech by the warden, Gershom Powers, who—leaving nothing to the imaginations of the newly arrived convicts—interpreted for them the meaning of incarceration: as convicted felons that had lost "the inestimable privileges of a free American citizen, of social intercourse, and the endearments of home and friends," the warden instructed them; now they were to be "literally buried from the world."[58] (Not incidentally the language of death, burial, Hell, and purgatory soon became prominent in the popular imagination of imprisonment, and in convicts' writings about the prison. Rituals of the Auburn stripe remained a lasting feature of commitment to a range of carceral institutions, and their twentieth-century incarnation was famously theorized by Erving Goffman, in the 1950s, as an effort to kill the prisoner's "personality" in service of his subjugation.)[59]

Afterlife: Civil Death in the Post-Contractual Era

In the decade either side of 1900 most states finally yielded to the sustained and large-scale efforts of workers, the trade unions, and the farmers' alliances to bring about the abolition of the nation's various contractual prison labor systems.[60] However, the penalty of civil death, whether in its statutory, doctrinal, or popular moral articulation did not simply wither away in the wake of the contract system's abolition. Rather, the convict's civil and political death and disabilities endured into the new century. In some states, including New York and Mississippi, the convict's civil death was reinforced in all three legislative, executive, and judicial arenas. (In New York and Mississippi the strengthening of political disfranchisement more or less coincided with the constitutional amendments that abolished the brutal system of contract prison labor.) Ironically, rather than delivering penal involuntary servants and "slaves of the state" from civil death and imbuing them with greater legal subjectivity, the abolition of contractual prison labor systems, coupled with subsequent legislation further restricting the scope of the "state-use" system of convict labor, carried the ironic consequence of deepening the convict's social burial.[61]

Ironically both the struggle to overthrow contract prison labor and that struggle's eventual victory in the 1890s and 1900s engendered a further hardening of the distinction between convicts and "honest" citizens, and further entrenched the idea that convicts, whether pre- or post-prison, naturally lost many or all the rights accorded freemen.[62] As late as the mid-1830s, workingmen's opposition to the contract prison labor system did not mark either convicts or prisoners as an alien and separate category of persons. But, as early as 1834, the rhetoric of the Workingmen's leader, J. Haskell, anticipated and exemplified the coming hardening of sentiment:

> [A]re not the most abandoned villains, thieves, and robbers sent to the state prisons, and when they are discharged, are they not thrown, with all their infamy and vices upon their heads, into the ranks of mechanics? Yes, sir, all the dregs and sediment of society of every occupation in the state, after passing and taking a degree at state prison, are made by your laws the associates of the mechanics.[63]

Particularly once the well-heeled reformers of the Boston Prison Discipline Society began insisting on the reformative virtues of putting convicts to productive labor (after the early 1830s) and ameliorating prison conditions, many mechanics called for the outright abandonment of the Auburn system in favor of a strict system of deterrence. By 1850 the deep-seated solidarity that many laboring republicans had demonstrably felt with their imprisoned brethren much earlier in the century (and even as late as the mid-1830s) had all but disintegrated.

The eventual victory of workers, organized labor, and the farmers' alliances over the contractual prison labor system (which occurred in most states following massive petition drives and, in some states, strike action, between 1890 and 1920) set in motion the collapse of the larger system of contractual penal servitude of which the contract labor system had been the fiscal, disciplinary, and ideological foundation. But it also had the long-term effect of buttressing the pronounced ex-communicative character of American legal punishment: for now, added to existing civil death (or disability) and political disfranchisement statutes, was excision from the productive sphere—precisely the sphere from within which organized American "citizen-workers" and the American Federation of Labor were staking their claims to certain fundamental rights and liberties, including the eight-hour day and a living family wage. So, although abolition and the ensuing collapse of prison industries more generally undoubtedly liberated prisoners from an extremely exploitative and violent penal system, it also helped, ironically, to deepen the social burial to which nineteenth-century civil death and disfranchisement statutes, prison laws and regulations, the everyday rituals of imprisonment, and the high walls of the prison itself had long treated the convict.

Surprisingly, given their emphasis on the rehabilitation of convicts through appropriate techniques of "socialization," progressive prison reformers (who assumed the mantle of reinventing prisons and penological doctrine in the wake of the abolition of the "old system") offered little relief concerning the legal status of convicts. They improvised the brave new rehabilitative penology of socialization, and substituted therapeutic and pedagogical disciplinary techniques for the older disciplinary regime of hard, productive labor. But they did not pursue systematic reform of the various statutes governing convicts' civil and political status. Nor did they test the constitutionality of civil death, and related civil disability, statutes in the courts.

The one case in this period that did touch upon the issue (*Anderson v. Salant* 38 R.I. 463 [1916]), did so merely as a by-product of the concerted drive by the National Committee on Prisons and Prison Labor[64] to terminate one of the last few contract systems still operating in the northern states (Rhode Island). It was not part of a larger strategy to gain rights for convicts or to otherwise challenge their civilly dead or disabled status.[65] The nominally therapeutic and managerialist prison system that eventually, in the 1920s and 1930s, emerged out of the progressives' reform efforts may have rendered obsolete the prisoner's practical and legal status as an involuntary servant; but it substituted in its place a status that no more conferred formal civil or political rights upon the convict than did its nineteenth-century antecedent. As the sociologist Nathaniel Cantor noted (in a paper presented to the American Academy of Social and Political Scientists in 1931), the rules and regulations to which convicts were by then subject were almost entirely created and enforced by the administrative arm of government. Unlike convicts in Europe, who were rights-bearing subjects whose rights were enforceable in a court of law, he observed, the American convict was almost entirely without legal rights. He opined:

> Thus we return, strangely enough, but under a different set of circumstances, to the position against which Beccaría successfully fought—placing the fate of criminals in the hands of state authorities with wide discretionary powers to be exercised over individuals rather than classes.[66]

In the mid-twentieth century, and particularly with the advent of the New Deal state, President Johnson's elaboration of the state under his War on Poverty, and the founding of what T. H. Marshall would call "social rights" (albeit that they were relatively weak in comparison with Western European social rights), the convict's civil death found new expression and fresh traction. State and federal laws and regulations (concerning, among other things, licensing, housing, labor, welfare, and student loans), while nominally nonpenal, effectively extended the penalty for crime beyond the prison and prison sentence proper and into civil society by barring persons with felony convictions from many of the entitlements. The patchwork of laws from the progressive era that accord professions certain rights of self-regulation and denied access to convicts remained intact. In effect, the convict's access to various economic and cultural resources was, relative to the expanded variety of those resources, more circumscribed than had been the case one hundred years earlier.[67] (A full exploration of these disabilities, many of which varied from state to state, falls beyond the scope of this essay but is the next step in the longer research project on the civil status of convicts to which my essay is a preliminary contribution.)

Arguably it was precisely the tenacious and malleable ideology of the convict's civil death with which prisoners (especially conscientious objectors),[68] the Nation of Islam, the leaders of the radical prisoner rights movement, the American Civil Liberties Union, and the Legal Defense and Education Fund of the National Association for the Advancement of Colored People did battle in the three decades following World War II. These various efforts, first to establish the prisoner's right to have rights and second to define and realize those rights, directly engaged the legacy of America's distinctive, nineteenth-century system of penal involuntary servitude.

Between 1953 and 1969 the Warren court breathed a few more degrees of legal life into *prisoners*, culminating in the Burger court's finding, in 1974, that "there is no iron curtain drawn between the Constitution and the prisons of this country."[69] However, at the same time that the U.S. Supreme Court and state courts were endowing *prisoners* with certain rights, and hence a degree of legal subjecthood, *convicts'* civil disabilities and exclusions (for example, in matters of licensing, housing, employment, welfare, and student loan laws and regulations) were proliferating at both the state and federal levels. In the 1960s the prisoner gained new rights, but the *ex-prisoner* remained a convict, and the convict became ever more constrained at law. Even though, by 1965, it was evident that the southern criminal justice system and convict disfranchisement laws disproportionately affected people of color, the Voting Rights Act of 1965 (which prohibited states from imposing qualifications and prerequisites based on race or color) did nothing to invalidate or trouble state convict disfranchisement laws. And, in 1974, the same year the Supreme Court ruled that the Constitution did not stop at the prison gates, it also ruled that disfranchisement of convicts did not contravene the Fourteenth Amendment.[70] (In 1985 the Court did strike down an Alabama convict disfranchisement law on the grounds that its intent was explicitly racially discriminatory—as was evident from the proceedings of the 1901 Constitutional Convention at which the disfranchisement article was added. This, to my knowledge, is the only instance where the court has struck down a convict disfranchisement law.)[71]

The intensity of the conservatives' response to both the radical prisoners' rights movement and the Court's steps to recognize prisoner's claim to constitutional rights, and conservatives' own mobilization, in the 1970s, of a new kind of rights discourse (specifically, the idiom of "victims' rights") in the service of the twin objectives of resurrecting the death penalty and substituting the "unforgiving" mass carceral state for the supposedly rehabilitative, progressive penal state might be usefully understood as the latest expression and reworking of a long, deep strain in American legal and moral culture: that is, the idea that the convict is a person unfit to share in the full fruits and protections of citizenship—even after the sentence of imprisonment (or punishment proper) has been carried out; that the convict is and ought to be a person socially dead (or severely disabled); that the convict ought rightly to be fully or partially civilly dead.

Conclusion

The legacy of nineteenth-century civil death law is arguably alive and well in our own massive and deeply punitive penal complex. It finds expression not only in law books and in the regulatory sphere but also in the workplace and mass culture more broadly. As Marie Gottschalk and others have persuasively argued, in American mass culture "felon" is a status-category that bears something approaching ontological weight, and whose mere utterance establishes, without argument and as a matter of course, that the bearer of that status rightfully occupies a different, and decidedly unequal, moral, economic, and legal universe to that of the non-felon citizen. Alongside the long-standing laws that perpetrate various civil, political, and economic disabilities on the "felon," a thicket of formal and informal rules and policies in the private sector that govern eligibility for mortgages, credit, and employment has bolstered the perimeter fence surrounding the economic, cultural, and related social resources upon which meaningful membership in a democratic society depends. Taken together, these norms and practices of exclusion subject the convict to a highly systematic, rationalized, and secular form of excommunication—unique among advanced industrial nations.[72]

Although clearly the heated controversies over crime and punishment that have periodically roiled American politics since the Revolution have been "infused with basic political questions about what should be the proper bounds of the state's power to imprison and kill" (as Gottschalk has put it),[73] we might also usefully consider the ways in which a different "basic political question" has been engaged in the debate over prisoners' rights. Perhaps not only the limit and extent of the nakedly retributive powers of the state (imprisonment and execution) are in question here, but so, too, are its distributive powers: in particular, the state's power to distribute and retract rights and legal personhood, on the one hand, and the various social resources that are critical to individual and collective security and thriving, on the other. Thinking through the material and symbolic relations between the distributive and retributive axes of state power in the penal sphere, both across the long nineteenth century of American penal history and in the more recent past, may help explain why the punitive turn in corrections after

1973 proceeded so seamlessly and thoroughly. The viciously exploitative system of involuntary servitude and civil disabilities to which American convicts were subject as punishment for their crimes is dead and gone. But that the "duly convicted" are separate and unequal in the eye of many laws and regulations—and the one class not protected by the Constitution's proscription of slavery and involuntary servitude—suggests that servitude's apparatus of civil death still thrives.

NOTES

I would like to thank Jacqueline Shine, Gary Gerstle, Carla Hesse, Jonathan Sheehan, David Lieberman, Alexander Cook, David Garland, Randall McGowen, Michael Meranze, and the Berkeley Legal History Workshop.

The source of the epigraph is Edward Coke et al., The First Part of the Institutes of the Laws of England; or, A Commentary upon Littleton. Not the Name of the Author Only, But of the Law Itself . . . Hæc Ego Grandævus Posui Tibi, Candide Lector (R. H. Small, 1853); 1st American ed. from the nineteenth London ed., 1832 [1628], 132a.

1. *Ruffin v. Commonwealth*, 62 Va (21 Gratt) (1871); *New York Times* (January 15, 1871), 1; (February 11, 1872), 3.

2. The guard's name in the court record was "Lewis F. Swats." In the *New York Times* report of 1872, it was "Lewis Schwartz" (February 11, 1872), 3.

3. *Ruffin v. Commonwealth*, 790.

4. Ibid.

5. Ibid.

6. Ibid.

7. A number of other "influential gentlemen" prevailed upon the governor to commute his sentence to life in prison. The archive casts no light on the petitioners' motivation or argument. Ruffin maintained his innocence throughout. It is possible they decided that the wrong man had been convicted.

8. Marie Gottschalk, *The Prison and the Gallows: The Politics of Mass Incarceration in America* (New York, 2006); Marc Mauer, *The Race to Incarcerate* (New York, 2006).

9. For a detailed discussion of the communitarian nature of most criminal trials and punishments in colonial America (bar those of slaves and accused heretics), see David Hall, *Worlds of Wonder, Days of Judgment: Popular Religious Belief in Early New England* (Cambridge, Mass., 1990); and Lawrence Friedman, *Crime and Punishment in American History* (New York, 1994). Although most of the colonies had disfranchised as punishment for crime, they had done so only for the most egregious crimes and for crimes relating to elections and voting; the franchise could also be regained.

10. Today legal disabilities vary by state but are numerous and wide-reaching. Most states exclude convicts from employment in law, real estate, medicine, nursing, physical therapy, and education, and six states bar convicts from public employment (Jeremy Travis, Amy L. Solomon, and Michelle Waul, "From Prison to Home: The Dimensions and Consequences of Prisoner Reentry," The Urban Institute, 2001, http://www.urban.org/UploadedPDF/from_prison_to_home.pdf (accessed May 9, 2010). Michael Pinard notes that the collateral consequences of conviction are so extensive that the American Bar

Association recently "adopted standards that urge jurisdictions to, inter alia, assemble and codify their respective collateral consequences, implement mechanisms to inform defendants of these consequences as part of the guilty plea and sentencing processes, require courts to consider these consequences when imposing sentences, and narrow the range of consequences" (Pinard, " An Integrated Perspective on the Collateral Consequences of Criminal Convictions and Reentry Issues Faced by Formerly Incarcerated Individuals," 86 *B.U.L. Rev.* 623 [2006]). For detailed discussions of the collateral consequences of conviction for crime, see *ABA Standards for Criminal Justice: Collateral Sanctions and Discretionary Disqualification of Convicted Persons Standard* 19-1.1, 3rd ed. (2004); Pinard, "Broadening the Holistic Mindset: Incorporating Collateral Consequences and Reentry into Criminal Defense Lawyering," 31 *Fordham Urb. L.J.* 1067, 1073 (2004); George P. Fletcher, "Disenfranchisement as Punishment: Reflections on the Racial Uses of Infamia," 46 *UCLA L. Rev.* 1895, 1897 (1999); Kathleen M. Olivares et al., "The Collateral Consequences of a Felony Conviction: A National Study of State Legal Codes 10 Years Later," 60 *Fed. Probation* 10, 10 (1996).

11. The close-run 2000 presidential election, in which thousands of Florida voters were prevented from voting on the grounds that they had criminal convictions, prompted significant scholarly attention to felony disfranchisement as well as to convicts' other civil disabilities.

12. In addition to a raft of civil penalties, no fewer than thirteen states had civil death statutes as late as 1970. Brian C. Kalt, "The Exclusion of Felons from Jury Service," *American University Law Review* 53 (October 2003): 65.

13. By unearthing some of the juridical lineages of legal punishment, the paper complements Marie Gottschalk's argument, in *The Prison and the Gallows*, that preexisting "state structures and ideologies . . . facilitated the incarceration boom" and suggests that American legal development played an important role in the making of the mass carceral state.

14. See for example, Friedman, *Crime and Punishment in American History*; David J. Rothman, *The Birth of the Asylum: Social Order and Disorder in the New Republic* (Boston, 1971); Louis P. Masur, *Rites of Execution: Capital Punishment and the Transformation of American Culture* (New York, 1991).

15. *Avery v. Everett*, 110 NY 317 18 (Andrews, J.), quoted in Opinion 393, Hamilton Ward, Attorney General, State of New York, June 18, 1930. New York State Archives, 429, Box 2.

16. Pollock and Maitland, *History of English Law* 433, 2nd ed. (1905), in L. F. Jr., "The Legal Status of Convicts during and after Incarceration," *Virginia Law Review* 37, 1 (January 1951): 105. For a discussion of the related, ancient legal categories of atimia and infamia, and their significance for political disfranchisement of American convicts and prisoners, see Katherine Pettus, *Felony Disfranchisement in America: Historical Origins, Institutional Racism, and Modern Consequences* (New York, 2005).

17. L. F. Jr., "The Legal Status of Convicts during and after Incarceration," 105.

18. James Q. Whitman is correct that the British government introduced the disciplinary system known as "penal servitude" into (domestic) English prisons in the 1850s and 1860s (Whitman, *Harsh Justice: Criminal Justice and the Widening Divide between America and Europe* [New York, 2003], 177–78). However, he overstates its similarities to the American penal system of the same period. English penal servitude was primarily punitive and was generally not profit-oriented. As punishing as the experience of hard labor could be in American prisons, it was primarily an economic activity (and, after 1876, a

large-scale economic activity) aimed at generating profit. Arguably civil death was not revived in English law because the English prison system, unlike the American, did not take the form of a highly profitable variant of involuntary servitude.

19. *Platner v. Sherwood, Johnson's New York Chancery Reports* 6, no. 118 (1822): 130–31; L. F. Jr., "The Legal Status of Convicts during and after Incarceration."

20. Michael Meranze, *Laboratories of Virtue: Punishment, Revolution, and Authority in Philadelphia, 1760–1835* (Chapel Hill, N.C., 1996); and W. David Lewis, *From Newgate to Dannemora: The Rise of the Penitentiary in New York, 1796–1848,* (Ithaca, N.Y., 1965). See also Larry Goldsmith, "Penal Reform, Convict Labor, and Prison Culture in Massachusetts, 1800–1880" (Ph.D. diss., University of Pennsylvania, 1987).

21. This claim refers only to convicted prisoners, not imprisoned prisoners awaiting trial.

22. Western Michigan Legal Services/Soros Justice Fellowship Program/Open Society Institute, "Is Your Criminal Record Holding You Back?" (June 2003).

23. Jeff Manza, Christopher Uggen, and Angela Behrens argue for the racial origins of disfranchisment laws. Their claim holds true for the New South: the South's Democratic Party saw convict disfranchisement as complementary to new voting laws that imposed literacy tests aimed specifically at black voters—and as a way of forging a "solid" white Democratic South in the wake of the Farmers Alliances, Knights of Labor, and Populist insurgencies. But the North's disfranchisement of convicts came almost seventy years earlier and was not primarily aimed at black convicts but rather at convicts drawn from the white laboring classes (and, subsequently, Irish and other immigrant populations as well). Although black men were disproportionately represented in northern prisons, they were still a small minority of the region's total prison population. That supporters of racial disfranchisement in the antebellum North sometimes characterized black men as criminal is not, in and of itself, sufficient evidence to support the claim that northern convicts were disfranchised on racist grounds. Jeff Manza and Christopher Uggen, with Angela Behrens, *Locked Out: Felon Disfranchisement and American Democracy* (New York, 2006), 41–68.

24. See, for example, Opinion 393, Hamilton Ward, Attorney General, State of New York, June 18, 1930. NYSA, 429 Box 2.

25. Between 1829 and 1875, 12.4 percent of Eastern Penitentiary's prison population was pardoned, and 12.5 percent was pardoned in Massachusetts between 1828 and 1866. Donald R. Walker, *Penology for Profit: A History of the Texas Prison System* (College Station, Tex., 1988), 101.

26. Kalt, "The Exclusion of Felons from Jury Service."

27. Alexis de Tocqueville, *Democracy in America,* trans. George Lawrence (New York, 1988), 96. For a comparative discussion of the "American system" in relation to European practice, see James Q Whitman, *Harsh Justice: Criminal Justice and the Widening Divide between America and Europe* (New York, 2003).

28. For a detailed account of contractual penal servitude—and the opposition it encountered—see Rebecca McLennan, *The Crisis of Imprisonment: Protest, Politics, and the Making of the American Penal State, 1776–1941* (New York, 2008).

29. New York's prison inspectors had been directed to adopt the contract system in 1817, but the law remained a dead letter until the construction of Auburn's famous cellhouse in the mid-1820s (Laws . . . Concerning January 1816, and Ending April 1818 (Albany, 1818), IV, 310–11, 315–16.JA 48th session (1825), Appendix C, p. 30. Quoted in Lewis, *From Newgate to Dannemora*.

30. Lewis, *From Newgate to Dannemora*, 180

31. McLennan, *The Crisis of Imprisonment*, 58–68.

32. Roger Panetta, "Up the River: A History of Sing-Sing in the Nineteenth Century," (Ph.D. diss., City University of New York, 1999), 278.

33. Lewis, *From Newgate to Dannemora*, 109, 186–187; Gustave de Beaumont and Alexis de Tocqueville, *On the Penitentiary System in the United States and Its Applications in France* (New York, 1974), 74, 277; McLennan, *The Crisis of Imprisonment*, 67–68.

34. Lewis, *From Newgate to Dannemora*, 110; Adam Jay Hirsch, *The Rise of the Penitentiary* (New Haven, Conn., 1992), 137; Mark Colvin, *Penitentiaries, Reformatories, and Chain Gangs: Social Theory and the History of Punishment in Nineteenth-century America* (New York, 1997), 95.

35. Report of the Directors of Connecticut State Prison (1844), 7. For a brief history of prison labor (and its antagonists) in Connecticut, see Alba M. Edwards, "The Labor Legislation of Connecticut," *Publications of the American Economic Association* (3rd series) 8, no. 3 (August 1907): 217–42.

36. Boston Prison Discipline Society, Thirteenth, Fourteenth, Fifteenth, and Twenty-Fifth Annual Reports (1838, 1839, 1840, 1849).

37. Indiana leased out all its state prisoners, for a two-year period, in 1849, and Ohio put hundreds of its state prisoners to work for just four private manufacturers. Boston Prison Discipline Society, Twenty-fifth Annual Report (1849); "Convict Labor in Ohio," *Mechanic's Advocate,* February 11, 1847, 85; David L. Lightner, *Asylum Prison and Poorhouse: The Writings of Dorothea Dix in Illinois* (Carbondale, Ill., 1999), 36. See also Dorothea Dix, "Memorial" (address to the General Assembly of the State of Illinois, February 1847), in Lightner, *Asylum Prison and Poorhouse,* 37–66.

38. Edward Ayers, a leading historian of southern criminal justice, notes that penitentiaries of the antebellum lower South contained almost no free black people. Four percent and 8 percent of prisoners in Tennessee and Kentucky, respectively, were black. In the upper South, free black convicts comprised half and one-third the prison populations of Maryland and Virginia, respectively. Ayers, *Vengeance and Justice: Crime and Punishment in the Nineteenth-Century American South* (Oxford, 1984), 61. For a meticulous and highly original study of the relationship between criminal law and slavery in the American South, see Thomas Morris, *Southern Slavery and the Law, 1619–1860* (Chapel Hill, N.C., 1996), 161–332. On the prison and slave plantation as mechanisms of social control, see Michael Stephen Hindus, *Prison and Plantation: Crime, Justice, and Authority in Massachusetts and South Carolina, 1768–1878* (Chapel Hill, N.C., 1980).

39. The Kentucky legislature turned the state prison at Frankfort over to a keeper who was directed to put the prisoners to hard labor, retain half the profit for himself, and pay the other half to the state. Keeper-lessees ran the Missouri state prison; Louisiana, Alabama, and Texas all put their convicts to contract labor, and Mississippi and Georgia put prisoners to work for state-owned enterprises (Ayers, *Vengeance and Justice,* 66–67).

40. Whitman, "Song of Myself," verse 37, from *Leaves of Grass* (1855). (In the 1840s Whitman ministered to prisoners at Sing-Sing and was appalled by the conditions under which they lived and toiled).

41. J. Thorsten Sellin, *Slavery and the Penal System,* (New York, 1976), 141–42; Ayers, *Vengeance and Justice,* 59–72; Orlando F. Lewis, *The Development of American Prisons and Prison Customs, 1776–1845* (New York, 1925), chaps. 17 and 20; Walker, *Penology for Profit.*

42. McLennan, *The Crisis of Imprisonment*, 90–97.

43. *Report of the Secretary of the Interior*, vol. 5, *United States Commissioner of Labor, Convict Labor in the United States* (Washington, D.C., 1887). This study (undertaken by Carroll D. Wright) was the most systematic of all prison labor studies conducted in the Gilded Age. However, it probably understates the full extent of prison industries and revenues, and underestimates the numbers of prisoners put to productive labor. Whereas Wright's study indicates that the prison system, on any day, held approximately 65,000 prisoners in 1885–86, according to the U.S. Census Bureau the reported total prison, reformatory, and jail population for the United States was 69,288 in 1880 and 95,480 in 1890. This suggests that Wright may have significantly undercounted the number of prisoners present in American prisons, jails, and reformatories in 1885–86 and, by extension, the number of prisoners put to productive labor. Moreover, several states did not submit full reports on their industries to Wright. (It is also true that the census takers for 1880 undercounted the prison population, as no data were available for prisons in ten states and territories [mostly southern], including Georgia, one of the largest southern states.) Margaret Werner Cahalan, *Historical Corrections Statistics in the United States, 1850–1984* (Washington, D.C., 1986), 29, 192.

44. According to the five commonly used historical inflation indexes, $29 million in 1886 is "worth" (in 2009 dollars) $684,630,000, using the Consumer Price Index; $643,740,000, using the Gross Domestic Product (GDP) deflator; $3,846,430,000, using the unskilled wage; $6,577,970,000, using the nominal GDP per capita; and 34,384,770,000, using the relative share of GDP. Source: Economic History Services, Wake Forest and Miami University, EHNet, http://eh.net/hmit/compare/ (accessed May 9, 2010).

45. *Report of the Secretary of the Interior*, 5:171.

46. Edmund S. Morgan, *American Slavery, American Freedom* (New York, 1975); and Eric Foner, *The Story of American Freedom* (New York, 1998), 3–28.

47. Foner, *The Story of American Freedom*.

48. Morris, *Southern Slavery and the Law*, 1–15.

49. Plato famously referred to slaves as "human property," observing that slaves are both objects of possession and human agents with the capacity to cooperate or resist, cast off, or subvert their enslavement. Their humanness is what made them, unlike all other kinds of property, "troublesome property."

50. Penal transports of the eighteenth century, to the contrary, were sold to private masters, typically for seven years.

51. Morris, *Southern Slavery and the Law*; Ariela Gross, *Double Character: Slavery and Mastery in the Antebellum Southern Courtroom* (Princeton, N.J., 2000), 3–4.

52. *Ruffin* has often been used to support the view that the courts took an absolute "hands-off" approach to prisons and prisoners in the nineteenth and early twentieth centuries. In my view, that claim overstates the courts' reluctance to intervene in the executive sphere of punishment and the prisoner's supposed absolute lack of rights. The courts did, in fact, occasionally hear prisoners' cases (including Ruffin's), which in and of itself constituted recognition of their right to an appeal; however, they rarely ruled in favor of prisoners. For a rejoinder to the absolute "hands-off" thesis, see Donald H. Wallace, "*Ruffin v. Virginia* and Slaves of the State: A Nonexistent Baseline of Prisoners' Rights Jurisprudence," *Journal of Criminal Justice* 20 (1992): 333, 340.

53. *Cunningham v. Bay State Shoe and Leather Co.,* New York Supreme Court (1881), reported in *American Law Review* 2 (December 1881): 811.

54. Warren E. Lewis, *Appellant, v. The State of New York*, Respondent [No number in original] Court of Appeals of New York, 96 N.Y. 71; 1884 N.Y. LEXIS 469 (1884).

55. Ibid. In the late 1880s and 1890s, as contract prison labor became the object of a series of exposés, critiques, and large-scale protests, a number of courts in both the North and South softened the positions found in *Ruffin* and in *Lewis*. In 1891 a Federal Court of Appeal ruled that a federal prisoner who was put to contract labor, and who was injured on faulty scaffolding that the contractor had erected and which the prisoner was compelled to work on, was in a master-servant or employer-employee relationship with the contractor, and so, entitled to compensation for "the pain and suffering that he may have been subjected to from the time of the accident up to this time, and which may be caused to him in the future" and charged the jury to take loss of earning capacity into account in their calculation of compensation. Justice Chiras, in *Dalheim v. Lemon et al.*, Circuit Court, D. Minnesota, Fourth Division, 45 F. 225; 1891 U.S. App. LEXIS 1733 (1891). Some state courts, however, stood firm: in 1890, for example, the Ohio Supreme Court ruled that no relation of master and servant existed between a contracted prisoner and his contractor: the plaintiff, a prisoner who had been severely injured when a poorly installed ceiling fan in the contractor's workshop fell out of its fixture, could not recover damages. *George W. Rayborn v. Alexander G. Patton*, State of Ohio, Court of Common Please, Franklin County, 1890 Ohio Misc. LEXIS 167; 11 Ohio Dec. Reprint 100 (1890).

56. For useful overviews of the history of prisoner litigation, see Jim Thomas, *Prisoner Litigation and the Paradox of the Jailhouse Lawyer* (Totowa, N.J., 1988); and John A. Filter, *Prisoners' Rights: The Supreme Court and Evolving Standards of Decency* (Westport, Conn., 2000).

57. Glen A. Gildemeister, *Prison Labor and Convict Competition with Free Workers in Industrializing America, 1840–1890* (New York, 1987); McLennan, *The Crisis of Imprisonment*, 115–34.

58. Gershom Powers, *Letter . . . in Answer to a Letter of the Hon. Edward Livingston* (Albany, N.Y., 1829), 13–14. For the complete passage, see Lewis, *From Newgate to Dannemora*, 114–15.

59. Erving Goffman, *Asylums: Essays on the Condition of the Social Situation of Mental Patients and Other Inmates* (New York, 1961).

60. For a detailed account of the abolition of the various contract prison labor systems, see McLennan, *The Crisis of Imprisonment*, 137–92. On Georgia and Mississippi, respectively, see Alex Lichtenstein, *Twice the Work of Free Labor: The Political Economy of Convict Labor in the New South* (London, 1996); and David M. Oshinsky, *Worse Than Slavery: Parchman Farm and the Ordeal of Jim Crow Justice* (New York, 1996). On the South as a whole, see C. Vann Woodward, *Origins of the New South, 1877–1913* (Baton Rouge, La., 1951); and Ayers, *Vengeance and Justice*.

61. Under the "state-use" model of prison labor, with which many states in both the North and South substituted for the contract system, the state assumed the functions of private capital as investor, producer, distributor, price-fixer, vendor—and consumer—of prison-made goods.

62. For a brief moment, in the early 1830s, when journeymen apprentices in cities such as New York first began organizing en masse against the use of prison labor in competition with the labor of free workingmen, protesting workingmen had not generally insisted

upon the existence of a deep moral distinction between imprisoned and free men. That changed dramatically after the anti-contract labor campaigns of the early 1830s were defeated, and as contractual prison labor became ever more deeply entrenched in the American penal system in the course of the 1840s and 1850s. Certainly, in the 1840s and 1850s, some critics of prison labor still took care not to denigrate the moral character of convicts, preferring to make strictly political and economic arguments against the use of convict labor in the trades. But many more asserted, whether directly or indirectly, the existence of a deep, unbridgeable, and moral divide between free workingmen and imprisoned men (McLennan, *The Crisis of Imprisonment*, 80–81).

63. Remarks of J. Haskell, *Workingman's Advocate*, May 9, 1835, 6. In the mid-1830s mechanics' resolutions sometimes referred to convicts as "worthless outcasts." See, for example, *Proceedings of the Mechanics' Meeting*, Buffalo, New York, January 13, 1834, *Literary Inquirer*, January 15, 1834, 2. However, this did not become commonplace until the 1840s.

64. The National Committee on Prisons and Prison Labor (NCPPL) was the leading progressive-era prison reform organization. Founded in 1909 by women workers of the Baltimore textile industry (which faced stiff competition, in a number of states, from prison labor), the group soon pursued the abolition of contracting. By 1915 a number of well-known progressives had joined—including Thomas Mott Osborne, Deans George Kirchwey and James C. Egbert of Columbia University, Julia Jaffray, Frederick A. Goetz, eugenicists Charles B. Davenport and Hastings H. Hart, Samuel McCune Lindsay, and a number of leading attorneys and judges (George Foster Peabody, William H. Wadham, and George Gordon Battle). On the NCPPL's origins, see Julia Jaffray, *New York Times*, March 22, 1936, N6, 1.

65. Battle and Kirchwey invoked E. Stagg Whitin's reasoning in his 1912 *Penal Servitude* to argue that the contracting-out of convict William Anderson's labor, with no remuneration for the prisoner, rendered him a slave, in contravention of the state constitution. *William E. Anderson v. Gabriel Salant et al.* [No number in original] Supreme Court of Rhode Island, 38 R.I. 463; 96 A. 425; 1916 R.I. LEXIS 8 (1916)..

66. Nathaniel F. Cantor, "The Prisoner and the Law," *Annals of the American Academy of Political and Social Science* 157 (September 1931): 25, 29, 32.

67. Gottschalk, *The Prison and the Gallows*, 22. European penal systems, Gottschalk points out, both aspire to a different penal ideal and practice a different penology.

68. See Desmond King, *Separate and Unequal: Black Americans and the U.S. Federal Government* (New York, 2007); Gottschalk, *The Prison and the Gallows*, 171–94.

69. *Wolff v. McDonnell*, 418 U.S. 539, 555–56 (1974).

70. *Richardson v. Ramirez*, 418 U.S. 24 (1974).

71. *Hunter v. Underwood*, 471 U.S. 222, 232 (1985). For a discussion, see Manza and Uggen, with Behrens, *Locked Out*, 33.

72. The recent work of James Q. Whitman (on the comparatively "harsh" justice of the American penal system relative to Western Europe) and Marie Gottschalk (on America's comparatively "unforgiving" politics and institutional culture of mass incarceration) confirms that American penal practice and politics have, more often than not, developed along a distinct trajectory relative to Western Europe and the British Commonwealth. As is well known, no other advanced industrial country, besides Japan, retains the death penalty today; as is less well known, not one advanced industrial nation carries the convict's civil penalties and the collateral consequences of crime to the extremes found in the United States.

73. Gottschalk, *The Prison and the Gallows*, 43.

About the Contributors

DAVID GARLAND is Arthur T. Vanderbilt Professor of Law and Professor of Sociology at New York University. He is the author of *Peculiar Institution: America's Death Penalty in an Age of Abolition.*

DOUGLAS HAY is Professor of Law and History at York University and co-editor of *Masters, Servants and Magistrates in Britain and the Empire, 1562–1955.*

RANDALL MCGOWEN is Professor of History at the University of Oregon and co-author of *The Perreaus and Mrs. Rudd: Forgery and Betrayal in Eighteenth-Century London.*

REBECCA MCLENNAN is Associate Professor of History at the University of California, Berkeley, and author of *The Crisis of Imprisonment: Protest, Politics, and the Making of the American Penal State, 1776–1941.*

MICHAEL MERANZE is Professor of History at the University of California, Los Angeles, and author of *Laboratories of Virtue: Punishment, Revolution and Authority in Philadelphia, 1760–1835.*

JONATHAN SIMON is Professor of Law at the University of California, Berkeley, and Faculty Co-Chair at the Berkeley Center for Criminal Justice. He is the author of *Governing through Crime: How the War on Crime Transformed American Democracy and Created a Culture of Fear.*

Index

biopolitics, 79–99; constitutional law, 93; death penalty, 81–82, 86–93, 98–99; definition, 83, 92; Europe, 90–92; Foucault and, Michel, 23, 74, 81, 91–92, 104n52; *Furman v. Georgia*, 74, 93–94, 96–98, 99; Great Society, 93; *Gregg v. Georgia*, 93; Harlan and, John, 95–96, 97–98; law, 86; *McGautha v. California*, 74, 93–96, 97–98, 99; politics of life, 87–88; race, 94; "socialization" of justice, 89–90; sovereignty, 79–86; United States, 90–92; U.S. Supreme Court, 74, 93–99; *Woodson v. North Carolina*, 93

Birth of Biopolitics, The (Foucault), 86

Bismarck, Otto von, 117

Blackstone, William, 138

Blok, Anton, 43

Bloody Code, 41, 49

Boston Prison Discipline Society, 208–209

Bramwell, George William Wilshere, Baron, 152

Brazil, 78

Brennan, William, 97, 98, 100, 104n66

Bright, John, 155

Britain: abolition of the death penalty, 61, 88, 112, 113–114, 119; death penalty offenses, 110; executions in, 60, 110; mass imprisonment in, 72; state violence, declining, 158. *See also* England; United Kingdom

Brown, Edmund "Pat," 167, 174–177, 180–183, 187

Brown v. Board of Education (1954), 168–170, 173, 183, 187

Brown II (1955), 169

Buller, Mr. Justice, 137–138, 148

Bush, George H. W., 186

Bush, George W., 12, 13, 14, 182

Bush administration, George W., 12–13, 72

Byng, Admiral John, 143, 162n32

Byrne, Mr. Justice, 154

Calhoun, John C., 170, 204

California: death penalty, support for, 182; death row inmates (2009), 8; executions in, 119, 181, 184, 185; Los Angeles County, 8; reinstatement of death penalty, 185

California Supreme Court, 104n66, 120, 167–168, 184

Camden, Charles Pratt, Earl of, 149

Camus, Albert, 58, 76

Canada, 61

Cantor, Nathaniel, 210

capital punishment. *See* death penalty

Caribbean countries, 9, 14, 17, 77

Chessman, Caryl, 175–176, 181

child rapists, 7, 17

China: concern about international opinions, 10; crimes eligible for death penalty, 15; executions in, 11–12; localized character of capital justice, 16; as retentionist state, 10–12, 14, 33, 77; UN's condemnation of death penalty, response to, 8–9

Christ, crucifixion of, 21

Christian, Justice J., 192–193, 194–195, 203–204

Christie, John, 154

civil death jurisprudence, 192–198, 208–212

Civil Rights Act (1964), 166–167

Civil Rights movement, 166, 168

civiliter mortuus, 194–195

clemency, 176–180, 182

Clinton, Bill, 186

Cobden, Richard, 110

Cohen, Esther, 36, 41, 45

Coke, Edward, 45, 46, 191

Cold War, 76–77

colonialism, 78

Connecticut, 5, 200

convicts, 191–219; American exceptionalism, 219n72; civil death jurisprudence, 192–198, 208–212; corporal punishment, 196–197, 198; disenfranchisement, 197–198, 211, 215n23; entitlements, 193; Europe compared to United States, 210, 219n72; forced labor for private contractors, 198–207, 217n43, 218n55; involuntary servitude, 201–205, 210; ritual degradation of, 207; Ruffin, Woody, case of, 191–193, 194, 203–204; as slaves of the State, 192; vs. "prisoners," "felons," 196, 211, 212

Cooper, David, 43–44

Cooper, Thomas Cooper, Lord, 154

Cooper v. Aaron, 171

Corzine, Jon, 5
Council of Europe, 61, 119
Crampton v. Ohio, 94, 95
crime: fear of, 158, 166–167, 183–184, 188;
    governing through, 169
crime control, 40–41, 50–51
Criminal Justice Bill (United Kingdom,
    1948), 153–154, 155
criminal justice system: rise of, 50–51;
    "socialization" of, 89–90; in United
    States, 72, 89–92
criminality, eugenicist *vs.* environmental
    notions of, 89
criminals, representations of, 46, 58, 88
Cuomo, Mario, 48

Dallas Morning Post (newspaper), 5
Damiens, Robert, 49
Dawson v. State, 6
death, significance of, 19
death penalty: alternative to, carceral punish-
    ment as, 194; alternative to, disenfranchise-
    ment as, 26; alternative to, life imprison-
    ment without parole as, 5, 25–26, 98, 111,
    186, 194, 196, 205–206; alternative to, trans-
    portation to colonies as, 132; as apolitical
    penal practice, 51; arguments favoring,
    115–116; assumed *vs.* chosen, 84; biopolitics,
    81–82, 86–93; circumscription of applica-
    tion of, 6–7; civil death jurisprudence, 194;
    colonialism, 78; commutation of death
    sentences, 49; crime, fear of, 158; crimes
    eligible for, 15–16; as cruel and unusual
    punishment, 6; definition, 30; Europe
    compared to United States, 2–3, 18–19,
    72–79, 91, 99–100, 108, 119–121, 123–124;
    "evolving standards of decency," 96, 98,
    104n66, 120–122; governance, modes of, 22;
    history in studies of, 19–26, 73–74, 78–79,
    106–108, 123–125 (*see also* death penalty,
    history of); human dignity, 100; legitimacy
    and authority *vs.* crime and punishment,
    25; legitimacy of, 47–48, 56–58, 61–62; local
    circumstances, history, 14, 16, 157–158, 175;
    mode/modality of, 65n14; NYU conference
    on (2007), 2–3; party politics, 52; penalties

extending beyond term of confinement as
    alternative to, 26; as a policy tool, 50–51;
    political crises, 141–147; politics of national
    identity, 17–18; power, 37–40; pro-death
    penalty sentiment, 7–8, 17; public opinion,
    121–122, 130, 182, 185; race, 78, 82–83, 158,
    181, 183, 186; Reagan and, Ronald, 168;
    reinstatement of, 5, 72–73, 98–99, 119,
    120–121, 184–185; religious justifications, 53;
    retribution, 63; sanctity of life, 114–115; sov-
    ereignty, 76, 99–100; state authority, 37–41,
    50–51; United Nations condemnation of,
    8–10; usefulness/functions of, 33, 37–42, 48,
    50–53, 57–58; victims' rights, 109, 114–115,
    122, 185; world's population subject to, 77.
    See also abolition of the death penalty;
    deterrence; execution methods; executions;
    retentionist states
death penalty, applicability of: arsonists,
    149; child rapists, 7, 17; collaborators, 118;
    cowardice and desertion, 153; decline in,
    30–32; drug offenders, 17; forgers, 40, 134,
    140–141, 145, 146; heresy, 70n87; juveniles,
    7, 11, 121; Luddites, 145–146, 147; mentally
    retarded, 7, 121; murderers, 70n87, 110,
    111, 113, 114–115, 131, 134, 148, 155; "petit
    treason," 38; pickpockets, 146, 149; politi-
    cal offenders, 38; profiteers, 144; property
    offenders, 112–113, 130, 131, 134–135; rapists,
    151; rebels/rioters, 142–145; sheep stealers,
    137, 146; shoplifters, 149–150; thieves, 151;
    traitors or national security violators, 15,
    38, 45, 52, 104n52, 131, 142, 144, 145
death penalty, history of, 30–71, 108–128;
    absolutism, 36–38, 57, 65n18, 66n24;
    American exceptionalism, 2–3, 14, 78,
    107–108, 125; ancient world, 64n1; con-
    tingent circumstances in, 123; criminal
    justice system, rise of, 50–51; early
    modern period, 30, 35–48, 66n21, 111–
    112; eighteenth century, 34, 38, 39, 40,
    44, 49, 108–110, 129, 132–140; England,
    36, 38, 39, 40, 47, 58, 66n24; Enlighten-
    ment period, 108–109; Europe, 34, 38;
    fifteenth century, 34, 36; fourteenth
    century, 36; France, 43, 44, 49, 58;

death penalty, history of (*continued*): late modern period (1960s on), 35, 58, 59–63; Middle Ages, 70n87; modern period, 35, 49–50; nineteenth century, 30–31, 35, 49–56, 58, 88, 110–111, 133–134, 140, 194; political structures, importance of, 124; secularization, 53–54; seventeenth century, 38, 47; sixteenth century, 34, 39; state formation in, 35–38; twentieth century, 60–61, 158. *See also* retentionist states

death penalty cases: clemency decisions, 176–180, 182; defense counsel, adequacy of, 6; judicial review, 15; juries, autonomy of, 95, 97; jury selection in, 6; in Los Angeles County, 8; moratoria on, 5, 6, 117; U.S. Constitution, 94–95; U.S. Supreme Court, 93. *See also names of individual cases*

Dei delitti e delle pene (Beccaria), 57

democracy. *See* liberal democracies

Democratic Party, 166, 215n23

Denmark, 61

Denning, Alfred Denning, Baron, 154

deterrence: effectiveness of, 63, 70n89, 180, 186; Reagan on, Ronald, 184–185

DiSalle, Mike, 167, 174–182, 187

Discipline and Punish (Foucault), 79, 81, 83

disenfranchisement: as alternative to death penalty, 26; of convicts, 197–198, 211, 215n23; criminal disenfranchisement, 197; felony disenfranchisement, 197, 214n11

District of Columbia, 200

DNA evidence, 5

Douglas, William O., 97

Doyle, John, 145

Eastern Europe, 16, 119

Eastern State Penitentiary (Pennsylvania), 199–200

Eighth Amendment, 6–7, 94, 96, 97

Eldon, John Scott, Earl of, 150

Elias, Norbert, 31, 55–56

Ellenborough, Edward Law, Baron, 149, 150, 156

Ellenborough's Act (United Kingdom, 1803), 149

Elmira Reformatory for Boys, 205

England, 129–165; abolition of the death penalty, 111, 149–155; absolutism in, 66n24; assize courts, 40, 132, 136–137, 161n17; Bloody Code, 41, 49; civil death in, 195; Common Pleas, Court of, 129; Crown Court, 136–137, 144; death penalty offenses, changes in, 132, 147–148, 151–152; eighteenth century, 39, 40, 44, 129, 132–140; Exchequer of Pleas, 129; executions in, 38, 39, 43–44, 68n52, 112–113; Georgian period, 146; Gunpowder Plot case (1606), 45; hanging in, 40, 132–133, 136–141; High Court, 136; high judiciary, 129, 130–131, 153–154, 155–156, 157; House of Commons, 130; House of Lords, 129, 130, 148; judicial influence on capital punishment, 136–138, 147, 157; King's Bench, 129, 136, 154; late middle ages, 36; Lord Chancellor, 129–130; Luddism, 145–146, 147; municipal justices, 161n16; nineteenth century, 58, 133–134, 140; Old Bailey cases, 40, 132–133, 136; pardons, 42, 132–134, 138, 141, 146, 177; parliamentary consensus, 130; political crises, 141–147; public opinion, 130; right to hear charges, 39; seventeenth century, 47; seventeenth and eighteenth centuries, 38; sixteenth century, 39; torture in, 152; Treason Act (1694), 39; United States compared to, 130. *See also* Britain; United Kingdom

Europe, 72–79; abolition of the death penalty, 118–119; biopolitics, 90–92; convicts, 210; eighteenth and nineteenth centuries, 34; race, 91; seventeenth century, 38; "socialization" of justice, 89–90; United States compared to, 2–3, 18–19, 72–79, 91, 99–100, 108, 119–121, 123–124, 210, 219n72. *See also* Eastern Europe; Western Europe

European Convention on Human Rights, 64n7, 119

European Union: abolition of the death penalty, 18–19, 61, 66n21, 72, 75–79, 124; UN's condemnation of death penalty (2007), 9

Evans, Richard: on Europe, 34, 38; on Germany, 36, 39, 46, 52, 53, 55, 58, 117; on sanctity of life as pro-death penalty argument, 114

Evans, Timothy, 154
"evolving standards of decency," 96, 98, 104n66, 120–122
Ewart, William, 110
execution methods: breaking on the wheel, 43; burning at the stake, 43, 45, 47; changes in, 31; decapitation, 15, 43; dismemberment, 45; drawing and quartering, 43, 47; the drop, 110; firing squad, 15; forms of, 42–43; France, 43, 60, 62; gibbeting, 67n46; guillotine, 110; hanging (*see* hanging); legitimacy of, 47; lethal injection (*see* lethal injection); by sword, 45, 110
executions: ceremonies surrounding, 36–38, 39–40, 43–47, 53, 55; decline in numbers, 110, 114; as display of power, 40–41; efficiency of, 54–55; hanging day crowds, 55; as law enforcement, 40–41; military executions for cowardice and desertion, 153; nineteenth century, 110–111; press coverage of, 56; public executions, 15, 17, 151; public view, withdrawal from, 55–56; race, 181; as religious events, 39–40, 47, 53–54, 56, 76; as representations of death and dying, 46–47; scaffold speeches, 44, 55; as spectacles, 43–47; status-based distinctions in, 42–43, 45, 53; as symbolic communication, 44–45; terms for, 41; as tragedies, 48; "witnesses" to, 55–56; worldwide variety in, 3–4, 15
executions in: Britain, 60; California, 119, 181, 184, 185; England, 38, 39, 43–44, 68n52, 112–113; France, 60, 110–111, 113, 118; Germany, 36, 39, 55, 117; Iran, 11, 15; Italy, 43, 110, 118; Netherlands, 43; Saudi Arabia, 10, 15, 17; the South, 8, 119, 121; United States, 8, 60
Eyre, Mr. Justice, 138, 145

Fairbairn, Nicholas, 157
Farmers Alliances, 215n23
Faubus, Orville, 167–168, 172, 173, 187
Fifth Amendment, 94, 95
First Part of the Institutes of the Laws of England (Coke), 191
Florida, 200–201

Foucault, Michel, 79–86; the biopolitical, notion of, 23, 74, 81, 91–92, 104n52 (*see also* biopolitics); *The Birth of Biopolitics*, 86; constitutions, 86; *Discipline and Punish*, 79, 81, 83; disciplines of the body, 79–80; *History of Sexuality*, 79, 81, 82; liberalism, 84–85; neoliberalism, 85–86; on nineteenth century France, 58; political economy, 85; race, 82–83; regulations of populations, 80; sexuality, 80–81; *Society Must Be Defended*, 82
Fourteenth Amendment, 94, 96, 211
France: abolition of the death penalty, 61, 62, 63, 88, 118, 123; Damiens, execution of Robert, 49; death penalty offenses, 110; execution methods, 43, 60, 62; executions in, 60, 110–111, 113, 118; nineteenth century, 58; penal reform, 113; scaffold speeches, 44; torture in, 109
Furman v. Georgia: abolition of the death penalty, 119–121; biopolitics, 74, 93–94, 96–98, 99; counterfactual history of, 122–124; "evolving standards of decency," 96, 98, 104n66, 120–122; reinstatement of the death penalty following, 120–121, 184; state sovereignty, reassertion of, 184

Gardiner, Gerald, 155
Gatrell, V. A. C., 38, 46, 57, 58
Geertz, Clifford, 66n21
Georgia, 8, 200
Georgia Supreme Court, 6
Germany: abolition of the death penalty, 60, 110, 111, 116–118; Basic Law (1948–49), 118; Christian Democrats, 118; executions in, 36, 39, 55, 117; fourteenth and fifteenth centuries, 36; Frankfurt Assembly (1848), 110; National Socialists, 117; nineteenth century, 52, 53, 55, 58; North German Reichstag, 117; Prussia, 49, 109, 110; scaffold speeches, 44; Social Democrats, 118; torture in, 109; transition from authoritarian regime to democracy, 16
gibbeting, 67n46
Goddard, Raymond Goddard, Baron, 153–154, 155–156, 158

God's vengeance, 21
Goffman, Erving, 207
"Going to See a Man Hanged" (Thackeray), 113
Goldberg, Arthur, 120
Gottschalt, Marie, 193, 212, 219n72
Great Britain. *See* Britain
Great Society, 92, 93
Greece, 59
Gregg v. Georgia: aftermath of, 4, 121–122, 184; biopolitics, 93; reinstatement of the death penalty, 98–99
Grose, Mr. Justice, 142
Gross, Ariela, 202
Gunpowder Plot case (1606), 45

Haltunnen, Karen, 54, 58, 70n87
Hamm, Theodore, 181
hanging: in England, 40, 132–133, 136–141; in France, 43; hanging day crowds, 55; indignity of, 43, 45; legitimacy of, 47, 58
Hanging Not Punishment Enough (Paley), 57
Harlan, John, 94–96, 97–98
Harris, Lou, 174, 187
Hay, Douglas, 25, 38, 41–42, 177
Hegel, G. W. F., 57
History of Sexuality (Foucault), 79, 81, 82
Hobbes, Thomas, 194
Hobhouse, Henry, 146
Homicide Act (United Kingdom, 1957), 154–155
Horsfall, William, 146
Hugo, Victor, 113
human dignity, 100
human rights, 59
Human Rights Convention, 124
humanity, affirmation of, 24
Humphrey, Hubert, 122
Hunt, Lynn, 43, 53
Hutchison, Kay Bailey, 6

Illinois, 5, 200
India, 8–9, 14, 15, 63
Indonesia, 10
Innocence Project, 5

International Covenant on Civil and Political Rights (ICCPR), 61
interposition doctrine, 166–190; abolition of the death penalty, 174–183; Brown and, Edmund "Pat," 167, 174–177, 180–183, 187; clemency decisions, 176–180, 182; definition, 167; DiSalle and, Mike, 167, 174–182, 187; Faubus and, Orville, 172; fear of crime, 166–167, 183–184, 188; post-New Deal governors, 166–169, 171–173, 174–183, 187–188; Reagan and, Ronald, 183–187; school segregation, 187–188; state sovereignty, 169–170, 184; U.S. Supreme Court, 170–171; Wallace and, George, 172–173
Iowa, 119
Iran: executions in, 11, 15; as retentionist state, 10–11, 14, 33; UN's condemnation of death penalty, response to, 8–9
Iraq, 12–13
Ireland, 61, 118
Islamic countries, 15, 16–17
Italy: abolition of the death penalty, 60, 61, 118; executions in, 43, 110, 118

Japan: executions in, 10; insensitivity to world opinion, 16; judicial review in, 15; as retentionist state, 14, 63; "unofficial" scrapping of capital punishment, 28n23
Jenkins, Roy, 119
Johnson, Frank, 173
Johnson, Lyndon, 166, 210
Johnson, Samuel, 33
Jowitt, William Jowitt, Earl of, 153–154, 156
judicial review, 15, 72
Judt, Tony, 75
juries, autonomy of, 95, 97
jury selection, 6

Kant, Immanuel, 57
Kennedy, Anthony, 7, 10
Kennedy v. Louisiana, 7
Kentucky, 48, 200
Kenyon, Lord Chief Justice, 138, 142, 144, 148
Kilpatrick, James K., 170–171
Klarman, Michael, 172–173
Klumpp, Edythe, 178–179

Knights of Labor, 215n23
Labour Party (United Kingdom): abolition of the death penalty, 88, 116, 118, 130, 147, 155, 156; fears, ending of, 158; Select Committee on Capital Punishment (1929), 153
Lamartine, Alphonse de, 50
Laski, Harold, 153
"last meal," 53, 56
"last rites," 53
"last words," 56
Latin America, 15
Laurent, Emile, 115
Le Blanc, Samuel, 146
League of Arab States, 71n113
Lee, Lord Chief Justice, 142
lethal injection: acceptance of death penalty, 62; *Baze v. Rees*, 6–7; in China, 11; in New Jersey, 4; in United States, 15, 62; U.S. Supreme Court on, 6–7
Leviathan, terror of, 21
Lewis, W. David, 196
Lewis, Warren E., 205
liberal democracies, death penalty in, 35, 40
liberalism, 84–85
life, sanctity of, 114–115
Lindsey, Richard, 178
Little Rock High School, 172
Lofland, John, 67n46
Los Angeles County, California, 8
Loughborough, Alexander Wedderburn, Baron, 148
Louisiana, 7, 200
Luddism, 145–146, 147
Lushington, Stephen, 110
Luxembourg, 61
Lynd, William, 8
Lynds, Elam, 207

Mackintosh, James, 110, 147
Madow, Michael, 54, 56
Maine, 200
Maistre, Joseph de, 37
Maliki, Nuri Kamal al-, 12, 13
Mansfield, William Murray, Earl of, 148–149
Marshall, T. H., 210
Marshall, Thurgood, 97, 98

Martineau, Harriet, 110
mass imprisonment, 72
Massachusetts, 200
McCain, John, 7–8
McElvaine, Charles, 54
McGautha v. California: biopolitics, 74, 93–96, 97–98, 99; dissenters in, 97
McGowen, Randall: English executions, 39; forgery prosecutions by Bank of England, 140–141; legitimacy of execution methods, 47; method of violence as a language, 45; prison and punishment, 69n82; religious justifications death penalty, 53
McLennan, Rebecca, 26
McVeigh, Timothy, 17
Medellin, José, 18
Meranze, Michael, 196
Merback, Mitchell, 43, 45
Mexico, 18
Michigan, 110, 200
Middle East, 77
Mill, John Stuart, 57, 113
Mississippi, 8, 208
Missouri, 200
Mitterand, Françoise, 118
M'Lane, Daniel, 131
modernity in Western culture, 24
Morris, Thomas, 202
Muhammad, John A., 8

Nation of Islam, 211
National Association for the Advancement of Colored People (NAACP), 93, 120, 211
National Committee on Prisons and Prison Labor (NCPPL), 209, 219n64
national identity, politics of, 17–18
Nebraska Supreme Court, 6
neoliberalism, 85–86, 100
Netherlands, 43, 44, 61, 118
New Deal: constitutional challenges and difficulties, 91; model executive, 178; post-New Deal political order, 166–169, 171–183; in the South, 187; style of governing, 182
New Hampshire, 5, 200
New Jersey, 4–5, 200
New Mexico, 5

defense of, 168, 176; civil rights, softening of, 166; interposition doctrine, 183–187; neoliberalism, 100

Reconstruction, 201

retentionist states: arguments advanced by, 9–10; China, 10–12, 14, 33, 77; cultural development, level of, 14–15; Greece, 59; Iran, 10–11, 33; Japan, 14, 63, 77; list of, 8–9, 14, 33; number of, 33, 64n9; Portugal, 59; Russian Federation, 104n52; Saudi Arabia, 33; Singapore, 33; Spain, 59; Sudan, 33; United States, 1–3, 32–33, 61, 63

retribution, 63

Rhode Island, 110, 200, 209

Richmond News-Leader (newspaper), 170

Riddle, Rose Marie, 178

Riot Act (Great Britain, 1713), 142, 143

Roberts, John, 7, 100

Romilly, Samuel, 147, 149, 150, 156

Roosevelt, Franklin, 180

Roper v. Simmons, 7, 10, 99

Ruffin, Woody, 191–193, 194, 203–204

Ruffin v. Virginia, 217n52, 218n55

Russell, John Russell, Earl of, 148, 151, 155

Russian Federation, 104n52

Ryan, George, 5, 182

Saddam Hussein, 9, 12–13

Sarat, Austin, 174, 182

Saudi Arabia: executions in, 10, 15, 17; insensitivity to world opinion, 16; as retentionist state, 14, 33

Savoy, 109

Scandinavia, 119

Schama, Simon, 55

secularization, 53–54, 76

Sharpe, James, 36, 44

Sidmouth, Henry Addington, Viscount, 140

Simon, Jonathan, 25

Singapore, 9, 14, 17–18, 33

Society Must Be Defended (Foucault), 82

"Sonnets upon the Punishment of Death" (Wordsworth), 53

South, the: contract labor system for prisoners, 200–201, 207; convict disen-franchisement, 215n23; executions in, 8, 119, 121; interposition doctrine, 169–170; massive resistance to civil rights, 171–172; New Deal in, 187; post-New Deal governors, 167, 168–169, 171–172; pro-death penalty sentiment in, 18

South Africa, 16

South America, 16, 66n21

South Carolina, 8, 197, 200–201

sovereignty: abolition of the death penalty, 9–10, 17, 23; biopolitics, 79–86; death penalty, 76, 99–100; interposition doctrine, 169–170, 184; power, 81; state sovereignty, 169–170, 184; U.S. Supreme Court, 74

Spain: abolition of the death penalty, 61, 63, 119; as retentionist state, 59; transition from authoritarian regime to democracy, 16

Spierenburg, Pieter, 44, 46

state, dignity of, 100

state authority, 37–41, 50–51

state formation, 35–38

Steiker, Carol, 119

Stephen, James Fitzjames, 113–114, 152

Stevens, John Paul, 7

Stewart, Potter, 97, 98, 121

Sudan, 14, 33

Susilo Bambang Yudhoyono, 10

Sydney, Thomas Townshend, Viscount, 148

Syria, 8–9, 14

Tennessee, 200

Tenterden, Charles Abbott, Baron, 150–151, 155

Texas, 5–6, 8, 18

Thackeray, William, 113

Thirteenth Amendment, 197–198

Thomas, Clarence, 7

Thorndike, John, 171

Tocqueville, Alexis de, 197

torture, 77, 109, 152

Townsend, John, 137–138

Treason Act (England, 1694), 39

Truman, Harry, 170

Tuscany, 49

United Kingdom: abolition of the death penalty, 61, 62, 130; House of Lords, 116; Royal Commission (1948–1953), 153, 154; Select Committee on Capital Punishment (1929), 153; United States compared to, 157–158. *See also* Britain; England; Labour Party (United Kingdom)

United Nations, 1, 8–10, 61

United States: abolition of the death penalty, 110, 119, 130; biopolitics, 90–92; colonial America, 47; crimes eligible for death penalty, 15; criminal justice system in, 72; death penalty, reinstatement of, 120–121; death penalty practices, variety in, 4–8; England compared to, 130; Europe compared to, 2–3, 18–19, 72–79, 91, 99–100, 108, 119–121, 123–124, 210, 219n72; executions in, 8, 60; insensitivity to world opinion, 16; judicial review, 15, 72; lethal injection, 15, 62; mass imprisonment, 72; neoliberalism, 100; Reconstruction period, 88; resistance to application of international standards, 10; as retentionist state, 1–3, 32–33, 61, 63; retributiveness, mood of, 122; "socialization" of justice, 89–90; United Kingdom compared to, 157–158. *See also names of individual states and* "South, the"

U.S. Congress, 74

U.S. Constitution: Fifth Amendment, 94, 95; Eighth Amendment, 6–7, 94, 96, 97; Thirteenth Amendment, 197–198; Fourteenth Amendment, 94, 96, 211; biopolitics, 93; death penalty cases, 94–95; proscription of involuntary servitude, 213

U.S. Supreme Court: abolition of the death penalty, 157; biopolitics, 74, 93–99; Burger Court, 211; circumscription of application of death penalty, 6–7; culture wars, 92–93; death penalty cases, 93; interposition doctrine, 170–171; on jury selection in death penalty cases, 6; on lethal injection, 6–7; sovereignty claims of states, 74; Warren Court, 92, 184, 193, 211

Valline, John, 145

Vermont, 119, 200

victims' rights: death penalty, 109, 114–115, 122, 185; as a discourse, 211

Virginia, 8, 200

Virginia Bill of Rights, 191, 203

Virginia Supreme Court, 191

Voting Rights Act (1965), 211

Wallace, George, 167–168, 172–173, 187

Waltham Black Act (United Kingdom, 1722), 150

Waltho, John, 137

Watkins, Craig, 5

Weaver, Vesla, 167

Wensleydale, James Parke, Lord, 152

West Virginia, 119

Western Europe, 44, 60–61, 72

Western nations, abolition of death penalty in, 33

Wethersfield State Prison (Connecticut), 200

White, Byron, 97, 98

Whitman, James Q., 219n72

Whitman, Walt, 200

Wilberforce, Samuel, 148

Willes, John, 143–144

Willingham, Cameron T., 6

Wilmot, John Eardley, 143

Wilson, Harold, 155

Wisconsin, 110

Wood, George, 146

Woodson v. North Carolina, 93, 99

Wordsworth, William, 53

Wright, Carroll, 201, 217n43

Zimring, Franklin, 122